Global Thirst

Water and Society
in the 21st Century

John R. Wennersten

To Bill & David
Best Wishes
John R. Wennersten

Schiffer Publishing Ltd

4880 Lower Valley Road, Atglen, Pennsylvania 19310

Schiffer Books are available at special discounts for bulk purchases for sales promotions or premiums. Special editions, including personalized covers, corporate imprints, and excerpts can be created in large quantities for special needs. For more information contact the publisher:

Published by Schiffer Publishing Ltd.
4880 Lower Valley Road
Atglen, PA 19310
Phone: (610) 593-1777; Fax: (610) 593-2002
E-mail: Info@schifferbooks.com

For the largest selection of fine reference books on this and related subjects,
please visit our website at:
www.schifferbooks.com
We are always looking for people to write books on new and related subjects.
If you have an idea for a book, please contact us at
proposals@schifferbooks.com

This book may be purchased from the publisher.
Include $5.00 for shipping.
Please try your bookstore first.
You may write for a free catalog.

In Europe, Schiffer books are distributed by
Bushwood Books
6 Marksbury Ave.
Kew Gardens
Surrey TW9 4JF England
Phone: 44 (0) 20 8392 8585; Fax: 44 (0) 20 8392 9876
E-mail: info@bushwoodbooks.co.uk
Website: www.bushwoodbooks.co.uk

Designed by Mark David Bowyer
Type set in AmplitudeComp-Bold / NewBaskerville BT

ISBN: 978-0-7643-3973-8
Printed in China

Contents

Acknowledgments

T his is a book about the important subject of water. I have tried to write an analysis that would not trip the reader over countless scientific studies, water polemics, and foundation and government reports. If I have succeeded, it is because I have benefited from the help and support of people truly concerned about the fate of our global waters.

Several years ago I had the good fortune to work with Dr. Jeffrey Stine of the Smithsonian Institution while I was a Senior Fellow in the Museum of American History. Jeffrey Stine was an excellent mentor and colleague. His insights, knowledge of the field of environmental history, and good humor continue to influence my work.

Along the way I have received help, information, and assistance from a number of people. At the Interstate Commission for the Potomac River Basin (ICPRB), I received perceptive support from Heidi Moltz, Cherie Schultz, Jim Cummins, and Curtis Dalpra. The ICPRB has constructed useful water flow computer models for understanding river systems like the Potomac.

During the writing and research of my recent book *Anacostia: The Death and Birth of an American River*, I was greatly aided by the insights of friends at the Anacostia Watershed Society. Since that time, Jim Foster, Robert Boone, and Jim Connolly have demonstrated on many occasions the multiple uses of litigation and publicity to protect our waters.

Keith Walker, a scientist at the University of Adelaide, Australia, made the complexities of the drought-stricken Murray River Valley comprehensible to me while Daniel Sarewitz of the Consortium for Science Policy and Outcomes at Arizona State University offered insights on how scientists think about water issues, climate change, and the general environment.

My son, Matthew Wennersten, and his wife, Dr. Malathi Velamuri, scrutinized critical portions of this manuscript and offered invaluable comments, especially on India. During a six-week stay in India, I had ample opportunity to chat with Malathi's father, Dr. V. Raghavendra Rao, a perceptive geologist who spent many years in Nigeria. Dr. Rao's perspectives on water and oil were as masterful as his bridge game.

My eldest son, Stewart, is a career officer in the United States Navy and has spent the greater part of his career at sea. Stewart continues to help shape my views on the power of the ocean and the redemptive capacity of water.

Ann Womeldorf gave the manuscript a critical reading. Her deft commentary helped me to write a better book.

Lastly, my wife, Ruth Ellen, has endured yet another book, replete with my mental absences. Ruth Ellen continues to remind me what I really should be about. I am forever in her debt.

"It takes 53 gallons of water to produce one glass of milk. It takes 64 gallons of water to produce an 8-ounce steak."

-- Peter Rogers, author, *Running Out of Water*

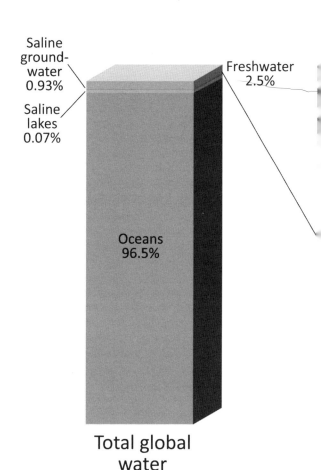

Saline ground-water 0.93%

Saline lakes 0.07%

Freshwater 2.5%

Oceans 96.5%

Total global water

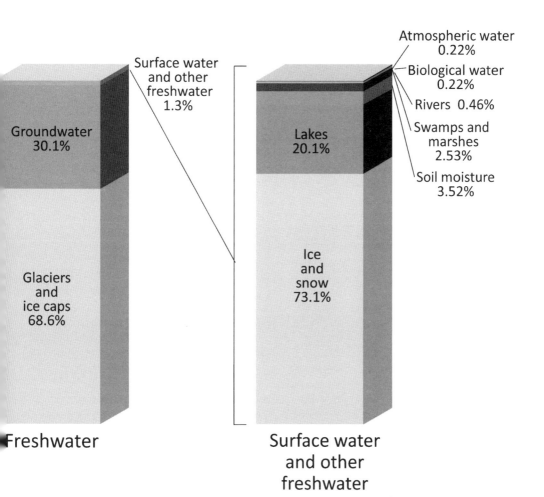

Atmospheric water
0.22%

Biological water
0.22%

Rivers 0.46%

Swamps and
marshes
2.53%

Soil moisture
3.52%

Surface water
and other
freshwater
1.3%

Groundwater
30.1%

Glaciers
and
ice caps
68.6%

Lakes
20.1%

Ice
and
snow
73.1%

Freshwater

Surface water
and other
freshwater

Courtesy of the United States Geological Survey.

Introduction
The Cruel Arithmetic of Water

W ater shapes the world's many different societies, a factor that is just beginning to be realized by social scientists and the general public. As scholars like Norwegian Professor Terje Tvedt have pointed out, water is a unique natural resource for two reasons: it is absolutely essential for all societies because we cannot live without it and it is always the same. Says Tvedt: "Whatever you do with water on the surface of the earth, it reemerges. You can destroy rivers and lakes, but you cannot destroy water itself."

Water is vital to all life on earth, yet it is such a commonplace substance. Colorless, odorless, and calorie free, water is central to everything from microbes to plants, animals, and humans. The composition of water seems simple: two atoms of hydrogen and one atom of oxygen. It is the most investigated of chemicals, though the least understood. By the standards of chemistry, H_2O could be a gas and not water. Either as a flowing liquid or as a flowing ice sheet, water sculpts the earth's surface over time and shapes the parameters of human existence. The quotidian work of water over the centuries, however, is not the stuff of the popular media. We take water for granted. In our daily lives, we expect that when we turn on the tap in our homes or businesses the water will flow. We fill our baths and hot tubs with the expectation that we can discard the wasted water when we are finished. That there will always be water is an idea strongly rooted in our subconscious. It is the major selfish conceit of the affluent West.

According to the World Commission on Water for the twenty-first century, half the world's population is living in unsanitary conditions without access to clean water. One billion of them have no access to safe water at all. Brian Appleton, a water expert for the United Nations, says that 5,000 children die every day needlessly from waterborne illnesses. "That's the equivalent of twelve full jumbo jets crashing every day," he argues. With urbanization and industrialization, the quality of rivers, lakes, and aquifers is deteriorating seriously — a development intensified in major proportions in the world since 1970. Further, the growth in population, increasing consumption, infrastructure development, and poor land use accelerate the problem. We need to think of the world's water supply as a giant glass and each demand for water as a straw in that glass. Today there are seven billion straws. At a minimum, the average inhabitant of the planet needs at least five gallons of water a day for drinking, cooking, and personal use. The weight of five gallons of water is about forty pounds. Thus, much of the labor of the planet is consumed in the drawing, lugging, and transport of water, in many cases by hand. We in America would be easily overcome by the myriad tasks of getting water the way they do in poorer societies of the world.

Awareness of water as an ecological concept is fairly recent, dating for the most part from the mid-twentieth century. The growing desertification of the planet and the disappearance of wetlands of the world have helped to give us a stronger environmental focus. Nothing concentrates the world's mentality on water like the prospect of global thirst.

It is only now in the first part of the twenty-first century that we are beginning to realize that water is the key component of climate change. Altered atmospheric circulation patterns and expanding arid land mass, as well as changes in patterns of rainfall and river flows, are beginning to place limits on public access to water — with the poorest countries becoming increasingly hostage to water problems, wide-scale poverty, and disease.

Water Cycles and Water Footprints

Drinking water is the preoccupation of all societies attempting to evolve and grow. Access to water reveals much about people, and managing water in today's crowded world constitutes one of the foremost public challenges to world governments. Water is the bloodstream of the biosphere; and the water cycle is much better understood than the origins of water itself.

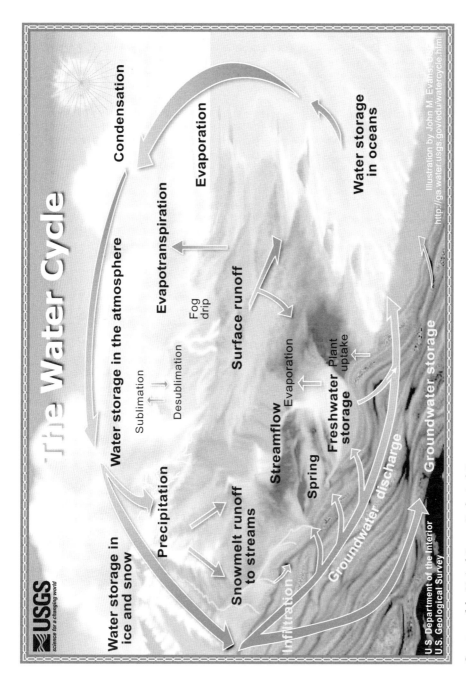

Courtesy of the United States Geological Survey.

Basically the water cycle consists of three elements: the seas; the clouds responsible for transference, condensation, and precipitation; and continental surface water (springs, rivers, and lakes) that run into the sea eventually. The water cycle of the planet is a closed system — we always have the same amount of water — but it is the quality and geographic distribution of that water across earth that becomes the problem. Most water supplies come from surface runoff through rain and, increasingly, this water is becoming impaired through pollution and/or industrial use. Trapped fossil water comes into the cycle only through human technological efforts. Until recently, it has been a bit player in the water story. All of us today, like it or not, live at the mercy of the water cycle and, increasingly, the human species finds itself confronting a new conflicted dependence on water cycles that have become less and less reliable.

Scientists currently are asking global political leaders and policy makers to think of their water resources in terms of a "water footprint" concept. A water footprint is the volume of freshwater required to produce a given product, measured at the place where the product is actually made. The water footprint, therefore, shows the extent of water use in relation to the consumption of people. For example, scientists calculate that it takes 960 liters of water to produce a glass of wine and 16,000 liters of water to produce a single hamburger. A cup of coffee to go with that hamburger requires an additional 1,120 liters of water. Of course this calculation includes the amount of water with the cow and coffee plants included.

In the United States, notes water expert Peter Rogers, we use about one hundred gallons a day for household functions like drinking, bathing, and sanitation. Yet, Rogers points out, that this is just "a small fraction of our water footprint." Currently our water footprint is calculated to be about 1,800 gallons per person per day, which, says Rogers, is "1.5 times the figure for the developed world and twice the world average."

When you calculate the vast amount of water consumed by food plants such as sugar (1,500 liters to produce one liter of product), you begin to have some idea as to the water content of things and their ecological cost. For some time, water experts have argued about the Earth's carrying capacity to support ever-larger populations. Would there be enough food on the planet to support a population of 8 to 10 billion people? It now appears that water is the key factor in limiting the Earth's food productivity. It is a commonplace fact today that water is facing heavy and unsustainable demands from users of all kinds. Farmers increasingly have to compete for water with urban residents and industry. The water footprint of nations will become a valuable tool in the future for international water management.

Meanwhile, in developing nations, water issues intensify everyday between the rich residents of overcrowded cities and their poorest neighbors. The World Water Forum, at its third triennial meeting in 2009 in Istanbul, Turkey, offered a grim assessment in its "Water In a Changing World" report. Despite promises of world leaders to follow the UN's lead in protecting and conserving water resources, it is still "business as usual" for the 5 billion, or two-thirds, people on the planet who do not have access to safe drinking water, adequate sanitation, or enough food to eat. Each year, the World Water Forum reports, the world is increasing by 80 million people who will add to the stress of our water resources.

People today have difficulty reacting to facts that contradict their worldview. In a series of recent studies at the University of Michigan, researchers found that when misinformed people were exposed to corrected facts in news stories, they rarely changed their minds. Facts, they found, rarely cured misinformation; facts actually made misinformation even stronger. Such is the case with the subject of water crises and catastrophes. Open any newspaper and you will find that climate change and the water crisis have millions of deniers. Few believe that there will come a time when the life of the planet, as we know it, will be riddled with catastrophic burn spots caused by droughts or overwhelmed by floods.

The exclusion of natural forces like water from society's historical understanding is not a benign academic problem, notes Terje Tvedt. Most modernization theories, posited by social scientists since World War Two, have tended to disregard the critical role of water in the process of social change. The modernization theory argues the notion, incorrectly, that all societies could develop in the same way if they had the same economic instruments. This disregards nature as a force or process of social change, Tvedt argues.

Looking at water through the critical lens of the twenty-first century, we see that our rivers are drying up. This is a matter of grave concern, as poignantly documented by British science writer Fred Pearce. Some of the world's largest rivers, including the Yellow, the Niger, and the Colorado, are drying up as a result of climate change, with potentially disastrous consequences for many of the world's most populous regions and cities of the world. The Rio Grande is drying up before it reaches the Gulf of Mexico; the Nile has been dammed to a modest flow; and reservoirs behind countless dams sacrifice millions of gallons of water to evaporation. Wetlands and floodplains down river dry up as water flow dwindles. In many parts of India, farmers, desperate for irrigation water, plunder their aquifers faster than rainfall can replace the withdrawn water. Scientists also predict that those rivers that have seen stable or increased flows, such as the Brahmaputra in South Asia and the Yangtze in China, could wither as inland glaciers melt and rainfall patterns change.

"Reduced runoff is increasing the pressure on freshwater resources in much of the world, especially with more demand for water as populations increase," says Aiguo Dai, a prominent water scientist. "Freshwater being a vital resource, the downward trends are a great concern." Regions facing the greatest threat include those dependent on the Niger in West Africa, the Ganges in South Asia, and the Yellow River in China. Further, large areas of the western United States could be impacted by the reduced flow of the Colorado River. In Australia, public authorities warn that parts of the Murray River are running so low that Adelaide could run out of water within two years. Today, more than a billion people lack access to clean drinking water and millions die annually from unhealthy water conditions. According to United Nations reports, two-thirds of the global population will suffer at least intermittent water shortages by the year 2025.

Oil may have been the defining resource of the twentieth century, but we are in a new century now and many consider it to be the "Century of Water." There are forecasts that within the next generation, water will, in certain critical but arid parts of the world, cost as much per barrel as oil. Water is in crisis in China, Southeast Asia, Southwest America, and North Africa — indeed, in much of Africa except the Congo, Niger, and Zambezi basins. Even in Europe there are shortages.

Drought is no longer a word alien to England, where water tables began dropping throughout the early 1990s. British colleagues write at how surprised they are to see the growing proliferation of irrigation companies in rural areas of their formerly well-rained country. Recently Thames Water, England's giant water utility, switched-on Britain's first desalination plant, which can pump up to 150 million gallons of water a day. The plant removes brackish water from the Thames and turns it into conventional water, a process more identified with water-starved nations in the Middle East than with England, the country that gave us the grass lawn.

In many parts of Europe, downstream towns and cities are beginning to feel the consequences of the careless alteration in age-old hydrological ecosystems as rivers suddenly rage out of control, wetlands dry up, and contaminants enter the groundwater. Yes, even in Europe there is a crisis in water supply and management, as groundwater tables sink and rivers are reduced to a trickle or increase to a destructive flood. Today's environmental news carries story after story of melting glaciers, dry streams, and unanticipated flooding. In Alpine, France, in the shadow of Mont Blanc, the town of Saint-Gervais is busily boring a large hole in the Tete Rousse glacier to relieve pressure on a large water pocket that threatens to send a wall of water, mud, and ice down on the chalets of Saint-Gervais.

Everywhere you look there are signs that the global water supply is in peril. Already Jordan, Israel, the West Bank, Gaza, Cyprus, Malta, and the Arabian Peninsula are at the point where all surface and ground freshwater resources are fully used. Morocco, Algeria, Tunisia, and Egypt will be in the same position within a decade. Here is something to consider: Very few major water systems are contained within one political entity. Many transborder water systems are in places where the political situation is already fractious and where water resources are increasingly scarce.

Rather than taking the dramatic action necessary to protect precious water resources, governments around the world are retreating from their responsibilities. Instead of acting decisively, they are bending to the will of giant transnational corporations that are poised to profit from the shortage of water. *Fortune Magazine* reports that corporations are rushing to invest in the water business. Giant water, energy, food, and shipping companies have plans to buy water rights, privatize publicly-owned water systems, promote bottled water, and sell "bulk" water by transporting it from water rich areas to markets desperate for more water. At the same time, to ensure maximum profits, these companies are lobbying to weaken water quality standards and pushing for trade agreements that hand over national water resources to foreign corporations.

In the United States, where some regions are already suffering from serious water shortages, corporations from Vivendi to Nestle® prepare to make a profit on water. Some corporate interests even want to sell bulk water from the Great Lakes, the world's largest freshwater system. The Great Lakes, meanwhile, have suffered from pollution, lost two-thirds of their extensive wetlands, and experienced a catastrophic loss of biological diversity. Only three percent of the shorelines is suitable for swimming. Yet these issues rarely receive the consideration they deserve in the popular media. In the West, our lives and our histories continue to play out as if life-support systems were stable. They are not, but getting to that cognitive moment means surmounting a lot of environmental and political misinformation promulgated by affluent elites.

Given the rampant growth of the world's population and metropolitan sprawl, there is an urgency to all the considerations about water in the twenty-first century. Reports on water issues, water scarcity, and water conflict have become a major cottage industry that fuels international commissions, university studies, think tank reports, state government bureaus, and countless task forces. Leading the industry are water policy analysts like Sandra Postel of the Global Water Policy Project, Maude Barlow of the Council of Canadians, and Peter Gleick of the Pacific Institute. All three write forcefully and cogently on water issues. Their work operates on the premise that if we can understand the evolution of environmental and social processes then we can develop the proper kind of sustainable approach to assure people of clean drinkable water. *Global Thirst* seeks to add a sharper and somewhat more pessimistic angle of vision to much of the work that has already been done and offer the lay reader a comprehensive view of what our water future may look like in the very near term locally and globally.

Furthermore, I realize now that when it comes to the subject of water and the satisfaction of the planet's monumental thirst, calamities seem to be coming to our water resources that border on the biblical. We seem to be ill-prepared for disasters whether they are hurricanes, drought, or the poisoning of our aquifers — or a catastrophic rise in sea levels for that matter. We bemoan the disasters that befall our society as acts of nature, but we do not seem inclined to do much that is proactive to forestall them. Risk experts tell us that it is natural not to take action against events with low probability of occurring. Thus, the once-in-a-hundred years perfect storm of a hurricane does not motivate us to plan for the havoc that it will cause. We just can't seem to get upset about a collapse or catastrophe that is years down the road.

Such thinking is as old as Noah's Ark. Noah, you may recall, was a lonely planner against the deluge that was to come. Risk analysts deal so much in the world of probability in terms of what they tell the public that it is difficult for the average man on the street to have a sense of urgency about some future catastrophe. Also planning for a catastrophe that may not happen is expensive. It involves marshalling of resources and the disciplining of populations. Now the recent drought events in the United States have been eclipsed by periods of good rainfalls in many parts of the country.

This convinces people that the long planning view for catastrophe in the form of record droughts many be unnecessary. It is very hard for anyone to be rewarded for preventing a low probability disaster. Also, there are so many risks and disasters in our modern world that to plan for them all would invite global bankruptcy. When you factor disaster possibilities in terms of anticipated costs over long periods of time, is it really worthwhile to spend the money? Most of us have short-term views. We can hardly think five years down the road, let alone decades. We certainly don't like to contemplate problems in terms of alternative outcomes. It requires serious thinking and planning.

Practically every plan to deal with the problems of global thirst involves efforts to deal with the extractive profit motive, cultural values, and questions of national and regional political hegemony. Developed nations will pay for drought and other problems with their affluent GNPs. At most they will be inconvenienced. In other areas of the world, when major droughts occur, the rivers will dry up, the land will die, and hordes of environmental refugees will be unleashed on the better-watered world.

In Jamie Uys' best-known movie, *The Gods Must Be Crazy*, a Coca-Cola® "Coke" bottle fell out of the sky on to a Kalahari Desert landscape in Africa and startled a bushman. The bushman thought at first that the clear bottle was water, but it was too hard. When he took the bottle back to his fellow bushmen, the bottle created strife and it was decided that since the bottle had fallen out of the sky from the gods it had to be returned to them.

I have often thought about that Coke bottle and what it means, even though I can't remember much of the plot of the movie. Water does not fall out of the sky. Coca-Cola® does. Yet, in this instance, the container is empty. In his own wry way, Jamie Uys informs us that despite a world needing sustainability and peace, much of our global consumer economy is as worthless as an empty bottle in the desert.

At this writing we are about to get schooled in what experts at the World Bank call "the grim arithmetic of water." We will have to calculate how to deal with global water shortages in the face of a projected population of nine billion people by 2050. It will force us to face up to who and what we are as inhabitants of the planet. Water shortages are part of an equation of distribution, wealth, and power; and we cannot always make water available where it is needed.

Several years ago I gave a public lecture at St. Mary's College of Maryland on the future of America's largest estuary, the Chesapeake Bay, in which I was especially pessimistic. At the time the Chesapeake, because of the high rate of fecal and nitrogen pollution and widespread anoxia or dead zones devoid of oxygen, seemed to me destined to become the mid-Atlantic's largest sewage lagoon. During a question and answer session, Tom Wisner, the noted Chesapeake folksinger and poet, jumped up and gave me a stinging retort. "You sir," he said heatedly, "have done us a disservice. You give us no grounds for hope." Without hope, he asked, how could people ever expect to change the conditions in which they find themselves? As an environmental affairs writer, I do not believe in "hope" as a social remedy. Hope is not a strategy. My task as a writer is to inform people about the environment in which they live. Thus, my concern is the "what is" of life and by providing that kind of information, a writer makes conditions for justice possible.

At the moment, like many people, I am following the aftermath of the earthquake and tsunami that devastated Japan's coast at Fukushima and staying in contact with American and Japanese friends in Mito in Ibaraki prefecture and in Tokyo who have been greatly shaken and traumatized by the seismic upheaval. The Japanese prepared for disaster with stringent building codes and seawalls meant to hold back quake-generated tsunamis. Apparently they did not prepare enough. All calculations were made on the basis of a 7.5 seismic event. An earthquake of 9.0 magnitude that hit the Japanese coast in March 2011 caught Japanese scientists and disaster planners completely by surprise. Meanwhile, Japan and its people endure. Japan will ultimately rebuild its shattered communities. Some populations, for a variety of social and cultural reasons, will be sustainable in the face of water-borne catastrophe. Others may not.

At this moment in time, our lives are captive to huge sweeping waves of political upheaval, demographic growth, and climate change that are transforming history and challenging us in myriad ways. It is these challenges and events that are the stuff of this book.

"And lo, I am parched with thirst and I perish. Give me quickly the cold water flowing forth from the Lake of Memory."

-- Jane Harrison,

Prolegomena to the Study of Greek Religion

Chapter One

Cool Clear Water

Water is the fundament of life, central to all human, animal, and plant activities. Water grows the food that we eat and supports our modern economies. Water is the most abundant resource on the planet. About 1,460 trillion tons of water covers 71 percent of the Earth's surface, but little is suitable for human consumption: 97.5 percent of it is saltwater. This leaves only 2.5% as freshwater — and nearly 70 percent of this small amount of freshwater is frozen in the icecaps of Antarctica and Greenland or lies in deep underground aquifers not accessible to human use. This leaves us with about one percent of all freshwater on the Earth as suitable for human use. Water is more valuable than many of us realize; and statistics like these currently prompt hydrologists to refer to water in the twenty-first century as "blue gold." Today we have seven billion people living on planet earth and each individual needs 2-1/2 liters of water a day in order to survive. We drink 6,600 gallons of water in our lifetime and about five times our body weight in water each year.

Thirst

Mankind has thirsted for water. Today, with diminishing or impaired water resources, that thirst has become global in consequence. Thirst — it does not get more basic. It is as primal as survival instincts go. In our more affluent West, we tend to treat thirst as a minor nuisance — something to be alleviated after a game of tennis or golf or a long walk. When we thirst, we do not fear for our death. Yet we can survive only a matter of days without water. Thirst is a nagging reminder of that fact and, thus, plays a crucial role in keeping us alive. We experience intense thirst following a five percent loss of our body water. Our thirst becomes almost unbearable by the time we lose seven percent and circulatory failure may ensue. While we can do without food for periods that exceed a month, we can do without water only for a few days to a week in an optimum climate. In a desert or dry zone, lack of water might induce death in a matter of hours. Water keeps us alive and healthy. It provides the necessary elements that keep the body fluid and functioning.

The urge to drink water is an instinct regulated in the human body by a feedback loop between the brain and other organs in the body. Given the fact that 60 percent of our body is composed of water, continuous dehydration can cause myriad problems such as seizures and renal failure. Scientists have been studying the neurological mechanisms of thirst for decades. Early on they discovered that the brain's "thirst center" was the hypothalamus, a mechanism deep in the brain that regulates appetite, body temperature, and sleep. When water levels diminish in the blood flow, the hypothalamus sends out a strong message: Drink something and drink something now! Once, while driving on vacation across the hot arid Spanish plains towards Zaragosa, my wife and I were overcome with such a thirst that we stopped at the first irrigated garden that we came to and danced in the spray, cupping our hands greedily to take and drink much sought after water on a dry afternoon. Our thirsty response to water was joyous and irrational.

As a boy, I watched *Death Valley Days* on television and sat enthralled by the stories of the old ranger about life in one of the hottest and most waterless regions in North America. Everything in the Old West seemed dried and shriveled. Also during this time, pop singer Vaughn Monroe and a western group, Sons of the Pioneers, soared to fame with a simple song — "Cool Water." The lyrics were so compelling that I vividly remember them: "All day I face the barren waste without the taste of water. Cool Clear Water. Old Dan and I with throats burned dry and souls that cry for water, cool clear water."

Later, as I traveled the southwestern United States and entered Phoenix, Arizona, I was astonished at the sight of neighborhoods and golf courses full of luscious green grass. A desert had been wastefully watered for aesthetic and recreational purposes. I had begun to understand the value of "cool water," how it was being squandered and how we were creating a thirsty society. Our knowledge of water and thirst has come a long way from the *Death Valley Days*. We are now living at a time when the future of all world economies will depend upon how we interact with water.

What is Water?

Considering how nearly every school child has heard some mythic story about water and the creation of the universe, it is remarkable how little we know of either the scientific origin of water or why it plays a central role in human affairs. Speculations on the origin of water on Earth continue to lack the kind of clarity one would expect of such an important subject as water. Until recently it was thought that water's origin lay in water-rich comets or meteorites that may have crashed into the earth's atmosphere and brought oceanic water to a vast dry spherical rock. This theory is no longer subscribed to by most astrophysicists, nor is the idea that volcanic activity, coupled with the vast heating and drying of the planet over the eons of time, may have caused vast temperature shifts conducive to the creation of moisture along the earth's crust. The most credible theory is one of vapor from fiery silicate magma combining with an excessively heavy CO_2 atmosphere soon after the formation of the Earth to release water into the atmosphere. This happened over four billion years ago.

Only in moments of keen self-awareness do we think of ourselves as water creatures. At birth our body is about 78 percent water and declines with the aging process by 18 percent between the ages of 30 and 80. Our blood is composed of 90 percent water and even our "dry as a bone" skeletal system is 33 percent water. Our brain is 85 percent water; and it is relatively easy to think of the role that water in this complex neural system plays in determining our mental health. The term "living water" in its ability to support life from its surface down into its deepest depths is more than just religious insight of pious Christians. Water is a sublime force in human life with the power to create and destroy. We ignore it at our own peril as it can be a very stern teacher.[1]

Given the centrality of water to human existence, it is understandable that humankind has taken care not to wander far from our water sources. Civilization has carefully settled over the millennia next to seas and river basins, and supplemented these with canals and dams. What happens at the level of great waters often magnifies what is happening on the atmospheric level in the form of rains and storms. Unfortunately man often leaves his negative imprint on water — from pollution to sewage to municipal waste and even nuclear radiation. Ruined waters have resulted in the loss of 20 percent of freshwater species. Human water diversions in the twentieth century resulted in the loss of over 50 percent of the world's wetlands.

The Taste of Water

How does water taste? Most of us recall a time when we drank water from a clear mountain spring or sampled cool water drawn from a deep well. The water had a clean crisp taste to it, redolent of mineral traces. Other times we reveled in the sheer tastelessness of cool water once it has passed a quick eye test for clarity. Our taste buds give definition to the water we drink. Is it salty, bitter, sweet, or sour? Water is both taste and sensation.[2] Most experts agree that water should have taste. There should not be the absence of anything. Absence of taste is what makes drinking distilled water so boring — all the chemicals have been boiled out of it. Water should have a positive taste, notes Arthur von Wiesenberger, an international water consultant. Wiesenberger believes that water should have certain minerals present — potassium, magnesium, calcium, and even small amounts of sodium — to give water its fullness. Many of us have tasted mountain water with a too high concentration of minerals that makes the water take on a tinny metallic taste.

In the 1960s, Wiliam Bruvold, a scientist at the University of California, Berkeley, conducted a series of studies on the importance of minerals to the taste of drinking water. His studies confirmed that certain combinations of minerals in drinking water were preferred to others in terms of taste. He also argued that removing minerals from water might reduce its drinkability. Writing in *Public Health Reports* in April 1964, Bruvold and his colleagues argued that the approval of water's taste is also determined by culture. In the western United States, because of mining and other industries, a growing population grew accustomed to high-mineral waters that were slightly brackish. It was not the best water they could taste, but it was the only water they had. The one mineral that made people avoid a local water source in the arid West was the presence of sulphate in the water. People also look at water in terms of its attractiveness. Notes Bruvold: coolness, absence of turbidity, and absence of color and any disagreeable taste or smell is of the utmost importance in public supplies of drinking water.[3] Often people like the water they grew up with because they have imprinted that taste.

In these days of environmental deterioration, people take their water seriously. Every February, hundreds of people travel to Berkeley Springs, West Virginia, for the annual Berkeley Springs International Water Tasting competition for the best municipal water in the world contest. In February 2010, a dozen judges examined and tasted 125 waters from twenty-four states and ten foreign countries. Also, bottled water came literally from all over the globe, including that of Brazil and China, to compete for a gold medal of "highest quality." Arthur von Wiesenberger served as water master of the event, which some called "the longest running and largest water tasting in the world." The public was able to taste the waters as well. Hamilton, Ohio, won first place for best Municipal Water 2010 and Ecoviva Water of Roscommon, Missouri, won a gold medal for best-bottled water in the world. Ecoviva also won an award for best packaging with a water bottle that is 100 percent biodegradable. These medals carry weight and give water companies the kind of bragging rights that can make a national success story. According to conference organizer Jill Klein Rone, "We consider it the Olympics of Water. In an age of oil spills and water pollution on a massive national and international scale, there is only so much clean drinking water. We need to protect it." Towards that end, Rone has a small theater group, The Ripple Effect, that produces a water drama for adults and school children to "bring awareness to water."[4] While the competition is good for business in the Cacapon Mountains in winter, none can gainsay the contest's seriousness of purpose — to alert the public to the need for better quality in water supplies, both municipal and private.

At the conclusion of the day-long water tasting came the famed "water rush," when the audience was invited to take bottles of water home as souvenirs. A large elegant display of water bottles disappeared in a matter of minutes as people rushed to get their share of free bottled water as mementoes of their water tasting in Berkeley Springs, West Virginia. As the conference wrapped up, tourists could see trucks and cars parked at the mineral spring at the town park. Men and women loaded gallons of Berkeley Springs water into plastic jugs. This delicious spring has flowed undiminished since colonial times when George Washington first surveyed the town.

Water: Cultural and Spiritual

Water forms the basis for much of the world's cultural and religious thinking. Over the centuries water has been a spiritual force and a symbolic explication of universal truths. The allegory of creation begins with divine intelligence and a swirling mass of water. *Genesis 6* records God creating sky and land out of separated waters. "And God said, Let the waters under the heavens be gathered into one place, and let dry land appear." Water is fundamental to the language, symbolism, and creation stories of all religions. In fact, water over the ages has become the metaphor for man's livelihood and spiritual development. It is a symbol of life and a means of cleansing, as well as purification, of the human body.

Because the Bible was written in an arid part of the world, it is not surprising that the people of the Old Testament were preoccupied with water. The scarcity of water was very serious and prophets like Elijah and Jeremiah preached that drought was the wrath of God. Conversely rainfall was a sign of God's favor and goodness.

The Bible also mentions polluted waters. Chapter 7 of the *Book of Exodus* speaks of one of the plagues of Egypt as turning the waters of the Nile to blood and, when the Israelites left the Red Sea and came to the land of Marah, they found the water to be polluted and complained to Moses. Later God allowed Moses to perform a miracle that turned the waters of Marah sweet. Since that time the troubled lands of the Middle East have been praying for additional miracles of sweet water in the desert wastes.

Thirst is so fundamental a Biblical problem that the Israelites called upon God numerous times to address it. In the *Book of Isaiah*, the prophet writes: "When the poor and needy seek water, and there is none, and their tongue faileth for thirst, I the LORD will hear them … I will make the wilderness a pool of water, and the dry land springs of water." Thus in the Old Testament water becomes a symbol of spiritual refreshment. It is hardly surprising that in the arid vastness Jeremiah describes God as "the fountain of living waters."

Turning to the New Testament, we find that water is closely connected with the gift of eternal life. In Chapter 4 of the *Book of John* there is this statement: "But whosoever drinketh of the water that I shall give him shall never thirst, but the water that I shall give him shall be in him a well of water springing up into everlasting life."

Finally, for both Hebrews and Christians, water is associated with baptismal cleansing for the forgiveness of sins. Orthodox Jews regularly go to a mikvah for immersion in water and purification in Judaism. The baptismal font is the keystone of Christian churches. Holy water is water blessed for use in certain rites, including baptism, blessings, dedications, exorcisms, and burials.

In Islam, water is important for cleansing and purifying. Mosques generally have pools of clear water for Moslems to wash themselves and become ritually pure before approaching God in prayer. Water in Hinduism has a special place because it is believed to have spiritual cleansing powers. To Hindus all water is sacred, especially rivers. There are seven sacred rivers in India: Ganges, Yamuna, Godavari, Narmada, Sindhu, Kaveri, and Saraswati. The Hindu story of water contains like others the destruction of creation by a great deluge. One man, Vaivasvata Manu, is rescued from drowning by a fish that had previously ordered him to build a large boat. The fish then towed the boat to safety by anchoring it in the highest of the Himalayas. Only Manu and his boat survived as the deluge swept away all living creatures.

Rivers appear frequently in the world's sacred traditions as symbols of divine influence and life's interdependence. They evoke an image of spiritual-intellectual energies cascading through the manifold planes of cosmic and individual life — linking us intimately with our spiritual source, nourishing and sustaining us, and flowing forth to connect us with all things. The symbol of the Great Life is "living water," which the Mandaeans call yardna (Jordan); one of their central rites is immersion in flowing water, i.e., natural rivers or man-made canals. Using enclosed or still water for this purpose is not permitted, for such water is considered to be stagnant or dead. The ancients realized that the rivers of life were not simply outflowing or downhill. All rivers must eventually return to their source. In the earth's ecosystem, most rivers empty into oceans and lakes, whose waters are drawn up by solar heating into the atmosphere, where clouds form to shed moisture again upon the earth, thereby completing the life-sustaining cycle.

Water plays such a key role in the New Testament of the Bible that it is difficult to understand any of the major events in the life of Christ without it. Water is the baptismal force that anoints all new souls in the faith. John the Baptist baptizes Christ. The Christian spiritual idea of water transmits a series of religious and cultural messages. Water symbolizes destruction, death, and burial, purification healing, redemption and regeneration.[5] In the *Book of John*, Jesus turns water into wine at Cana, saying that water leads to a spiritual transformation, and in his ministry Jesus often spoke of giving man living water, which is the source of eternal life (*John* 2:1-11 and 4:10-14).

One of the most interesting theological speculations deals with the words of Jesus on the cross: "I thirst." While religious divines interpret those two words as a longing to be caught up in God's majestic force, scholars can also speculate that on the cross Jesus succumbed to one of life's most elemental forces. Roman soldiers gave him a taste of water mixed with sour wine, a kind of Gatorade at the time, for him to slake his thirst before death. New York forensic pathologist Frederick Zugibe argues that throughout his final ordeal leading up to his crucifixion at Mt. Calvary, Jesus suffered from extreme dehydration caused by Jerusalem authorities and Roman soldiers.[6]

Water and Myth

Water plays an important role in many legends and myths. There are many mythological water beings and gods, stories of heroes that have something to do with water, and even stories of continents lost below the swirling oceans. According to one Egyptian myth, a chaos of churning water called Nu rose up and in its turbulence created the first sunrise and the Nile River. Thus in myth does the creation — the earth and its fullness thereof — begin with water in stories that transcend the boundaries of time, geography, and ethnicity. According to Iroquois legend, gigantic water animals came into the swirling floods, diving down into the vast depths to bring mud to the surface, which they used to create a continent that would be eventually called North America.

Indian mythology contains tales of Lemuria, a hypothetical lost continent located in the Indian Ocean, which supposedly had records of the origin of the human species. A popular German spiritualist named Helen Blavatsky, who was one of the founders of the Theosophist movement, claimed in the 1880s to have seen an ancient text, "The Book of Dzyan," that recorded the existence of this lost continent.[7]

In Cameroon, they tell stories of Jengu, water spirits who were mermaid-like with long woolly hair and acted as water intermediaries between the living and the spiritual world. These Jengu could cure disease of the sick who were immersed in their waters — an ancient form, perhaps, of pagan baptism. Meanwhile, the Greeks wrote of the Nereids, nymphs of the sea who always helped sailors during rough storms.

The waters of the earth also had their dangerous side. In Biblical mythology, the waters of creation held the Leviathan, an evil sea creature associated with Satan and all the forces of chaos in the creation. In Hebrew, Leviathan simply means whale. However, in modern literature, Herman Melville's *Moby Dick* conjured up again the evil nature inherent both in the whale and man's pursuit of it. Further, the most vicious of the water spirits was the Uncegilla, the mighty water snake of Native American (Lakota) mythology. She polluted rivers and subsequently flooded the land with saltwater so nothing could grow. Perhaps this was a mythological foretaste of the problems of irrigation practices in dry lands.

Water Speculations

In every culture water forms the basis of human speculation on the beginnings of earth and how the lands and seas took shape. Water is synonymous with life: fertility, birth, and growth. Philosophers from Socrates onward have seen water as the great unifier and connecting force in humanity. From water comes our survival, our health, and our prosperity; and from the beginning of time humans have used water for many purposes, including drinking, irrigation, fisheries, industrial processes, transport, and waste removal. Water is also the essential part of the geologic cycle for the creation of soil out of storm sediments for the building of new lands and continents.

All great civilizations have been either water-based or water-oriented. Thus it is surprising how little attention water receives in history books. As early as five hundred years before the birth of Christ, the Chinese were measuring rainfall and, by the fourteenth century, had elaborate systems of measurement to predict the onset of floods on the Yellow River. Similarly Egypt's educated classes measured the Nile's water with instruments that came to be called "nilometers."

However, it was not until the seventeenth century that Europeans began to understand the balance between water evaporation and the levels of oceans and rivers. The first book on the subject of hydrology in Europe at this time was *On the Origin of Springs* in 1674 in which Pierre Perrault advanced the notion of balance in the water cycle. By showing that precipitation was sufficient to sustain the flow of rivers, Perrault used his new "science of hydrology" to refute ancient Aristotelian theories that held that the flow of springs and rivers resulted from either underground discharges or return flow from seawater.

In the nineteenth century, noted evolutionist Charles Darwin posited that the first form of life was ocean-born and that human life emerged slowly from the planet's waters to evolve from other forms into its current shape. Such a theory shocked polite Victorian society on both sides of the Atlantic because it contradicted the idea that God in a providentially centered universe created man whole.

Thanks to the hydrologic cycle, we drink and bathe in the same water that rained once on the dinosaurs. By this I mean that water is constantly being recycled and evaporated on the planet. The Earth has more than enough water for personal use, agriculture, and industry. The problem with water rests in its distribution. While the hydrologic cycle guarantees the same amount of water for the planet, it does not always place water in the same area. Nor does it guarantee that water will not be used, polluted, or diverted. Communities draw water from surface waters like rivers, lakes, and reservoirs. These replenish over time. Groundwater or aquifers are more problematic. Fossil water is water that has been underground, trapped over the millennia. It can be drawn down, but not replaced. Other aquifers can be replenished, but it is a long process. In most areas of the world, it is groundwater that poses the problem because it is like drawing down a bank account that cannot be refurbished. When the water is gone from the aquifer, it is gone. Thus, in the saga of the hydrological cycle, there is always water. Yet it is often gone from where it is most needed — in the dry or desert areas of the world.

Water Karma

For Professor Ruth Levy Geyer, a bioethicist teaching at Haverford College, water is an intoxicating subject. "I can stare endlessly at the sea and not get bored, and I can swim for hours in a placid lake and not get winded," she says. Professor Geyer has been under water's spell since her childhood when she learned her body was over 60 percent water that transported life throughout her system. The fact that she was drinking the same rainwater that fell from the sky that George Washington or the ancient Biblical hero Noah drank left her emotionally charged. Says Professor Geyer: "We spend our first nine months afloat, so it is not surprising that some of us remain amphibious throughout life. And suppose the relation is reciprocal. Suppose water feels an affinity for us?"[8]

This idea is one of the major insights of Dr. Emoto Masaru, a Japanese scientist and author of books on the relationship between science and the spirituality of water. Trained in Magnetic Resonance Analysis, Masuru has devoted his life to understanding the mystery of water. In his experiments with water crystals, Masuru exposes water to different words, pictures, or music and then he freezes the water and examines the aesthetics of the resulting crystals with microscopic photography. Masuru claims that the crystalline shape of water from a pure or contented source will be beautifully shaped when frozen. Polluted water crystals will show definite distortions. At present Masuru has little credibility with scientists who claim that his experiments cannot be replicated in double blind studies. That does not prevent Masuru, however, from having a large following. His book, *The Hidden Messages In Water*, has wide currency among the water conscious global readership.[9]

For those heavily into "the karma of water," this substance in its primal form is a mirror to human consciousness that can be whatever a dreamer perceives. While I find such thinking to be a bit goofy, I nonetheless prefer to let these ideas speak for themselves in periodicals like *The Spirit of Ma'at*.[10] These water theorists may be on to something when they claim water has a cleansing power and that our rivers can heal themselves if we cease polluting them. According to *The Spirit of Ma'at*, "there are movements that water can make to energize it to a point of consciousness. And there are some that de-activate the water, leaving it just a molecule without life." Using Emoto Masuru's theory, I would have to approach a vessel of bottled water with karmic apprehension. Bottled water (and I will have more to say on this subject later in Chapter Six) in many instances has been found to contain fecal coliforms, estrogenic materials, and a mix of chemicals from plastic bottles themselves far above what state authorities permit in tap water.

Water and Health

In recent times our notion of "health" has taken on a broader definition that goes beyond medicine and health care into the expanses of exercise, diet, and water replenishment. We now are aware of the importance of water in allowing the organs of our body to fulfill their responsibilities with the help of nutrients arriving within blood, lymph, and other secretions. Few of us drink as much water as we should. The prospect of drinking six full eight-ounce glasses of water each day is a daunting one.

According to the Mayo Clinic, no single water consumption formula fits everyone. Water is your body's principal chemical component and it is wise to think about the water that you drink. The best tactic is what the Mayo Clinic refers to as the "replacement approach." The average urine output for adults is about 1.5 liters or 6.3 cups a day. You lose an additional liter through sweating and various kinds of exercise. So if you drink two liters of water a day along with a normal diet, you will replace your lost fluids.

There are a lot of "health gurus" that claim populations in developed countries are walking around dehydrated and unhealthy. Yet most of us get enough water from our food and beverages. If you go to the bathroom fewer than four times a day, you are probably drinking too little water. If you run to the bathroom so much that it seems you cannot get any work done, you may be drinking too much water. In sports, overconsumption of water leads to depletion of sodium in the blood and "water intoxication" that can cause either fainting spells or death. Once a rare occurrence at sporting events, it is becoming more prevalent as participation increases and more individuals are entering stressful endurance events.

Falling Waters

A number of years ago, my wife and I were hosts to a group of visiting Japanese women whom we had come to know when we worked at a Japanese university in Ibaraki Prefecture near Tokyo. In addition to wanting to see the normal tourist sites of Washington and New York City, the Japanese women surprised us with their strong desire to visit Niagara Falls. As they had been very good to us during our stay in Japan, we decided to rent a van and take them to this famous landmark, once the honeymoon destination of many Americans. At the falls we boarded a tour boat to see, first-hand, the power of water rushing over Niagara. Our boat ride near the falls resulted in a good soaking as the flimsy plastic rain capes the tour guide gave us did little to protect us. Fortunately it was a hot summer day and we dried off quickly. The Japanese ladies said that they believed water has the power to refresh and engender spiritual growth. When we lived in Japan, we regularly went to Fukuroda Falls. Located in the town of Daigo, Fukuroda Falls is rated as one of the country's three most popular and beautiful waterfalls. Fukuroda's visitors stood transfixed as they watched the power of falling water. Thus our experience at Niagara Falls gave me an opportunity to think about water as I waited for the Japanese ladies to complete a post-Niagara shopping expedition for souvenirs. Niagara Falls prompted me to wonder why such an important landmark had degenerated into such a tourist town. Everything about the town of Niagara Falls, New York, had a run-down feel to it as if the city had seen better days and was now easing into decrepitude. Certainly the honeymooners have long ceased coming, and the view of the majesty of Niagara Falls is far better from the Canadian side.

Most of us prefer water as an amusement rather than a mystical experience. Each year water parks all over the world attract millions who wish to ride rollercoasters that will crash through water or ride a zip wire that allows them to drop into a deep swimming pool. Some, like those in England, operate under enclosure and are year-round pleasure spas. Others like Ocean Park in Hong Kong are so famous for their aquatic amusements and pleasures that they become a global tourist destination in itself.

There are times, however, when thoughts of water give me a certain sinking feeling. Years back, during a canoe trip on the lakes of the Adirondacks, my sons persuaded me to join them in a jump off a twenty-foot cliff into a deep pool of a mountain lake. I had to prove myself to my sons and their friends as they had already made the jump and were egging me on. Bracing myself with a final dosage of courage, I stepped off into the air and it seemed an endless time before my body sliced through the water. The water in this pool was nearly forty feet deep and, in my affrighted state, it seemed to take forever before I rose though curtains of soft bubbles to reach the surface and the applause of the raucous teenagers. For me, it was indeed a unique sub-aqua experience that I care not to repeat.

Experiencing Water

In what ways do we personally experience water? Of course we drink it in its common form in beverages like coffee, tea, wine, soda, and beer. We drink millions of gallons of bottled water as well and litter the countryside with plastic water containers. We wash ourselves in it in a variety of ways for cleansing and physical relaxation. Most of us can recall those various times when we experienced the pure sensual lingering delight of a shower or bath. One water aesthete, Merle Flannery, writes that water allows her to concentrate on sensual harmony as shower water flows over her naked body. She describes her experience with water and its outcome in an evocative manner that reveals a different dimension of the spiritual side of a shower: "The feeling of being moved by the water becomes more and more intense until the skin of my body bursts: I am soaring weightless and breathless with the water and in the water as I dip and sway. The water shatters me completely. My body is an exultant, joyous, and boundless flow of energy."[11]

While most of us may not quite have Flannery's exultation in the shower, the experience of water and washing is pleasant most of the time. Water sports in the summer have remained attractive certainly since the Romans took themselves off to seaside mansions in antiquity, and when we think of our experiences at the ocean in the summertime we remember laughter and the feeling that swimming allows us to be in a profoundly different world.

Water has seductive powers. I recall the joyous pleasure of floating suspended in the Jefferson "Pool of Mineral Water" at The Homestead in the Virginia Blue Ridge Mountains where President Jefferson once bathed. As I floated in the water I enjoyed the primordial feeling of womb-like buoyancy and security. It is sometimes said by lifeguards that the person who learns how to float gives herself over to trusting water and trusting life itself. Sometimes we can have too much water. Movie buffs recall the famous choreographer Gene Kelly splashing and dancing in the iconic 1952 Hollywood musical film, *Singing in the Rain*. The set for the movie required so much dancing in water that Gene Kelly contracted a serious cold and fever.

Water can be fearsome as well. Think of crashing waves and Pacific riptides on the beaches of Puerto Vallarta, Mexico, or the menacing, engulfing tsunamis devastating Japan's and Thailand's shores. An almost instinctual fear of drowning is always in the back of our minds when we enter water. Recently we have been conditioned to the horror of water with the nightmare of huge tidal surges crashing down upon the city of New Orleans and drowning its inhabitants in 2005 during Hurricane Katrina. Water works out its own destiny for man.

Our fundamental problem with water is that we never view nature directly, but through a particular "mind set" or cultural paradigm. This behavior blocks out some portions of the environment while bringing others sharply into focus. Unfortunately the focus on water that we see today, primarily in the dominant cultures, is on water as an economic object — a commodity to be bought, sold, and traded just like cotton, soy beans, or oil. We don't see the pastoral, restorative, spiritual, or healing variant of water. That the simple flow of water in a stream could have a tender beauty was well known to nineteenth century landscape artists, but not to us in the West. Here we have a proclivity towards burying our streams in pipes and culverts. Surprisingly, in the United States, "watershed" (the land area that drains a specific body of water) is a relatively new word in common environmental parlance. Additionally, we must take note that there is a certain overture of hustle to the subject of water. Thus, when we think of water, we ask: Who gets it? When do they get it? How much do they get? Whatever lofty sentiments we may have about water, we are forced to realize that these questions matter a great deal in contemporary society.

Today we deal with problems of "consumptive water," that is not returned to streams after use. Even though we know that water will be a critical limiting resource for many regions of the world in the near future, we are dealing with the idea of water as a buyable commodity. Against this paradigm, concern for humanistic or moral consideration is but the small change of legal argument. Changing thought processes that are part of an organized philosophical system is difficult. Some social analysts argue that we, at least in the West, are at the beginning of a new environmental ethic where nature has as much "right" as human society. We shall see how that plays out.

For years in the developed countries, not much thought was given to the subject of water. Until recently, newspapers and media accounts of the environment were devoid of any critical account of water problems and thirsty nations. Thus water and human consciousness have suffered from a cultural disconnect that only now is finding a remedy. In an age of diminishing waters, we find that we all live downstream — and we all gather at the common well of survival.

Water Technology

History is waterlogged. Both scientists and anthropologists acknowledge that few of our water technologies are modern creations. They have been with us over the millennia. From earliest times human societies have faced the challenges of supplying themselves with adequate water supplies. In antiquity, society gathered and used water employing three principal techniques: irrigation, drainage, and impoundment (dams), but it has only been since 1900 that dams have become a worldwide phenomenon. The only areas of new developments in the modern era have been in water treatment and waste disposal.

Egyptian paintings from fifteenth century B.C. depict sophisticated water filtration devices to remove sediment from the Nile for public drinking. We often overlook the fact that the Egyptians were the first people to record their technology for treating water, which, in the ancient pictographs, was important both in this life as well as in eternity. For the ensuing centuries pure or clear drinking water was often regarded as unimportant. It was not until 1804 that John Gibb, a Scottish businessman, built a water facility to supply his town of Paisley. Shortly thereafter Gibb pumped drinking water to customers in Glasgow.

In 1806, a water treatment plant in Paris began pumping drinking water that was filtered through sand and charcoal by use of horse-powered pumps. In the nineteenth century, the water visions of the Egyptians of antiquity were at last on their way to becoming common currency in the West.

Irrigation as a water technique in farming dates back to 5000 B.C. and became extensive mostly in Mesopotamia, the Indus Valley of Pakistan, the Nile Valley of Egypt, Morocco, and Iran. Ancient farmers developed ingenious methods of irrigation using groundwater and the collection of surface runoff. They also had a sophisticated well technology for their own domestic uses. Indians of the American Southwest practiced irrigation and had flourishing communities in what is today New Mexico. Chinese civilization was located principally in the Yellow and Yangtze River basins. Aztecs in the central valley of Mexico practiced a system of agriculture known as Chinampa or "reed basket" irrigation. This process consisted of the construction of numerous canals and high spots in lakes and swamps planted with willow trees to control erosion. Long fingers of dry land alternated with canals, which was perhaps one of the earliest examples of agricultural swamp reclamation. It was enormously successful and Chinampa sustained a very large population long before the coming of the Spanish conquistadors.

Irrigation, however, presented the same problem in antiquity that it presents today — soil and water salinity that ultimately results in ruined and abandoned fields. Salinity continues to haunt agriculture in arid areas today. Salinity refers to the presence of soluble salts in soil and water that can take the form of sodium chloride, calcium, magnesium, carbonate, bicarbonate, and sulphate. Salinity occurs as a problem for irrigation farmers when the concentration of soluble salts through evapotranspiration is high enough in the soil to impede plant growth. Salinity exacts many economic and environmental costs. These include damage in farm productivity, decline in water supplies for drinking and industrial use, as well as damage to biodiversity and aquatic systems. While most soils have some degree of salinity, the problem is compounded through irrigation. Irrigation in sandy or "leaky" soils increases the amount of groundwater discharge as the water table rises. Evaporation and plant uptake remove water leaving the salt to accumulate in the soil.

The great civilizations of Mesopotamia were severely compromised by the problem of salinity. Poorly drained soils in arid areas during the Sumerian dynasties from 3100 to 1700 B.C. led to a build-up of salt in the soil that ruined agricultural productivity and led to a population decline of 60 percent, making the balance of power between the rival empires of Sumer and Akkad difficult to maintain. The Sumerians, more affected by salinity in their land than the Akkadians, gradually disappeared as a culture. Sumerian as a language survived only in pagan liturgy. Contaminated water in ancient Sumeria shows how easily a society could be destroyed by its water problems.[12]

Unlike the ancients who knew little of the chemistry of soil, modern irrigation farmers try to mitigate salinity by reducing groundwater rises. Today farmers avoid over-irrigation, monitor soil moisture, and use deep-rooted crops like alfalfa and other pasture crops to minimize drainage. In the Imperial Valley of California where irrigation crops constitute a billion dollar industry, farmers install expensive leaching pipes about six feet underground throughout their fields to collect and drain the salt washed or leached from the soil.

Hydraulic Vision: Canals and Technology

Given the centrality of water in the human experience, it is hardly surprising that water should be harnessed for industrial uses. The hydraulic vision of society dates back to the slave labor systems of the Pharaohs who used engineered watercourses to tap the wealth of the Nile. Egyptian canals date back to Pharaoh Pepi I Meryre (2332-2283 B.C.), who ordered a canal built to bypass the cataract on the Nile near Aswan. The oldest canals were irrigation ducts that date to 4000 B.C. in Mesopotamia in what is modern day Syria and Iraq. The Romans built aqueducts for the transport of water from mountains to distant cities that today are still considered the great marvels of civilization. In China, the emperors built the Grand Canal of China — some 1,115 miles long — to carry the Emperor Yang Guang between Beijing and Hangzhou. It was built out of original parts of a canal that dated to 486 BC. In China, canals became important connections for river transport and were important devices of political unification and economic development. Because of differences in elevation and natural obstacles, canal building became one of the first hydraulic sciences. Locks, boat lifts, and aqueducts allowed boats to be floated between two levels. In Britain and the United States, canals were important eighteenth and nineteenth century precursors to the Industrial Revolution. Canals facilitated transport and halved the price of coal in England in the eighteenth century for the new network of steam and water-powered textile mills.

In fact, between 1760 and 1820, a "canal mania" prevailed in Europe and North America. Hundreds of canals were built with either wage or slave labor in Britain and the United States. The sweat of Irish immigrants and African-Americans constructed many of the canals in the United States. By 1750 European society had reached the point where it had the capability to cut down forests, alter the earth, and transform Europe's natural cycles. This transformation was made possible by water, specifically a vast network of canals that transformed Europe and spurred the agricultural and industrial development of the eastern United States. Canals provided a variety of waterpower for mills. In Lowell, Massachusetts, for example, a canal system of 6.7 miles provided stream flows of over 10,000 horsepower to run the city's textile mills.

Canals also opened up the wilderness areas for settlement in North America and allowed countries, particularly France, Britain, and the United States, to ship goods by canal boat cheaply over long distances. In Europe, canals linked all of the continent's river systems — Rhine, Rhone, and Seine, and Saone with the North Sea. By this time there were plenty of political leaders, engineers, and visionaries who saw that the key to a region's economic development lay in the connection of rivers with a network of canals. Canals and rivers provided a good network across the country. All were fairly close to the sea and enabled goods to flow throughout the year. Also the rivers were not much given to silting. Elsewhere in the world, where rivers were either wild or uncontrollable, waterpower was not as easily used.

Professor Terje Tvedt of the University of Oslo argues that water played a fundamental role in the Industrial Revolution that is often overlooked by historians. According to Tvedt, the structure of the water system can adequately explain why the Industrial Revolution began in Britain. The early Industrial Revolution was stimulated by the power of water mills and bulk transport of goods by canals. Tvedt says that social structure is excessively relied upon to explain the Industrial Revolution. Water has to be taken into account both in the understanding of the Industrial Revolution as well as the evolution of human history. "Since World War II, the dominant theories relating to the international economic system have, without exception, disregarded the role of nature." Economic instruments alone cannot account for development.[13] Looking at areas with profound water scarcity we see areas of stunted modernization.

In our frenetic age of modernization and growth, canals are used in real estate developments to link homes with navigable waterways. Civilization yesterday and today flourishes around rivers and major waterways. Large metropolitan centers like Rotterdam, Paris, London, New York City, Shanghai, Chicago, and Singapore owe their success in part to their easy accessibility to water and the resultant expansion of trade. Canals lost their utility with the advent of railroads that triumphed in the battle of price and distance. Fortunately, many of these canals have been saved by historical preservation societies and serve as an unending source of water-borne enjoyment for tourists who relax in slow-moving canal boats through the countryside of England, France, and western New York. Canals also have been built to facilitate the passage of large ships. The Welland Canal in Canada, the Suez Canal in Egypt, and the Panama Canal are well-known water highways in the modern age. Canals have defined the growth of cities like Venice, Delft, Brugge, and Birmingham in England. In fact, Venice's twenty-six miles of canals served as a standard for the building of canals in St. Petersburg, Russia, Hamburg, Germany, and Fort Lauderdale, Florida.[14] Today canal aqueducts remain engineering marvels. Along the Erie Canal in New York and the Chesapeake and Ohio Canal in Maryland, one can still see how these stone aqueducts traversed rivers and valleys. In Wales, United Kingdom, one can still see the famous Pontcysyllte aqueduct that spans the valley of the River Dee.

The canals of yesteryear have been replaced with huge engineering hydraulic projects capable of pushing water and money over mountains and across deserts. The fullest flowering of hydraulic society today can be observed in the arid lands of the American West. Blessed with an abundance of earth and sky but cursed with a scarcity of water, the American West has long dreamed of harnessing all its rivers to produce unlimited wealth and power. Since the time of Mormon settlement in Utah, Americans have been damming, diverting, and controlling streams and rivers to create a hydraulic society in the great American desert. The fullest expression of this concept is the Colorado River, which has largely been harnessed to satisfy the nearly insatiable water demands of farmers and city dwellers in Colorado, California, and other Western states. While we will return to this subject in Chapter Seven, it is worth noting at this point the words of Donald Worster, in his *Rivers of Empire*. This hydraulic society is "a social order based on the intensive, large scale manipulations of water and its products in an arid setting. It is an increasingly coercive, monolithic system ruled by a power elite based on the ownership of capital and expertise." Worster notes that along with wealth has come massive ecological damage and growing class conflict. Currently, water in the West, despite all the hydraulic dreams of politicians and businessmen, is increasingly a scarce resource, inadequate to the demand and declining in quality.[15]

Slouching Towards 2025

If demographic projections hold true, almost 8 billion people are scheduled to populate the Earth by 2025. According to the International Food Policy Research Institute, total global water withdrawals in 2025 are projected to increase by 22 percent over world water consumption in the base year 1995. Will water be able to sustain this demographic increase? Over the coming decades the area of land devoted to farming worldwide will grow but slowly, as the sheer size of the increase in the world's industrial production leads to major increases in total industrial water demand. The developing world will pay the highest price for this water crisis with severe consequences for food production. Already many countries in the developing worlds are net food-importing countries; the inability of these countries to feed themselves economically and safely will get worse. As food grows more expensive due to scarcity and water problems, the impact on the real income of poor consumers will be reflected in growing malnutrition, fuel inflation, and severe pressure on the currency reserves of poor countries.

In the future one thing is certain: water prices will rise. Prices will be forced upward by scarcity and exponential industrial use. Efficient programs of water use in developing countries are hampered by the business-as-usual approach, political corruption, and a low technology base. Agricultural economists currently project a ten percent increase in the price of rice, the global food staple, by 2025 in areas of the world characterized by declining incomes and diminishing water resources. Thus, water and the price of rice may fuel international conflict in the near future. The World Commission on Water projects a dismal scenario: "With water becoming increasingly scarce, continued high flow diversions would become self-defeating. Excess extraction speeds the recession of ecological systems and lowers water quality finally reducing the qualified water supply for human uses."

While Americans tend to focus on their own water problems — either too much or too little — water conflicts continue to be a main theme worldwide. For example, the conflict between the Israelis and the Palestinians is not just about religion and politics. It is also about water, as any hydrological map of the region will tell you. Countries in the Middle East with the least access to water are experiencing some of the fastest growth in population. When the oil runs out in Saudi Arabia, its society will still have a pressing need for water. The availability of water is at crisis levels already in parts of China, India, and various African countries. While not yet a critical issue before the man on the street in the West, the politics of water resources matters a great deal.

There are, however, natural limits to the world's water supply. We are coming up against something that hydrologists have begun to call "peak water." Briefly stated, "peak water" is a concept borrowed from the oil industry. It means that the world is approaching or has even passed the maximum production of water. "Peak water" means that we are now running up against natural limits to availability of human use of freshwater. The net result may be hardship and constraints in water usage that leads to global economic deterioration. Even though modern medicine gives us better control over waterborne maladies like dysentery and cholera, we really have not progressed that much. Fecal coliform, that nasty sewage toxin, bedevils us today. If Dr. Jekyl is the benevolent and efficient manager of water, Mr. Hyde is the sewage monster waiting to infect the planet. Extreme events like droughts and floods will grow in intensity throughout the globe and bring in profound water problems for coastal cities in terms of a host of new waterborne pathogens.

During the past century, the world's population has trebled and water use has increased six-fold. These changes have come at great environmental costs: half of our wetlands disappeared at the end of the twentieth century, countless rivers and lakes in the world are now too polluted for swimming and fishing, fish are either endangered or carriers of toxins that may be carcinogenic, and 20 percent of the world's fish are endangered. Meanwhile, the most polluting industries on the planet move to the outskirts of cities in the developing world and place horrendous pressure on water resources.

Suffice it to say, as we move closer to the year 2025, sixty percent of the world's population will be urban and this makes urban water quality an issue of the utmost importance. The United Nations Environment Program (UNEP) has developed a number of scenarios to help understand the world's future water problems. The UN projects the following: nearly seven billion in sixty countries will face water scarcity by 2050. Water scarcity won't hit all the regions of the world the same way. North and Sub-Saharan Africa will be the regions most threatened. By the year 2025, it is estimated that nearly 230 million Africans will be facing water scarcity, and 460 million will live in water-stressed countries. Further, the UN estimates that climate change will account for at least 20 percent of the global increase in water scarcity. In the near future, millions of people from arid parts of the planet will be on the move seeking to slake their thirst.

Conclusion

As the new century progresses, control of water — who will provide it and how its quality will be assured — will become an increasingly important and divisive issue in the United States and around the world. In the United States, heretofore a water-abundant nation, water is up for grabs because of failing water companies, rapid urban growth, and the continued exponential use of technology in industry and agriculture. Today huge multinational water companies are buying out small inefficient and expensive municipal systems everywhere. For years the public relied on an older image of municipal water companies being unparalleled in terms of access, low cost, and quality. Now reality is setting in. In the name of business efficiency, and with higher water standards being imposed by governments, corporations are buying up the water. I discuss this issue more fully in Chapter Six. In the United States, at least, this comes at a time when the political right has launched an unprecedented ideological attack on the public sector for being weak, inflexible, inefficient, and costly. As water becomes increasingly privatized, it crosses racial, class, and political lines. The notion of water as a public good becomes replaced with water as a private resource for sale, much like oil. For those of us nurtured in a time of water and air being ultimate public goods, the future is scary. Once water is privatized, say critics of corporate water, what does a community have control of?

Here in the twenty-first century we are at the beginning of a nasty global fight over the access to and control of water. Our future is problematic and we may well struggle and "face the burning waste without a taste of water. Cool clear water."

"The fact is that our water supplies are vulnerable and there is nothing we can do in the near future to 100% assuage the risk."

-- Dan Kroll,

Securing Our Water

Chapter 2

Water and Global Conflict

I n 1995, Ismail Serageldin, the World Bank's vice president for environmental affairs and chairman of the World Water Commission, stated bluntly that it was time "to ring the alarm bell for the impending water crisis." He predicted, "The wars of the twenty-first century will be fought over water." Although he was roundly criticized for this opinion, he refused to disavow it and has frequently asserted that water is the most critical issue facing human development. Former UN Secretary General Boutros Boutros Ghali has said something similar about water wars; so did Jordan's late King Hussein, who had obvious cause to mean it, having more than his share of argument with Israel over the River Jordan. Egypt has more than once threatened to go to war with Ethiopia over diversions of the Nile.

Argues Serageldin: How are we going to have enough water to supply an additional three billion people on the planet in the twenty-first century? Looking at Egypt, his own country, Dr. Serageldin noted that "the rich will manage to insulate themselves in any situation," but where will Egypt get the additional 1,000 cubic meters per person of water a year to service its own growing population? Water has become a Malthusian subject and gloomy news seems the currency of environmental prediction these days.[1]

In January 1992, over five hundred delegates from one hundred countries attended the International Conference on Water and Environment in Dublin, Ireland. Towards the close of the session, delegates called for new approaches to water problems in what came to be known as "the Dublin Principles" for water and sustainable development. High-minded and recognizing the need for concerted action, the delegates supported a series of resolutions, the most important of which read: "Water development and management should be based on a participatory approach, involving users, planners, and policy-makers at all levels."[2] Cynics argued that this was more the language of a cop-out than principle. Unfortunately the delegates could not come up with system-wide approaches for monitoring and regulating water use. Simply put, national rivalries tend to undermine conference agreements; and most countries see their thirst for water in the short-term when many of the problems concerning water require long-term planning.

Water Conflicts Worldwide

The struggle to have access and control of water resources today is the major fact of life in countries dependent upon Himalayan snow melt and aquifers like Rajasthan, in Africa's Sahael, Bolivia, and Central America. Water conflicts need to be seen in the context of rapid population growth and environmental scarcities like arable land. Often ruling classes in countries have the power to rewrite legislation regarding property and water rights to their own advantage. Mauritania is a good example. In the 1970s and 1980s, the prospect of drought and food shortages prompted the Mauritanian government to build a series of irrigation and flood control dams along the Senegal River. With greater access to water, land values along these dams escalated sharply. In the words of one recent study, the Mauritanian government "controlled by white Moors of Arab origin quickly took control of these water resources by changing the laws regarding land ownership and abrogating the traditional rights of black Mauritanians ... Scarcity-induced resource capture by Moors in Mauritania helped ignite violence over water and cropland in the Senegal River basin, producing tens of thousands of refugees."[3] Thus, long-term issues like water scarcity and accompanying population problems can slowly tear a nation's social fabric apart and may result in overt wars and guerilla operations like Peru's Shining Path, which threatened water utilities.[4]

Water scarcity is already hindering the economic growth of many poor countries. Today, access to river water is a matter of life and death. In addition to being a requirement for economic growth, water is a component of a nation's military strength. More than 40 percent of the world's population lives in 214 river basins shared by more than one country. Some basins have more water conflict than others. The Nile is a good illustration. Egypt has long had turbulent relations with its upstream neighbors, Sudan and Ethiopia. Militarily Egypt is much more powerful than both of its neighbors and over the years Cairo has threatened war to guarantee an adequate supply of the Nile's waters. Despite its control of the Nile, Egypt has become increasingly vulnerable on the water issue, especially since the democratic uprisings in Cairo in 2011. Affected by environmental factors, water availability flowing to Egypt along the Nile has been significantly reduced, making Egypt increasingly dependent upon the political dynamics of the region.

A 1988 futuristic article in the *U.S. News and World Report* described a frightening scenario where a war erupted in the Middle East in the fall of 1993 in a desperate struggle for dwindling water supplies. Iraqi forces, attempting to smash a Syrian blockade, launched massive attacks on the Euphrates River Valley. Syria answered with missile attacks on Baghdad. Of course, the envisioned scenario never occurred, but water security conditions in the Tigris Euphrates basin are unstable and the potential for water wars still looms in the background of that region. Significantly, this magazine article is still cited with currency by security agencies dealing with Middle Eastern affairs.[5] Water has become a key element in the balance of power between Syria, Israel, Lebanon, Iraq, and Turkey at a time when political upheavals in the Middle East are disturbing the social economies of the Middle East. Uprisings in Libya, Yemen, Tunisia, and Egypt rattle the nerves of water resource managers in the region.

One of the most perplexing trouble spots in the story of water conflicts resides on the Asian subcontinent. India has built a huge dam on the eastern end of the Ganges — the Farakka Barrage — with harsh flooding and drought consequences for downstream cropland, fisheries, and villages in the nation of Bangladesh. Given the fact that Bangladesh is one of the weakest countries in the world economically, it has little political or military leverage in dealing with India other than being reduced to mendicant status and begging for an equitable approach to Ganges River management. A lot is at stake insofar as most of Bangladesh is at sea level and susceptible to massive flooding by the Ganges and by storms and typhoons. Lack of dependable water flow from the Farakka Barrage has resulted in the out-migration of thousands of Bangladeshi environmental refugees in to India's Bengal region. This has caused numerous resettlement problems and has placed great stress on the local Bengali environment. One can easily point to similar developments along the Mekong Delta and the Euphrates.

Poisoning the Border

In California, the city of San Diego has an ongoing problem with Tijuana, Mexico, over massive outflows of raw sewage along the coastline. This represents a highly visible and serious challenge to the environment of San Diego's coast. At stake are the future of San Diego's beaches, shoreline for real estate development, and the public health of the citizens of San Diego. Currently raw sewage from Tijuana flows at the rate of 13-15 million gallons a day. The situation has gotten much more serious due to the uncontrolled development of Tijuana without a reliable sewage infrastructure. Toilet waste washes up on Imperial Beach next to San Diego, a transnational water problem that is beginning to be seen in other parts of the world. Surfers at Imperial Beach have long complained of "surfer's nose," a runny nasal system caused by water containing e-coli in the nasal passages. The surfers know the water is polluted, but the waves are just too good to be missed. Imperial Beach first issued a sewage quarantine in 1959 and, since the 1980s, the Playas de Tijuana treatment plant, located one mile south of the border, has discharged, by itself, about one million gallons per day of raw sewage into the ocean due to leakages and system failures.

Until recently problems with "renegade" water flows have been under the radar of public opinion, but that situation is rapidly changing as municipalities issue health alerts and quarantines. At Imperial Beach, these quarantines in the past have lasted as long as 146 days, from January through August, dampening the summer's tourism and economic activity. Today beach closings along this section of the California coast due to Tijuana's fecal tides are not short-term. Permanent metal signs encased in concrete warning citizens against entering the water have replaced old wooden signs announcing "temporary" beach closings. Imperial Beach, once a famous site for surfing champions, is now part of the general cesspool that flows from Tijuana down the Tijuana River, through the heavily polluted estuary and thence to the sea.

In 1998, the International Boundary and Water Commission completed construction of a bi-national water treatment plant to clean Tijuana's impaired waters. However, this has been hampered by the explosive economic growth of Tijuana resulting in whole neighborhoods without sewers and sewer systems. Many hillside shanties have outdoor gravity toilets that are not regularly emptied. In the view of Juan Vargas, a San Diego city official, by the time the 25-million-gallon-a day treatment plant came on line the flow of Mexican sewage exceeded its capacity. Despite the willingness of the United States and Mexico to develop joint treatment facilities, renegade sewage continues to fuel public ill-will in California towards Mexico. In addition to illegal immigration, Hepatitis A has become part of the transnational conflict.

In similar fashion, Singapore has sewage pollution problems with Malaysia, and countries along the Danube River in Europe are constantly arguing over sewage discharges. Watercourses, notes Robert Percival, are "cheap and convenient vehicles for waste disposal" around the world. One of the chief difficulties to developing effective transnational sewage policies is that "upstream dischargers have little incentive to be concerned about downstream water quality. If wastes can be cheaply discarded in a manner that imposes the environmental consequences on someone else, dischargers have little incentive to be concerned about downstream water quality."[6]

Sometimes the construction of a single dam in a major river basin can make a poor country a major player in water contests. In 1984, the Itaipu Dam opened. It was a joint undertaking between Brazil and Uruguay with Uruguay getting 90 percent of the 94.68 billion KWH of hydropower annually generated. Located along the Parana River (one of the longest water systems in South America after the Amazon), the Itaipu Dam is second in size to China's Three Gorges Dam and is changing the ecological face of much of South America. Itaipu demonstrates how hydroelectric power may be a central planning and economic development issue in countries in the watershed ranging from Bolivia to Argentina. These countries are currently subject to wild swings in the global commodity and currency markets; therefore, building more dams generating more power along the Parana River may be the only economic certainty to which these nations can cling. This will no doubt fuel a "dams race" in the region much like the "arms race," as other countries in the region challenge Paraguay's hydro-hegemony.

The Specter of Water Terrorism

International water conflicts are further compounded by the specter of terrorism. In this watery context, what we mean by terrorism is relatively straight-forward: the Federal US Code defines terrorism as "premeditated, politically motivated violence perpetrated against non combatant targets by sub-national groups or clandestine agents, usually intended to influence an audience." Damage or destruction of a nation's water supplies or to its water quality infrastructure is a growing concern. The potential for water terrorism is not new. In fact, water terrorism is the stuff of history.

The English words "river" and "rivalry" derive from the Latin "*rivalis*," which relates to theft or appropriation of river access. There are biblical accounts of the fight over water. When Abraham and his followers entered the land of Canaan, the Philistines sabotaged the water wells. Later the Israelites fought amongst themselves over access to water and named the conflicted wells, as translated from Hebrew, "Contention" and "Enmity."[7] Early in the history of the Middle East, the Sumerian Kingdoms in the Tigris and Euphrates valleys used war as a kind of environmental terrorism. In the period 2450 to 2400 BC, Urlama, King of Lagash, diverted water from boundary canals and irrigation ditches in his realm to deny water to the neighboring city-state of Umma. His son Urlama II subsequently used the same tactic in his conquest of the city Girsu in Sumeria. During the many wars that Athens fought against its rival city-states on the Peloponnesus, Solon commanded his troops to put the poison hellbore (rye ergot) into the local water supply of the besieged city of Cirrha in the period 600 BC. As late as the eighteenth century, it was considered a convenient military tactic for armies to attack the water systems of their enemies. In the United States, water terrorism was not unknown in the American West. Between 1907 and 1913, angry California farmers dynamited the aqueduct system that they believed was stealing their water for the growing city of Los Angeles.[8]

It was during World War II that national policy makers first became aware of the various dimensions of water terrorism. In 1941, J. Edgar Hoover, director of the Federal Bureau of Investigation, warned: "It has long been recognized that among public utilities, water supply facilities offer a particularly vulnerable point of attack to the foreign agent, due to the strategic position they occupy in keeping the wheels of industry turning and in preserving the health and morale of the American populace."[9]

Since September 11, 2001, a growing segment of national leaders and scientists has worried about terrorist attacks on water supplies that will threaten the environment and possibly cause significant loss of life. In nearly every developed nation today water infrastructure systems extend over vast areas whose ownership and responsibility are both public and private.

Mindful of the 9/11 attacks, dam operators in countries ranging from the United States to India have operated under heightened concern for the security of their facilities. In most countries the key issues are: 1. How to develop international protocols protecting water facilities, especially drinking water reservoirs; and 2. How to fund and operate risk reduction activities at these facilities in a time of global financial retrenchment.

The vulnerability of water supplies in the United States and other countries to potential terrorist or malicious acts has been well-documented by agencies like the US Army Corps of Engineers, the Environmental Protection Agency, the British government, and the Indian Ganges River Project. In 2002, the FBI issued a series of public warnings regarding possible terrorist attacks against American targets. According to a report by the Center for Defense Information, "The effort comes after the discovery that al-Qaeda terrorists have been investigating ways to disrupt the U.S. water supply on a massive scale." The FBI feared that pathogens like Cryptosporidium, a protozoan able to survive water treatment plants, could reach the water taps of citizens. In the spring of 1993, a large outbreak of this waterborne disease in Milwaukee caused more than 400,000 illnesses (diarrhea) and fifty to one hundred deaths from customers drinking the water.

The CDI also warned against acts of vandalism by terrorists in water plants aimed at disrupting the water purification process. Said David Isenberg, a consultant on water terrorism projects: "While some of the scenarios being sketched these days are undoubtedly plain old fear mongering by utilities seeking a greater share of the homeland security budget pie, the danger is real."[10] In a public statement issued in 2006, Britain's former Secretary of State for Defense John Reid warned of coming "water wars." Reid predicted that violence and political conflict will become more likely as watersheds turn to deserts and water supplies and mountain melt are poisoned. Calling the global water crisis a national security issue for the West, Reid argued that Britain's armed forces should develop military strategies to handle global water conflicts. The growing water crisis in Darfur, noted both Reid and Prime Minister Tony Blair, was the warning sign of an unfolding global water conflict.

Both Reid and Tony Blair articulated a stark assessment of the potential impact of rising temperatures and diminished water resources. Reid warned of increasing uncertainty about the future of the countries least equipped to deal with flooding, water shortages, and valuable agricultural land turning to desert.[11]

In 2008, former Prime Minister Gordon Brown's Labour Government came out with a new strategy to protect Britain from water wars and water terrorism by charging its super intelligence agency MI5 to monitor and abort attacks on water and power facilities. The British government also began to access computer and personnel records for individuals in key water industries. According to a published report, this effort came as "part of Gordon Brown's new national security strategy, expected to identify a string of new threats to Britain — ranging from future 'water wars' between countries left drought-ridden by climate change to cyber-attacks using computer hacking technology to disrupt vital elements of national infrastructure."[12] India continues to remain on alert against "water jihadists" who threaten to blow up dams and contaminate public water supplies. This is part of a long-standing conflict between India and Pakistan over access to the water reserves of the Indus River.[13]

Nuclear terrorism against water facilities remains the ultimate fear in the West. Currently, writes Harvard policy analyst Caitlin Talmadge, it is next to impossible for a terrorist group to have the scientific expertise to prepare and detonate fissionable materials against a specific water target. What is possible, she notes, is that a government seeking specific water objectives could give a nuclear device to a small terrorist group and deny any connection with the subsequent nuclear blast.[14]

Water scientists such as Dan Kroll say that the easiest terrorist technique for inflicting mass casualties would be to orchestrate a simple back flow using a cheap hardware store pump working at 80 pounds per square inch pressure to start a siphoning effect that would draw toxins into water pipelines. The point of toxic entry could be as simple as a fire hydrant or a domestic residence.[15] Water can also be targeted for the casual entry of poisons. Terrorists can easily place a chemical or biological agent into local water supplies and pipelines or water treatment facilities. Sewage treatment plants, so essential for removing human waste toxins, are especially vulnerable to attack by a disciplined cadre of terrorists who could invade small municipal plants, shut down processes, and flood our river courses with toxins that could unleash a cholera epidemic. Poisoning our water, however, would be temporary as water is a powerful element and most toxins cannot survive long as waterborne threats. Indeed, water treatment plants can usually handle most dangerous substances introduced into our waterways. For example, ozonation, chlorination, and ultraviolet radiation, as well as the sun's powerful rays, can destroy most biological pathogens.

In 1972, two members of a terrorist group, "The Order of the Rising Sun" were arrested in Chicago after they were discovered with 30-40 kilograms of typhoid cultures that they planned to use to poison the public water supply of Chicago, St. Louis, and other cities. They were part of a neo-Nazi group dedicated to creating a new master race in America. Health authorities down-played the threat, citing that this terrorist plan would not have caused serious health problems owing to chlorination of water supplies.[16] The problem with this kind of water terrorism is more in the public fear it causes among resident populations than the actual threat to public health. Public perception, these days, to nearly any terrorist threat is just barely above the threshold of hysteria, and public officials are very much aware that 9/11 has left a powerful imprint in the human psyche of developed nations in the West.

While water engineers long planned for violent disruptions to public water supplies, these contingencies revolved around earthquakes, violent storms, and mechanical failures. Until quite recently little attention was devoted to assessing vulnerabilities for terrorism. When water plants re-calibrated their computer systems in response to the perceived crisis of Y2K impacts on their computer systems on January 1, 2000, they did not make detailed plans to incorporate sufficient procedures to address any type of terrorist activity.

During the Clinton Presidency, the Environmental Protection Agency developed plans to protect the nation's critical infrastructure against terrorist acts. Specifically, these efforts focused on the 340 large community water supply systems that served more than 100,000 persons. The EPA also began to disseminate alerts to drinking water and wastewater plants about the hazards and vulnerabilities to their operations that had been detected by their inspectors.[17]

In the United States, the EPA, in concert with the Homeland Security Agency, has taken a number of steps to develop scientific research tools that can be used to respond to attacks on water systems. Specifically, the EPA conducts a needs assessments of water facilities in helping national security agencies to develop security protocols for the protection of water plants. Currently the EPA is focusing on protecting "critical assets," such as public health institutions, government and military bases, as well as utilities serving areas with large populations. Additionally, in 2005, the EPA developed the Water Sentinel program that can serve as a model for all water utilities. Its purpose is to test and demonstrate contamination warnings at drinking water utilities and municipalities. Thus far most government programs have been geared towards protecting larger utilities and municipalities against water terrorism. Small facilities, however, may be much more vulnerable because they have minimal security.

In 1999, bomb attacks in Lusaka, Zambia, destroyed a large water pipeline that cut-off water for the city of 3 million and frightened the general population. In 2002, terrorists from Morocco plotted to contaminate the water system of Rome, Italy, with a cyanide-based chemical. Lethal potassium cyanide concentrations were discovered in a water tank at a Turkish Air Force base near Istanbul. A Kurdish terrorist group claimed credit. Also, there have been threats by terrorist or national groups to blow up dams in Tajikistan,

Zimbabwe, and South Africa. Since 2003 al-Qaeda has regularly issued threats to poison the drinking water in the western cities of the United States.[18]

In Europe, most water resource protection plans revolve around the prevention of cyber terrorists from hacking into important water engineering systems like the flood control gates in the Netherlands and the tidal surge gates of the Thames River in England. Computer experts in the British Royal Air Force, however, are quick to point out that a teenage hacker with a computer at a kitchen table is more likely to temporarily disrupt a dam or reservoir system than any terrorist with either dynamite or biological weaponry.

Views on water terrorism are mixed. In an important analysis, the Center for Strategic and International Studies in Washington concluded that the threat to water and electrical infrastructures by cyber-terrorists was likely to result more in attacks of "mass annoyance" rather than in serious loss of life. From strategic military perspectives "attacks that do not degrade national capabilities are not significant." Further, most water supply facilities continue to rely on technology not easily disrupted by network attacks. Armed terrorists attacking and disrupting a specific water facility would have the best chance of success, the report concludes.

The Center agrees with an American Water Works Association assessment that "physical destruction of the system's components to disrupt the supply of water is the most likely source of infrastructure attack." Most infrastructures in large industrial countries are resistant to cyber attack. Thus the Center for Strategic Studies argued, "The sky is not falling, and cyber weapons seem to be of limited value in attacking national power or intimidating citizens." The center, however, did caution that things could change. "Vulnerability could increase as societies move to a more ubiquitous computing environment when more daily activities have become automated and rely on remote computer networks."[19] In the context of modern social life and culture in the West, however, public impatience with even a single day of disruption of water and electricity "sets a very high standard for security." As Peter H. Gleick, of the Pacific Institute, and others have noted, "Even a plausible public threat has the potential to cause fear and anxiety." Thus Gleick argues that the best possible defense against water terrorists is to have "public confidence in water management systems, rapid and effective water quality monitoring, and strong and effective information dissemination."

Many water districts, especially those in rural and small town areas of the United States, lack the financial means to undertake ambitious monitoring programs in defense against water terrorists. New tools may have to be developed that are both affordable and accurate for these districts. At this writing, many water districts are overly preoccupied with revamping their sanitary waste treatment plants and retrofitting antiquated water lines in their areas. Large federal appropriations may be necessary to help them deal with new problems of water security. Gleick notes that one of the best strategies today is to bring water issues to public attention through widespread environmental education campaigns.[20]

For the foreseeable future terrorist attacks on water supplies of modern western nation states will probably focus on physical attacks on water infrastructure — an attack on a dam, a hydroelectric plant, or a sewage treatment facility. While most of these assaults might produce minimal disruption, water authorities take seriously terrorist threats against large dam projects. As Peter Gleick notes, "A major dam failure can kill thousands of people and even more modest damage might interrupt power generation or affect some important water-system operation."[21] Since the passage of the Bioterrorism Act by Congress in 2002, Congress has mandated that water community systems serving over 3,300 individuals perform systematic vulnerability assessments for potential terrorist threats, including poison contamination.[22]

While the industrial west remains worried but relatively safe from the depredations of water terrorists, it is another matter entirely in developing nations. In August 2002, Israel agreed to buy about 1.75 billion cubic feet of water from Turkey's Manavgat River annually for the next twenty years to alleviate the nation's growing water shortage and ensure the success of an arms deal with Ankara. The water would be shipped to Israel in specially designed tanker ships. The quantity was believed to be enough to satisfy about 7 percent of Israel's annual need for potable water. Soon after the deal was negotiated, terrorists from al-Qaeda struck Istanbul with a deadly ferocity. To show their outrage over this water deal, al-Qaeda bombed two synagogues in Istanbul and attacked the British consulate. Twenty-seven people were killed, including the British consul, and 450 wounded. Subsequently, al-Qaeda reported that they had also planned to attack the water and power facilities of the American consulate. However, the terrorists complained that it was so well guarded that not even a bird could fly over it.[23] The bombings put Turkey on full military alert and troops were placed along the miles of canals and aqueducts that carry water to Turkish farms and communities.

As we have seen, a well-publicized threat against a dam or water supply may generate even more success in harming the public than the real act of terrorism itself. Meanwhile, the following vulnerabilities are worthy of mention: terrorist groups could access large underground sewers for the purposes of placing explosives beneath buildings or city streets; explosions in sewers could cause the collapse of roads, sidewalks, and adjacent structures and easily kill pedestrians; and damage to wastewater facilities prevents water from being treated and can harm down river communities. It is uncertain at this writing just how much damage terrorists nationally and internationally can do to both water infrastructures and the water supply itself. Many experts believe that the physical destruction of water systems or the disruption of water supply is a much more likely scenario than bioterrorism or chemical contamination.

Remote control of a water or sewage plant is not merely a hypothetical concern, however. Wire reports for *Ionizer Magazine* state that in 2008, "a frustrated computer hacker, seeking retribution for being fired, caused treatment plants in Queensland, Australia to overflow. The break-in caused millions of gallons of raw sewage to be dumped into creeks and parks on the Sunshine Coast, a popular tourist and holiday destination."[24]

The simple destruction of a railroad car containing chlorine gas destined for a water treatment plant could cause massive deaths and havoc in a community. Many community leaders remain concerned about water plants that continue to use chlorine gas in their treatment facilities when other purifiers like sodium hyperchlorite are easily at hand. Chlorine remains the favorite purifier because of its strength in combating e-coli and neutralizing other contaminants. Currently the US Department of Transportation requires all water plants to have emergency isolation devices to contain chlorine gas leaks from railroad cars. Also, the financial cost of converting their water treatment plants from chlorine gas to alternative disinfectants can range anywhere from $650,000 to $13 million.[25]

The Jordan River Basin Conflict

The Jordan River Basin is a key example of conflict over water that includes politics, propaganda, armed might, and water terrorism. Jordan and Palestine rely extensively on water from the basin that is controlled primarily by Israel. As a freshwater resource, the River Jordan is vital for most of the population of Israel, Palestine, and Jordan, and, to a lesser extent, Lebanon and Syria. Sharing this water resource involves the issue of water rights, water use, and water redistribution. Water that is used upstream for drinking can hardly be reclaimed for the same purpose, and even storing water for later release causes undesired effects in downstream states. Since water is a scarce resource to every country in the region, access to enough water to meet the demands of households and economic sectors is a main concern for all governments involved. Currently the countries in the Jordan River basin have enough access to the river for drinking water and washing. The sticking point is the amount of water available for industry and commercial agriculture.

The demand for water is rising, due to population growth and economic development. Israel, Jordan, and Palestine are already facing a situation where water consumption is close to exceeding the renewable amount available. Water saving measures, water recycling, or desalination are adequate measures for the short-term, but fail to fill the expected gap over the long-term. In candid moments hydrologists argue that the water capacity of the Jordan River is a zero sum game. If one country gets additional water, another loses. The overuse of water resources as a result of pollution and population growth have seriously affected relations between Jordan, Israel, and Palestine. In 1999, when Israel faced a looming water deficit due to drought, it halved its annual water allocation of 2 billion cubic feet of water to Jordan. This led to water rationing in Jordan and a near break down in diplomatic relations between the two countries before water allotments were increased. Jordan is plagued by escalating populations that are stretching water availability beyond sustainable levels. Meanwhile, Jordan now articulates an "hydraulic imperative," which Israel fears will be nothing more than a Hashemite grab of resources.

The Jordan River is 251 kilometers (156 miles) long and, over most of its distance, flows at elevations below sea level in a northern extension of the Great Rift Valley. Its waters originate from the high precipitation areas in and near the mountains in the north, flow through the Sea of Galilee and Jordan River Valley, ending in the Dead Sea, at an elevation of minus 400 meters, in the south. Downstream of the Sea of Galilee, where the main tributaries enter the Jordan Valley from the east, the valley bottom widens to about fifteen miles (24 km). The need for water and the continuing hostility between Israel and the surrounding Arab states has made the Jordan River the centerpiece of Middle Eastern conflict.

Water problems in the Jordan River valley predate the founding of Israel. Before World War One, Arabs struggled with the Ottoman Empire for funds and technology for irrigation in the region. After World War One, the British administered what was then called TransJordan and began to develop plans for both the utilization of riparian (surface water) and groundwater in 1922 and 1928 by draining marshes and improving the flow of the river. In 1935, Zionist settlers in the Galilee prepared a plan for the transfer of water from the Jordan River to the Galilee to open up farmland. This kind of planning factored in a large Jewish immigration to the region and Palestinians demanded that the British Minister of Colonies cancel the sale of new lands to the immigrants. This settlement and water issue led ultimately to the partition of Palestine between the Palestinian Arabs and the Jews and a quota set for further Jewish immigration.

To examine critically the water problems of the Jordan Valley, the government of TransJordan commissioned a British engineer, Michael Lonedis, to study the river and serve as Director of Development in the region. His study was published in 1939 and was the first comprehensive analysis of the available water resources of the Jordan River and the irrigable land in the Jordan Valley. The study and others that followed argued the case that the waters of the Jordan

River basin could not be taken out of it for the benefit of land outside of the basin for irrigation until all the lands of the basin were irrigated. This study frustrated Zionist plans for irrigation of land distant from the river and gave the Palestinians a strong claim to a large share of the river's water. These water studies and the water projects that followed became the major conflict between the Arabs and the Jewish settlers. At stake was a key issue: could Zionists take water from the Jordan River at Arab expense to irrigate as much as possible its arid south and make more room for Jewish immigrants?

During World War Two, water problems of the TransJordan captured the attention of the United States. Because of Arab history of cooperation with the Nazi German government during the war, the United States Department of State considered the Arab League a volatile mixture of nationalism and violence. After the Nazi surrender, the Arab League made the decision to engage in a military campaign to prevent the establishment of a Jewish state in Palestine. What the Arab league had not prepared for was its military setback of 1948, the establishment of Israel, and its diplomatic recognition by the United States.

The decade of the 1950s was marked by repeated military clashes involving Syrian soldiers dug in at the Jordan River watershed on the Golan Heights and Palestinian guerrillas in the refugee camps of Gaza. Water conflict flowed into an already cooked porridge of anti-Semitism, Arab nationalism, and public fear in both the Palestinian and Israeli sectors. Clashes involving riparian rights to the Jordan were especially violent in 1952-53. The Arab response in the international media remained constant during this time: The Arab League "utterly refuses consideration of any joint project to utilize the waters of this river (the Jordan) with the enemy Israel." Throughout the 1950s US Ambassador Eric Johnston sought Egyptian mediation for a water agreement and continued to woo both the Arab League and Israel towards a joint management of Jordan's waters that would be identified in specific water withdrawals by all parties. However, in 1956, Britain invaded the Suez Canal, which ended all attempts by the Egyptians to serve as water brokers for fair use of resources in the Jordan Valley.

In the years after the founding of the nation state of Israel, reliance of that country on the resources of the Jordan River grew to over 50 percent of its water needs. This part of the Middle East has between 250-400 mm of regular rainfall, an amount that makes regular agriculture difficult. Thus, after 1948, farmers in Israel relied heavily on the Jordan River to irrigate their farms. In the early 1950s Israel created the National Water Carrier, which combines a system of giant pipes, open canals, tunnels, and pumping stations. Most of the water works in Israel are combined with the National Water Carrier, reaching a length of about 130 kilometers (80 miles). Building the carrier was a considerable technical challenge as it traverses a wide variety of terrains and elevations. These new waterways helped Israel open up more land to agriculture and settlement in what heretofore had been scrubland and desert.

To Arab nations, especially Syria and Jordan, the National Water Carrier became a symbol of the reckless expansionism of a country they considered to be a rogue nation. In 1955, Syrian artillery fired on an Israeli construction team working on the Carrier. US President Eisenhower, in an effort to diffuse the situation, sent Ambassador Johnston to mediate the water conflict. The negotiations dragged on for two years, and the only fruitful result was a cease-fire agreement. Tensions over water use of the Jordan however continued. In the early 1960s, following more than ten years of a Cold War over water, the Syrian government began to divert the Banias River, a tributary of the Jordan River. The action jeopardized Israeli water resources and the Israeli army and airforce attacked the diversion site. These actions were major issues that led to the outbreak of the Six-Day War in June 1967 with Israel against Syria, Jordan, and Egypt. During the fighting, Israel captured the Golan Heights and the site of the headwaters of the Banias River, which enabled Israel to stop the diversion of the Banias by the Syrians. Israel also gained control of the West Bank, the Jordan River, and the northern bank of the Yarmouk. With the Six-Day War, Jordan lost significant access to the Jordan River and its plans to expand usage of the river's waters had to be terminated.

Since that time, water has been a key component in Israel's strategic planning. Today Israel's National Water Carrier is an immense hydraulic siphon that extends from the Sea of Galilee in the north to Beersheba in the south near the Egyptian border. These pipelines and waterways take water from the Jordan River far south into the desert, diverting the Jordan's waters in ways similar to how the state of California siphons off the Colorado River for its immense urban and agricultural requirements. Since 1967 Israel has also tapped the aquifers of the region to service its growing settlements, further antagonizing Arabs because these underground water sources are underneath the West Bank and the Gaza Strip. In the Golan, water coming from the Golan Heights keeps north central Israel green, to the annoyance of the Syrian government, which still claims the land and water of the Golan.

Conflict between Israel and the Arab states remains well-nourished by water issues. In 1990, King Hussein of Jordan commented that water was the only issue that could take him to war with Israel. Water conflict in the Jordan River basin has been rooted in the fact that the Arab countries consider the State of Israel to be illegitimate. Connected to these declarations, the Arab states have persistently denounced the unilateral diversion of the Jordan River as completely illegal. The Israeli response has been that the surrounding Arabs nations were never willing to let Israel exist in peace. (The few water agreements operational between Israel and Jordan consist of some summer transfers of water to Jordan and cooperation over water access to the Yarmouk River, which flows into the basin from Jordan.) These historical disagreements intertwine with the dispute between Israel and Jordan in which the Jordan River plays a main role. In the southern part of the Jordan River, the water is a mix of highly saline streams, underground tributaries, and sewage that has caused Israel unanticipated difficulties with the western Christian world. It is in this area of the Jordan River known as Qasr al-Yahud, which is a hallowed spot, where Christians believe that John the Baptist baptized Jesus Christ. Currently, it is too filthy for human use and environmentalists hope that their warnings about the condition of the southern Jordan will prompt Israel to improve the river's water quality in this area. With its mix of cloudy greenish water, it bears little resemblance to the waterway of Jesus' time, notes environmental reporter Janine Zacharia.[26]

In order to understand the core of the conflict between Israel and Jordan about the Jordan River, it is important to note the different perceptions of water between the two countries. Jordan, as part of the Arab world, perceived the water problem as part of the Arab-Israeli conflict. Therefore, for Jordanians, water was always a matter of Arab national pride.[27] For Israel, as a young country, water seemed to be an integral part of territory and a necessary resource for agricultural survival and industrial development. The struggle for freshwater in the Middle East continues today, though well below yesterday's threshold of violence and anger. Meanwhile, low level threats to water supplies by terrorists are fairly constant. Palestinians have destroyed water supply pipelines to Israel's West Bank settlements. The Israeli government often retaliates by blocking water tanker deliveries to Arab communities in the occupied territories.

The Peace Treaty of 1994 between Israel and Jordan allowed for building a Red-Dead Sea Canal, but little else regarding the channeling of freshwater in the basin. The water of the lower Jordan is mostly brackish recycled irrigation water. Currently there is a lack of a basin-wide riparian agreement between Israel and her neighbors, and organizations like the United Nations are hopeful that sometime soon an agreement will be concluded on water projects to be monitored and administered. Jordan, Syria, and the Palestinians suspect Israel's water projects and believe that they are taking more than their rightful share.

Another issue needing to be addressed is water rights for Palestine. Israel's rising industrial and technologically oriented population has a growing water thirst that has led the country to control groundwater in its occupied territories with severe restrictions on water draw for the Palestinians. This control of water resources has led to the rapid decline of Palestinian agriculture in the region. Without dependable water supplies, the children of Palestinian farmers now must seek work as day laborers in Tel Aviv and elsewhere. In this context, some see Israel's denial of groundwater to the Palestinians of the West Bank as a violation of human rights.[28] Thus do water problems contribute to the growing frustration and alienation of the Palestinian population. Mutual reliance by Israel and Palestine on the West Bank Mountain Aquifer, which rests atop the border of the West Bank territory and provides nearly all of Palestinian water and one-third of Israel's supply, is a constant source of friction. Israeli officials, cognizant of a future water crisis in the region, fear that they will ultimately become dependent on Palestinian-controlled water sources. Since 1999 efforts at satisfactory water cooperation have proven to be ineffective most of the time.

The tentative peace process of the 1990s gave hope for a water solution, but recent developments, both in the West Bank and in the Jordan Basin itself, have brought a cloud over the water planning process. In this part of the world the "Dublin Principles" on water and sustainability are seen as a cruel joke. Without political peace on international borders and land rights, the water issue probably will never be solved. Currently Israel does not recognize Palestine as what it calls a "legitimate riparian" in the region.

Since 1967, Israel's control of water in the Jordan River Basin has not been seriously contested.[29] For tourists traveling in the Middle East, Israel seems to be an hydraulic miracle insofar as the Israelis have made the desert bloom. The latest water news from Israel focuses on its new huge seawater purification plant at Hadera. This gigantic desalination facility is part of a $US500 million plan to build a string of desalination plants along the Israeli coast. The Israeli government says that this will lessen this nation's dependence on the water of the Jordan River and hopefully mitigate a source of conflict for Israelis, Palestinians, and other Arab states. With desalination, Israelis will be able to rely less on an increasingly antiquated National Water Carrier that has been in operation since the 1950s.

Desalination plants along the coast have a stronger hydrological rather than political argument, however. After years of massive Israeli water withdrawals from the Jordan and local aquifers, the Sea of Galilee, a main source of water for much of Israel, has in recent years reached record lows. Israeli scientists are hopeful that desalination will allow the Sea of Galilee to come back to its previous levels. Desalination, though, is an expensive process, a prerogative of oil-rich Arab states and modern developed nation-states. Scientists fear that desalination's by-products, especially iron nutrients, will harm marine life in the Mediterranean. Meanwhile, the Palestinian Water Authority and other Arab communities have stated that they will not explore alternative water technologies until the Jordan River and its aquifers are returned to their control. Israeli's current hydro-technology plans do not allow the Palestinians access to its seawater purification plants.[30]

A number of years ago my family and I traveled in a cramped bus across the desert from Cairo towards the Suez Canal. As we crossed the Israeli border, a customs guard examined our passports and then said, "Welcome to Israel where you can drink the water and flush the toilets." The stark contrast of traveling across a desert filled with abandoned junk and dilapidated villages to a country of neatly planted farms and gushing fountains and watercourses could not fail to make a dramatic impression on us. Were the Arabs just lazy or inefficient or were there deeper issues at stake?

At that time we did not contemplate the transnational imbalance of technical and monetary resources in maintaining the hydraulics of a desert nation. Nor did any of us seem interested in challenging the efficacy of irrigating a desert in the first place. Once in Tel Aviv, we noticed a prevailing environmental lifestyle more reminiscent of Italy than the Middle East. We gave scant thought to the morality of taking water from other countries in the Jordan River basin against their will.

Conclusion

Everywhere you look, there are signs that the global water supply is in contention. Already Jordan, Israel, the West Bank, Gaza, Cyprus, Malta, and the Arabian Peninsula are at the point where all surface and ground freshwater resources are fully used. Morocco, Algeria, Tunisia, and Egypt will be in the same position within a decade. Here are a few items worthy of review: Very few major water systems are contained within one political entity. Many transborder water systems are in politically fractious places and where water resources are increasingly scarce, these scarcities are contributing to increased incidences of violence in the world. Water conflicts affect Western national interests by provoking migrations and encouraging powerful landowners to exploit weaknesses in the country's environmental laws in order to seize land and aquifers from poor people and indigenous farmers. Even developed nations have their share of transnational water problems. Protecting water resources from the pollution of another country is quite challenging because of the diversity of sources of water pollution and variations in the natural conditions of waters.

In the past conflicts over scarce water resources seldom led to war. Today terrorist organizations are smaller and more likely to resort to more extreme measures. In the future, however, water may be the essential trigger that ignites hostilities in and among nations.

"When the well's dry, we know the worth of water."

-- Benjamin Franklin

Chapter Three

America:
Polluted and Parched

Something In the Water

Water pollution comes from many sources, the chief culprits being sewage and industrial waste. Between 1936 and 1969, the Cuyahoga River in Cleveland caught fire several times because of its high levels of inflammatory waste. Public indignation over the pollution of the river flared only after the Cuyahoga had ignited for the tenth time and was the subject of international press coverage. Many environmentalists point to this event as one that got the ball rolling for the passage of the Clean Water Act in the United States in 1972.

While it is now uncommon for rivers to catch fire owing to industrial pollution, our waters are still being polluted, which could eventually lead, pessimists say, to the death of our habitat. While we are aware of these problems, most of us choose to ignore them because we feel that they do not affect us directly. When it comes to coping with pollution, there is a kind of psychological disconnect. We are content with business-as-usual, hoping that pollution will be somebody else's problem. The problem with this assumption is that it is wrong. Water pollution is here and we have to deal with it. Also, we are entering an age of water shortage in the United States. We have to deal with that as well.

Water problems, long a point of tension in the arid American West, are now becoming common on the Atlantic seaboard. Along rivers like the Connecticut, the Potomac, and the Chattahoochee, communities are experiencing either polluted water or not enough water at the right time. Even under normal weather conditions, reports the US NOAA Weather Service, Americans on the East Coast can expect future water shortages with significant economic, social, and environmental impacts during the summer and fall months.

America's population is growing fast and water consumption is at an all-time high. (American average water consumption is over 159 gallons a day while one-half the world's population lives on 25 gallons.) Some towns are literally running out of water, says Betsy Otto, senior director for river advocacy at Washington-based American Rivers, a non-profit conservation and environmental advocacy organization. "They haven't paid much attention to the problems of supply and demand."[1]

Water scientists are quick to point out that we have lived in North America with the idea of water as a public trust, something that could be relied on now and in the future. It is an idea that ties in with Judeo-Christian ideals about creation and the enduring sanctity of water. Now we are beginning to see just how fragile our water resources can become.

According to recent studies by the Natural Resource Defense Council, nineteen American cities have polluted drinking water systems serious enough to pose health risks to some residents.[2] Today, the typical glass of urban drinking water contains a witch's brew with parts of arsenic, lead, pathogens, cancer-causing by-products of chlorine, and rocket fuel per chlorate. Many urban sources of tap water are not adequately protected and cities are not altogether forthcoming about what is in the water.

Washington, DC, is a case in point. Over the past decade the city has been less than truthful about lead-tainted tap water. After a lengthy battle, Marc Edwards, a Virginia Tech Environmental Engineering professor, forced the Federal Center for Disease Control to admit that it had misled the public about the risk of lead in the District of Columbia's drinking water. Edwards' campaign took six years, during which time he argued that the Center for Disease Control's benign reports on lead levels in drinking water were being used across the country as a reason to relax concern about lead in the water.[3] Lead is especially toxic for small children and pregnant women. Too much lead in the human body can cause serious damage to the brain, kidneys, nervous system, and red blood cells.

Also, because Washington draws its water from the high-effluent Potomac River, it puts very high levels of chlorine in the drinking water — a not altogether healthy choice. The chlorine used to reduce the risk of infectious disease may account for a substantial portion of the cancer risk associated with drinking water. In a 1992 study that made front-page headlines and was reported in the July issue of the *American Journal of Public Health,* researchers at the Medical College of Wisconsin in Milwaukee found that people who regularly drink tap water containing high levels of chlorine by-products have a greater risk of developing bladder and rectal cancers than people who drink unchlorinated water. The study estimates that about 9 percent of all bladder cancer and 18 percent of all rectal cancer cases are associated with long-term consumption of these by-products. This amounts to over 20,000 new cases each year.[4]

Scientists now tell us that there is something in the Mid-Atlantic waters that we had least expected in our Bay and rivers. That something is called endocrine disruptors, and Dr. Vicki Blazer, a fisheries biologist at the US Geological Survey, found high concentrations of intersexed fish in the Shenandoah River, Monocacy Creek, and the south branch of the Potomac in West Virginia. As estrogen levels increase in water from disposed drugs like birth control pills and urine from hormone-treated livestock, male small-mouthed bass respond as if they were female. Dr. Blazer has found males attempting to lay eggs. They had both male and female sex organs. In 2003, these disturbing findings were in the upper reaches of the Potomac River. Now we are finding endocrine disruptors throughout the Mid-Atlantic. Environmental scientist Eugene P. Macri reports that the Susquehanna River, for example, is a "toxic soup" with chemicals and endocrine disruptors. Environmental agencies in Pennsylvania have failed to see the cumulative effects of endocrine disruptors in the Susquehanna watershed, Macri argues. "Contrary to the myth (about the river's good health) engendered by the Pennsylvania Fish and Boat Commission, the Susquehanna is a dying ecosystem."

Basically, endocrine disruptors are found in agricultural chemicals and consumer products that regulate internal functions of the body, like estrogen from birth control pills routinely flushed in urine into our waters. Endocrine disruptors are a diverse group of several thousand chemicals used in everything from pesticides to cosmetics and pharmaceutical products that send signals that can block hormones and disrupt the body's normal functions. Also endocrine disruptors come in many forms especially in pesticides like atrazine, 2.4-D, lindane, and permethrin. These disruptors mimic hormones, which can interfere with reproductive systems.

"These chemicals are rooted in our lifestyle choices," notes Dr. Blazer. In local pharmacy stores in the Chesapeake Bay watershed, virtually all shelved personal care products from shampoos to nail polish and sunscreen contain pthalates, which, in significant build-up, can cause birth defects and breast cancer. Pthalates in your shampoo cause sex problems in frogs and may be part of future environmental problems in human endocrine systems.

Endocrine disruptors in the water are hardly a Mid-Atlantic matter as the drinking water of 41 million Americans is contaminated with pharmaceuticals.[5] Chemical trash in the oceans and river systems elsewhere has led to pseudo-hermaphrodite polar bears with penis-like stumps and panthers with atrophied testicles. The same trend of intersexed fish is now observable in fish and wildlife populations in the Mediterranean.

How much of a synthetic chemical does it take to disrupt hormone levels and do lifelong harm? Scientific studies of synthetic hormones conducted by Dr. Earl Gray at the Environmental Protection Agency indicate that synthetic chemicals can disrupt testosterone in males and interfere with fertility. What does endocrine disruption mean for people? The results from experimentation wildlife studies indicate that we all may be at risk. Currently, however, scientific uncertainty (the need for more research to document findings) plagues any conclusions. Scientists are quick to point out today that with new pollutants entering our water systems, we really don't know what safe levels are. Humans have differing genetic susceptibilities. "This is the dilemma when we look at toxins in the water at parts per billion," says Dr. Robert Lawrence of the Johns Hopkins University School of Public Health. "Humans are long lived species and we are beginning to see a disturbing amount of genital abnormalities in male babies like hypospadias, undescended testicles, and impaired fertility influenced by endocrine disruptors."

Right now, says Lawrence, "the burden of proof is on those who say that levels of endocrine disruptors in the water are too low to be harmful. We need to take into account that endocrine disruptors have a capacity to synergize with other toxins and become harmful over time. Parents should be very careful in terms of what kind of drinking water they give to their young children." Dr. Lawrence adds that we need strict law enforcement procedures for water treatment and not mere monitoring. "Ten new chemicals per day are being manufactured globally that end up in our water system. Testing can't keep up. It's scary, very scary." We know enough to fear that in a solitary glass of water may lurk a number of ways to lose your fertility.

With significant numbers of our fish populations showing signs of ill health due to exposure of endocrine disrupting chemicals, we ought to take an interest in at least educating ourselves about the risks of human exposure, urges the Natural Resource Defense Council. In her book *Our Stolen Future*, Florida endocrinologist Theo Colbourn argues: "Humankind is now approaching the fourth generation of individuals born with the products of modern chemistry in their bodies."[6] Today scientists estimate that almost fifty percent of the American people will develop diabetes. Asks Colborn: "Does no one realize that the pancreas is an endocrine gland that can be harmed by chemicals that interfere with glucose metabolism and insulin?" Profit from chemicals is trumping public health, she says. It is an established scientific fact that drugs are not wholly absorbed or broken down by the human body. Significant amounts of drugs and medications pass through the body as urine, which is how pharmaceuticals enter our water resources — as toilet waste. Currently many urban public utilities are dependent upon rivers as a source of drinking water for their cities.

So far the Environmental Protection Agency has not regulated the presence of pharmaceuticals in drinking water. The problem is twofold: 1. There are no laws in existence today to protect consumers from increasingly dangerous chemical contaminants in the water supply; and 2. Water companies traditionally deal with the sanitation of wastewater and do not have the technology to remove most pharmaceuticals from drinking water. The pharmaceutical problem is at too low a threshold, they argue, and they do not want to embark on expensive technological upgrades. Meanwhile, in a national test of thirty-five American watersheds conducted by the Stroud Water Research Center, twenty-eight were found to be contaminated.

The report also mentioned "deep water aquifers" near land fills, feedlots, and other contaminant sources in twenty-four states were also found to contain pharmaceuticals. This means that even in rural areas of the United States, drugs are in the water. As we yearn for clean fresh water, we increasingly have water cocktails that contain hormones, painkillers, antibiotics, anti-convulsants, anti-depressants, and drugs for cancer or heart disease. Pharmaceuticals are designed to have an impact on humans at very low levels of concentration. Over time they may cause unanticipated changes in the human body. We live in an age of cancer and skyrocketing infertility; and it should not surprise people that drugs in the water supply might have adverse human effects. Drugs given to animals are also entering the water supply. Reports the *Environmental News Network*, "nobody knows the level of risk that may be associated with the chemical cocktail of pharmaceuticals now being found in the water supply. ... The EPA sticks its head in the ground over pharmaceutical pollution."[7]

According to a recent report by the US Geological Survey, about 105 million Americans receive water from public water systems across the United States that rely on groundwater pumped from public wells and increasingly have chemical contaminants like pesticides, gasoline hydrocarbons, and manufacturing additives. As these contaminants enter groundwater, they are mixed together. The US Geological Survey points out, "Mixtures can be a concern because the total combined toxicity of contaminants may be greater than that of any single contaminant."[8] Scientists are also now beginning to find "incidences of bladder cancer in the United States that are directly related to drinking water from the tap."[9]

The ongoing recession in the United States may have a disastrous impact on water use in the industrial heartland of the Midwest, and Detroit, Michigan, is an excellent case in point. Currently Detroit's water utility supplies 20 percent less water today than it did in 2003. The reason is obvious: a steep decline in industrial activity and population. Although Detroit has seen its core population of 800,000 wither by 10,000 residents annually, a lot of people have remained. They are poor and jobless and they have water problems that resemble developing nations. With a shrinking city, the public utility has been forced to raise water prices and many poorer residents are now unable to afford the service. As thousands of Detroiters have had their water service cut, they are adopting informal and illegal solutions to gain access to drinking water.

In some neighborhoods, notes Maureen Taylor, chair of the Michigan Welfare Rights Organization, "They run a hose through the window of their window to a neighbor's house." She also pointed out that like sub-Saharan Africa, people in Detroit now roam the city with large plastic canisters in search of cheap or free water. According to the Detroit Water and Sewage Department, more than 42,000 residences have lost their connection to city water since 2005.

In 2008, the average monthly water bill for a residence was $28. In 2010, for the same amount of water, citizens of Detroit paid $83, nearly a 200 percent increase. With half the population unemployed in some areas of the city, authorities anticipate a lot of garden hose networks to obtain much-needed water. Detroit's financial crisis may take years to work out. Until prosperity returns, garden hoses and plastic containers will be an urban icon of a new kind of thirst in the American heartland.[10] Detroit residents also have to worry about the various toxics from the automobile industry that have seeped into the groundwater. As oil enters the Michigan watershed through auto-exhaust contaminated rain, there is much to be concerned about. One drop of oil can ruin 25 liters of drinking water.

There is also another dimension to thirst in the city. Urban sprawl covers the ground with impervious surfaces like concrete and asphalt and prevents the replenishment of aquifers and groundwater supplies. Thus, even in the "wet" regions of the mid-Atlantic, state, city, and county officials are beginning to factor the "too many people and not enough water supply" issues into regional planning. The fundamental problem with so many American communities is that they have been so well-watered for so long that they have difficulty believing that they are now living in an age of potential scarcity. In many areas of the East Coast, homeowners are forced to double and sometimes treble the depth of their wells in order to obtain groundwater for their needs. Currently water withdrawals threaten many streams and tributaries in New England. As New England's population grows and expands beyond its urban centers, development places serious pressure on water resources. "We have seen Ipswich, Massachusetts, and Fenton, Connecticut, literally dry up during the hot summer months," says Steve Angers, a member of Massachusetts Blue Ribbon Task Force on Water Management. The region needs to take serious steps, Angers warns, to make sure that New England streams are not dewatered.[11]

In Maryland, during 2006-2007, a number of municipalities responded positively to water shortages. The town of Frederick, whose growth recently outstripped the local water supply, appointed a "water czar," Charles W. Boyd, to coordinate water planning with regional utilities and state agencies so that the county could rely on a secure water base. During its crisis, the city had to pump water from the Potomac River to meet the shortages caused by its growth. Essentially Frederick's water problems were caused by booming residential growth in the past decade that saw a 31 percent increase in population, a 33 percent increase in households, and a 20 percent increase in jobs. At the same time Frederick's leaders failed to plan for the water needs of a rapid-growth urban municipality. Residents of Frederick believed simply that it was impossible to run out of water in a water-rich region. Developers postponed new housing construction because they were unable to get connected to water, and outside Frederick, residents in the countryside were forced to dig expensive wells deeper in the earth to chase a receding aquifer. Meanwhile, the town of Aberdeen,

Maryland, planned to construct a desalination plant to convert the brackish waters of the Chesapeake into potable water.[12]

Thirsting for Western Waters

Water scarcity is increasingly becoming an acute problem for California's 36.5 million citizens. During winters with reduced precipitation, depleted snow pack produces less freshwater melt to fill the state's rivers. Forecasters in Denver currently predict that by 2035 there will be 35 percent more people in Colorado and 15 percent less water available in the Colorado River basin.[13] Something will have to give. In the West, the best dam sites have been taken and few reliable water supplies remain unclaimed. Denver's southern suburbs rely on water from an increasingly diminishing underground aquifer.

The Colorado River is a gusher as it flows through the Grand Canyon, but it is a mere trickle by the time it reaches the US-Mexican border. Like many rivers the Colorado is shrinking as agricultural and industrial uses deplete even more of the West's supply of freshwater. The snow and ice masses in the Sierra and Rocky mountains are diminishing as the arid West's freshwater reservoirs. The Metropolitan Water District of Southern California publishes an information picture that resembles the gas gauge of an automobile. Only it is a water gauge. From three quarter's full in 2006, this "water tank" is now verging on empty. Mono Lake nearly became a dry alkali desert bed owing to the tremendous water needs of Los Angeles. By 1982 the lake had lost over 30 percent of its 1941 water surface area. Because of public outcry over the potential loss of the geologically oldest lake in North America, Mono Lake came under the special protection of the California State Water Resources Control Board. Today Lake Mono's water level is approaching its nineteenth century level.[14]

Meanwhile, two iconic rivers of the great American West remain in bad shape: the Colorado and the Rio Grande. Although the United States has a treaty with Mexico to deliver Colorado River water over the border, it is hard pressed to do so in providing Colorado River water that meets treaty requirements. Simply put: all of the Colorado River is used up essentially by farmers and increasingly by cities along the Colorado. The water goes off to Southern California and Phoenix and Tucson, Arizona. A dry Colorado River delta is what Mexico gets most of the time.

The same goes with the Rio Grande: it is neither Rio nor Grande when it reaches Mexico. It essentially dries up around El Paso, Texas, 550 miles from the sea. The Rio Grande riverbed is dry for nearly 180 miles below El Paso before tributaries from Texas and Mexico replenish the last run of the Rio Grande to the Gulf of Mexico. However, this second Rio Grande is not much use to water-starved farmers seeking a reliable supply of irrigation water. The predicaments of the Colorado and the Rio Grande are part of a growing global phenomenon where some of the world's most important and longest rivers simply are not reaching the sea.

In Nebraska, parched pastures and barren fields bring home the fact that drought often makes areas of the state as dry as the moon. Grazing lands dry up in Arizona and animals in the wild thirst for water as well. Survival rates for young elk since 2002 have been exceedingly low. Meanwhile, in the Midwest, there is serious public concern about the strain placed on groundwater supplies by the emerging biofuel corn industry. Matters came to a serious head in Granite Falls, Minnesota, when, in its first year of operation, an ethanol plant depleted the groundwater so much that it had to begin pumping water from the Minnesota River.

As large areas of the West have been more or less in drought since the 1990s, the impact of no water accumulates and carries over. With even more serious droughts a western possibility, and given population growth, the existing water infrastructure becomes inadequate. It is not global warming, some climatologists say. The droughts are caused by rapid population growth and unwise agricultural choices like growing rice and cotton in the arid lands of California and Texas. All across the United States regional water systems cannot keep pace with metropolitan growth.

Unless consumption habits change, a generation of Americans will be looking skyward (for the sign of water) for relief from a new era of 1930s-style dustbowls. In 2009, Texas state climatologist John Nielson-Gammon said, at least nine of the 254 counties in Texas — the nation's most drought-stricken state — are suffering through their driest conditions since modern record-keeping began in 1895. In the decades ahead, Texas will only get hotter and drier, like the rest of the globe, says Nielson-Gammon. "We're going into territory we haven't seen in millions of years." This Texas A&M professor was appointed state climatologist by then-Governor George Bush. The current governor of Texas, Rick Perry, has never consulted Nielson-Gammon on the subject, preferring political nostrums to scientific evidence.[15]

Conservatives in Washington target wetlands as areas that could be developed for real estate interests, which could ruin a strategic link in the hydrological chain. Wetlands improve the quality of surface and groundwater supplies — and ultimately tap water. Wetlands also absorb heavy metals, nutrients, and sediments that adversely affect the water supply. Shallow ponds in Southwestern United States filter 20 to 80 percent of the water that goes into the Great Plains or Ogallalah aquifer. Many western states get their drinking water from this aquifer. The loss of ponds to developers and agribusiness interests means that contaminants ultimately end up in tap water.

Dixie's Drought

In 2007, the Southeast found itself to be one of the most rain-starved regions in the United States. Although the drought caused no public health threat, it did link America's fast-growing suburbs with very real water situations around the world as nations struggle to maintain reserves of potable water. Vacationers and recreational boaters noticed the water problem in 2007 when many of the lakes built for electric power plants like Lake Martin in Alabama became shallow mud flats in places. Drought in the South caused major losses in 2007-2008 to field crops like corn and soybeans and wheat. Adding cotton and hay to this list, the total loss in the Southeast was more than $1.3 billion. Further, low lake levels forced power companies like Duke Energy and the Tennessee Valley Authority to reduce their generation of hydroelectric power and turn to coal-fired plants that were more expensive and polluting for the production of electricity.

When rivers flow through fast-growing urban areas, a kind of grim zero-sum arithmetic takes hold as municipalities calculate for themselves and not for their fellow-citizens downstream. The Regional Water Planning District of North Georgia estimates that Atlanta will outstrip its water supply in ten years if water consumption is not curbed. Further, the depleted Chattahoochie River, which flows through Atlanta, is so heavily polluted with sewage and other toxins that by the time it flows to Alabama its usefulness as a public water source is seriously impaired.

Currently in the region mandatory restrictions on outdoor watering have been effective in the short-term during drought and surcharges on excessive water use seem to have worked. Although many Southeastern cities have tried to educate their citizens about conserving water, it is not until they are hit in their wallets that they begin to see the realities of their water problem. The Southeast's population continues to mushroom with retirees, workers, and immigrants. Pauling County, Georgia, outside Atlanta, for example, saw its population swell by 49 percent from 2000 to 2006.

Such growth has a profound impact on available water resources. According to Daniel Clodfelter, co-chairman of North Carolina's Environmental Review Commission and a member of the state legislature: "The population growth (in North Carolina) alone is going to make it impossible for us to assume we can always count on water for all purposes for all times." In 2009, Senator Clodfelter sponsored the Water Resource Planning Act. This law will make it harder to transfer North Carolina waters from one river basin to be used in another. In short, it would prevent more affluent and expanding communities from hijacking state water resources to the detriment of the general population.[16]

Throughout the South, during times of severe drought, there is fear that sparse water could force the shutdown of nuclear reactors. Nuclear reactors need billions of gallons of cooling water to operate and, during times of drought in the region, many of the water levels in lakes and rivers are getting close to the limit set by the Nuclear Regulatory Commission. We may see water levels decreasing below intake pipes. While this may not cause blackouts, this can result in increased energy costs as utilities buy from other sources.

As the South in 2007-2008 confronted severe water shortages, cities placed restrictions on lawn watering and car-washing operations. The drought in Georgia became so bad that Governor Sonny Perdue pleaded with his citizens to limit their water use. "I encourage all Georgians to make their dry lawns and dirty cars a badge of honor," he said."[17] In Atlanta, a sort of "water rage" began to be felt. An Atlanta TV station named and shamed a millionaire after it was revealed that he consumed sixty times more than the average Georgia household. During this time the level of Lake Lanier, an important water source, dropped seventeen feet.

Drought is having political consequences in the southeast, pitting Alabama and Florida at loggerheads with Georgia over a state plan for withdrawing water from Lake Lanier for Atlanta's metropolitan drinking water. This would severely disrupt the flow of the Chattahoochee River, which supplies water to towns in Alabama and Florida and whose flow is key to the survival of freshwater mussels and sturgeon species. The three states have feuded since 1989 over how to divide the water, but the drought exacerbated the problem. Meanwhile, Florida seeks legal control over Lake Lanier and the Chattahoochee and Flint Rivers, and this isn't likely to make water discourse any easier. Rains in 2006-2007 alleviated the problem briefly, but, in the fall of 2007, La Nina, a climate condition, diverted seasonal rains north and west — the hurricanes that usually dumped heavy rains on the region failed to materialize. By mid-February 2008, nearly all of the Southeast remained abnormally dry.

The irony of Lake Lanier outside of Atlanta was that it was not originally intended to be a public water reservoir. It was originally authorized by the federal government and built by the US Army Corps of Engineers to provide hydroelectricity and flood control. However, since 1990, Florida, Georgia, and Alabama have all been fighting for use of the water in Lake Lanier. Federal law mandates that when a river flows between two or more states, each state has a right to an equal share of the water. This has not happened. Atlanta's sprawling metropolitan development has produced a raging thirst for the water of Lake Lanier. After a bitter fight in federal court in July 2009, a federal judge from Minnesota (chosen as an arbiter from a neutral state) ruled that Congress never authorized Lake Lanier to be used as a source of the water supply for metropolitan Atlanta. Critics of the decision predicted a FEMA-style water disaster for Atlanta in the next drought if the decision was upheld. Meanwhile, Tampa, Florida, offered rebates of up to $100 on low-flow toilets, which use 1.6 gallons per flush instead of the older models that use 3.5 to 7 gallons per flush. By the end of 2005, Tampa had replaced 33,765 toilets for an annual savings of 434 million gallons or one day of peak water consumption in a busy Eastern metro-area like Washington, DC.

Resource wars are supposed to happen someplace else, not in our own country. People in the United States usually do not think of themselves as water poor or that the term "resource wars" might be applied as a description that is going on in their city or region.

Erik Hagen, a former hydrologist at the Interstate Commission on the Potomac River Basin, noted that what we are seeing are "water problems along the East Coast prompting some forward-looking planning." Regional authorities along the Potomac have planned for drought through water retention dams. Without reserve releases from retention dams, on a peak day, the three DC metro water utilities along the Potomac can suck out about 85 percent of its volume at the time.

Issues of water, growth, and land use are increasingly flowing to the forefront of multi-regional political discourse. In addition to linking the availability of water supply to metro-development, planners and politicians have to look at other ways to meet the demand for water that will support development. Also, academic institutions, city government, domestic and international non-profits, and corporations are working together to solve metropolitan water problems like those of Atlanta, but also to address the same kind of access, conservation, and water quality issues. This work is still in its initial phase, but failure to plan for the water problems of the future may lead urban areas on the Atlantic seaboard to the parched reality now being confronted by our Western states and many countries around the world.

Most of us would recoil in shock if we had to experience the water problems of those who live in Orme, a small, coal-mining town tucked in the mountains of southern Tennessee that has seen better days. Many of its residents are elderly, the average per capita income is around $15,000, and by 2007 sporadic water supply became the norm. Tiny Orme ran water collection drives and sought donated bottles of water from residents in surrounding communities. In the fall of 2007, water was so scarce due to drought conditions that the town had to ration water use to a few hours a day. Each evening Orme's 140 residents waited for Mayor Tony Reames to make a short drive from his house to a nearby water tower that contained the town's precious reserve of water. He opened a valve and the citizens filled buckets and water jars, did laundry, took showers, and washed dishes before the faucets ran dry, and then waited for the next evening. Few people in this bucolic mountain village ever envisioned a time when their wells and water supply would run dry. The drought of 2007 in the Southeast disabused them of that feeling, Some residents caught water draining from their air-conditioners in buckets to flush toilets since their spring-fed water source ran dry in August.

Once upon a time, a waterfall supplied the town with water. Now that source is gone and Orme, like a figure in a Tennessee Williams play, is dependent upon the kindness of strangers for its water. Orme never embraced the developing world; however, the developing world's water problems have embraced it.[18] Fortunately for Orme, in the midst of its suffering, it received a federal grant to install a water line to a town in nearby Alabama. Soon water drawn from the Tennessee River three miles away may again flow in Orme 24-hours a day, yet Mayor Tony Reame cautions about the lessons learned. "If it can happen in Orme, where we had a waterfall, it can happen anywhere."[19]

Water scarcity typically conjures up visions of drought and thirst, writes water expert Sandra Postel. The important fact to note, though, is that since the 1990s water tables in the United States have been dropping due to escalating water consumption. Around water-starved cities there is growing competition for access to water between rural and urban interests. If we use 1950 as a base water use year in the United States, water consumption in America increased over 50 percent by 1990.[20]

We have not yet touched upon the effect of water scarcity on the agricultural South. As Lester Brown has questioned, "At what point does water scarcity translate into food scarcity?"[21] Droughts in the South have had a marked impact on harvests in the region especially that of corn, soybeans, and garden-quality agricultural staples that need regular rainfall or dependable irrigation. Currently it takes a thousand tons of water to produce a ton of grain. It is worth noting that in the United States close to 19 percent of agricultural energy use, in the form of gas and oil, is for pumping water. Americans, accustomed to having a dependable supply of food, whether from 3,000-mile travel sources or locally, may well have to adjust to changing environmental conditions that impact on their consumption behavior.

The Potomac:
Last Chance Watershed

The Potomac River is one of the most storied and studied rivers in America. Although it lacks the romance and grandeur of the Hudson and the Mississippi, it is the nation's river, closely identified with Washington, DC, and our democratic heritage. The Potomac watershed is the land drained by the river; on a map, it is shaped like an eastward pointing crescent. The watershed covers 14,670 square miles and four states — 39 percent in Virginia, 26 percent in Maryland, 24 percent in West Virginia, 11 percent in Pennsylvania — and a small portion in Washington, DC. The Potomac watershed has eight major rivers and tributaries. This region has four major physiographic provinces: the Coastal Plain or tidewater, the Piedmont where the first mountain range is encountered, the Appalachian province, and the Allegheny plateau to the west.

Until its recent problems with pollution and sedimentation, the Potomac watershed has been remarkably fecund in fish and wildlife. Although this watershed is still predominantly rural, it is rapidly urbanizing. The environment of the 385-mile-long waterway and its watershed are as problematic as any political imbroglio on Capitol Hill; in this river system, scientific research and political agendas intersect often with intriguing and occasionally controversial results. Conservationists often refer to the Potomac as the "Last Chance Watershed" because it is at high ecological risk. The scientific record on the past and current conditions of the Potomac River reads like a frustrating story of short bursts of improvement within a longer time curve of development, degradation, and decline.

Starting in 1890, when the Potomac achieved notoriety for the stench of its sewage within yards of the White House, until 1965, when President Lyndon B. Johnson labeled it "a national disgrace," the river was largely a conduit for urban sewage from the rapidly expanding metropolitan capital nexus. Population growth and the demand for real estate resulted in polluted waters, wetland loss, and groundwater contamination.[22]

In the 1970s, widespread public concern over algae, sewage contamination, and sediment problems led to a much-heralded cleanup of the Potomac. The Federal Water Pollution Control Amendments and the Clean Water Act passed by Congress were geared toward making the Potomac and other rivers into "swimmable-fishable waters." Since 1990, however, new problems have affected the river. Storm water overflows are now the principal cause of high fecal coliform concentration in rivers like the Potomac. Other sources of fecal contamination are faulty septic tanks and livestock and pet feces.

However, the most worrisome of the new stresses on the Potomac come from rampant population growth in northern Virginia and the relocation of problematic poultry agribusiness to the upper watershed of the Potomac in the Eastern Panhandle of West Virginia. Thus, despite best efforts, the Potomac still constitutes a threat to human health. Swimming and other water-contact sports are risky activities. In 1997-1998, the Potomac was named one of the twenty most endangered rivers in the United States by American Rivers, the nation's leading river conservation group. One of the great ironies of federal life in Washington is that the Congress daily flushes its waste into the river while also daily commuting across bridges that allow it to view the river. Yet it seems particularly obtuse when it comes to guarding its own water supply.

"Washington," says Jim Dougherty of the DC Sierra Club, "has always been the tale of two rivers, what you would call the white river and the black river." The Potomac is blessed with green spaces, monuments, and fancy residences. The Anacostia, a small eight-mile-long river that feeds into the Potomac, he reflects, "has been home to jails, incinerators, and power plants." In the past, the Anacostia River was treated as a sewer. Large segments of the population along the river were also treated as part of the sewage problem as urban redevelopment in the 1960s took thousands of people from Southwest Washington and dumped them into a human disposal site called Anacostia.

Currently, the Anacostia River waterfront is being developed with a new baseball stadium, condos, and office buildings as part of Washington's revived civic consciousness. Meanwhile, the city copes with a semi-decrepit sewer and water system while baseball fans sit in expensive box seats to cheer on the Washington Nationals. At these games, Tom Arrasmith, of the Anacostia Watershed Advisory Committee, passes out business cards that identify him as a member of the Anacostia Swimming Club, an ironic reminder of the work still to be done to make local rivers swimmable.

The river is cleaner, though, than it used to be. Sewer overflows along Watts Branch are now referred to in the past tense and isolated Anacostia neighborhoods will be connected with a trolley system. The city percolates with housing and condo construction, and the District thus far seems immune to the recession that plagues other areas. Yet many people along the Anacostia River fear that all this progress will come at too great a price. Swelling housing prices and gentrification make it hard for working people — white and black — to remain in the city. A clean river may "clean out" the black population by encouraging neighborhood gentrification.

If you stand at Haines Point and look out at the mouth of the Anacostia River as it flows into the Potomac, you see a waterfront scene of considerable beauty. However, at the river's edge, opportunity flows into poverty and the future is a lot less certain than waterfront developers would have us believe. Just two short decades ago there were places in Washington where poor blacks had to get their drinking water from a neighborhood public pump.

Similar problems to the Potomac's can be found in other watersheds. As reliance upon groundwater for drinking water has increased in Delaware and Pennsylvania, state authorities are concerned about leaking underground storage tanks, landfills, septic systems, and drainage from abandoned hazardous waste sites. Along the Susquehanna, serious sewage contamination problems and acid mine runoff bedevil local water sources. Groundwater in Delaware is impacted by nitrate contamination, particularly in the agricultural areas of Kent and Sussex counties. High nitrate levels in underground sources of drinking water are a potential health concern. Synthetic organic compounds, such as cleaning solvents and degreasers, have been detected in Delaware's groundwater, primarily due to leaking underground storage tanks, landfills, septic systems, chemical spills and leaks, and abandoned hazardous waste sites. Elevated dissolved iron concentrations in well water and saltwater intrusion are also groundwater concerns. The protection of the quality and quantity of the State's aquifers is a key concern of public officials, particularly given the fact that reliance on groundwater for drinking water supplies has been increasing in Delaware.

"Frack Jobs" and Water

The Appalachian Mountains of North America contain rich methane gas deposits that historically are related to the opening up of the coalfields in the region after 1890. These fields contain billions of cubic feet of natural gas and are viewed as a much cleaner and reliable energy source for American consumers than oil products. Yes, gas is clean energy. However, the problem is in getting the gas out of the ground in the fields of Pennsylvania, New York, Alabama, and West Virginia. The current technology in use is something called hydraulic fracturing, a common engineering technique used to stimulate the production of oil and natural gas. Typically chemically-treated fluids are injected underground at high pressures. The shale formations fracture or break and the gas or oil moves freely out of the formation. The injected fluids are called "a frack job"; and a single operation can require five million gallons of water. The water injected is full of chemicals to dissolve sand and other minerals and the water that flows back to the surface often contains benzenes, heavy metals, and other chemicals that put aquatic life at risk. Frack water is stored in retaining ponds with plastic liners, but often the liners have tears that allow the "fracked water" to seep into aquifers.

The problem with fracking is twofold: the natural gas industry has been allowed to protect the chemical composition of the water as a trade secret and fracking water is exempt from Safe Drinking Water Act regulations. This piece of Washington legal casuistry was done in 2005 with the implementation of the Energy Act, which exempted gas exploration from federal water safety laws. This is often referred to as the "Halliburton Loophole," after the company that developed the process, and came about when ex-Halliburton president Dick Cheney was Vice President of the United States. It was a very valuable gift to his old company and a damning one for safe drinking water in the gas fields of Pennsylvania.

There are a number of cases in the United States where hydraulic fracturing has turned the well water of homes into a stinking brown cocktail. Communities are at risk wherever coal beds contain large amounts of methane gas that can be profitably mined by this process.

Currently the center of the major natural gas fracturing industry can be found in the Marcellus gas fields of Pennsylvania. Named after the Marcellus Shale found in north and central Pennsylvania, the Marcellus field has been a financial bonanza to energy companies and owners of farms in the state. The Marcellus Shale gas field, located more than a mile beneath much of Pennsylvania's land mass, has the potential to be the second largest field in the world, behind only the South Pars/Asalouyeh field between Iraq and Qatar. In BTUs, the domestic fields could produce the equivalent of 87 billion barrels of oil, enough to meet world demand for three years.

Gas is environmentally popular as a replacement for coal because it releases only half as much carbon into the atmosphere and can slow global warming.

The technology, however, is new and there has not been much research done on the long-term impact of fracking in terms of polluted water, declining wild life populations, and deforestation. Gas companies have bought up the mineral rights in Pennsylvania in a frenzy reminiscent of the Oklahoma Land Rush. Many farm owners are getting royalties on leased mineral rights. The state of Pennsylvania, desperate for revenue in recession times, has also sold gas permits to allow the companies to drill for gas in the 2.3 million-acre Pennsylvania state forest. In 2008, for example, the state of Pennsylvania sold off mineral rights to 74,000 acres of forest for $166 million to replenish its starved revenue coffers and Governor Ed Rendell unloaded an additional 32,000 acres for mineral leases for $128 million. Thus, while the Gulf Coast of Louisiana and Florida battled a toxic tide of oil spill drifting ashore from an underground British Petroleum well, years of work in reforestation and rural revitalization are put at risk for gas leases, putting gas well pads that are ulcers on the landscape and leeching brown liquids into water wells.

Also at issue is the gargantuan withdrawals of stream and groundwater by gas companies for drilling and extracting methane gas. This is perfectly legal, but a major concern to environmentalists who see the specter of drought as something that must be factored into the hydraulic equation tapping the gas fields of the Eastern United States. New York State has been far more cautious in its approach to natural gas and has declared a moratorium on drilling in the Marcellus until it knows exactly what the social and environmental costs will be. Meanwhile, in Pennsylvania, complains the Audubon Society, "outraged professional resource managers have been sidelined by big-money politics."[23] In the West, residents of Colorado find methane from gas-drilling in their drinking water while in West Virginia, New Mexico, Virginia, Wyoming, and Alabama residents have reported changes in their water quality or quantity following fracturing operations of gas wells near their homes.

Dimock, an impoverished enclave in Northeastern Pennsylvania, has had more than its share of problems from fracking. In 2009, some 8,000 gallons of dangerous drilling fluids from a well site manned by Cabot Oil and Gas seeped into a nearby creek where a large fish kill was reported by the state department of environmental protection. The drilling fluid manufactured by Halliburton was described as a "potential carcinogen." This incident was one of a host of environmental woes that have come to Dimock as a result of gas-drilling and fracking. Methane and other chemicals are contaminating drinking water wells. While methane in the water is harmless to drink, the gas can bubble up through the water and become gas again.

Methane gas fumes built up in the home of Norma Fiorentino, a few hundred yards away from a gas well she had permitted to be leased on her property. Somehow, from fracking, stray gas leaked into the aquifer and slipped into Fiorentino's well. When a motorized pump turned on in her well house, it flicked a spark that caused a blast on New Year's morning that tossed aside a concrete slab weighing several thousand pounds. Later Fiorentino worried that if the gas that had built-up in her well house had collected in her basement, it would have killed her. One homeowner in Dimock had so much gas in his water wells he was advised to open his windows to take a bath. This was not an isolated case. A spark ignited the natural gas that collected in the basement of Richard and Thelma Payne's suburban Cleveland home, "shattering windows, blowing doors 20 feet from their hinges and igniting a small fire in a violent flash. The Paynes were jolted out of their bed, and their house lifted off the ground." In Clearfield, Pennsylvania, a natural gas well operated by Forbes Energy of Alice, Texas, exploded in the spring of 2010, sending gas and polluted water 75 feet into the air. There was high underground methane pressure and if the gas had been ignited, the nearby Punxsutawney Hunt Club would have been consumed in a fireball. According to environmental groups, "a string of documented cases of gas escaping into drinking water — not just in Pennsylvania but across North America — is raising new concerns about the hidden costs of this energy tide and strengthening arguments across the country that drilling can put drinking water at risk."[24] A single fracking well can cough up a million gallons of wastewater laced with carcinogens like benzine and radioactive elements like radium.

Drilling for natural gas, authorities in Ohio and Pennsylvania point out, can break through the tight seals of geologic layers that separate gas from the surface. When a drill bit sinks down, it breaks the seal and a gusher of water and gas ensues that can contaminate aquifers. Gas companies argue that they take utmost efforts to prevent contamination by resealing the bore with concrete, but in many cases gas-drilling companies fail to build proper cement casings without filling all the gaps. If the concrete leaks, drilling fluids and gas get out. When you pump 46,000 gallons of water, sand, and chemicals into a bore well during fracking, you have the possibility of leaks into the aquifer, despite all the cement that is placed in the bore afterwards. Sometimes "over pressurized conditions" occur, resulting in an invasion of natural gas through cracks in the shale.

Ironically, as the Environmental Protection Agency tries to investigate hydraulic fracturing's effect on the environment, the United States Congress is seeking to put funding limits on EPA water and air investigations. The gas companies think that all the criticism of their welling operations is misguided and misinformed. Gas explosions and contaminated water wells, they argue, are rare events, like plane crashes. If well operators put too much concrete in the bore, they risk collapsing the well. Not enough cement and you get methane leaks. The problems for residents in the Marcellus Shale country are how to draw a balance between protecting the natural gas wells and protecting their groundwater from methane and other chemicals.

Drilling for natural gas in the Marcellus Shale continues in Dimock, Pennsylvania. Many of the town's 1,300 residents have fallen on hard times and they need the royalties from the gas wells that they have leased on their property. Pennsylvania is at the forefront of the nation's gas-drilling boom, with gas leases expanding at the rate of 4,000 a year. More wells are currently being drilled in Pennsylvania than any other states except Texas. There are currently more than 1,000 Marcellus Shale wells in Pennsylvania alone. In 2011, the Pennsylvania Department of Environmental Protection estimated that drilling produced 19 million gallons of wastewater a day, far more than all the state's waterways combined can safely absorb.[25]

Given the increasing appetite in America for low-cost energy to fuel our restless consumption engine, there will be little backing away from dangerous energy technologies. In 2010, Pennsylvania voted for natural gas and economic opportunities, but the environmental price tag can be very high with unknown dangers to public safety. Many safety experts believe the possibility of contaminated drinking wells is too close to home for environmental experiment.[26]

The question, however, is what impact natural gas and probably oil drilling operations will have on growing water needs of nearly 50 million people who live in the urban corridor between Washington, DC, and New York City. Polluted waterways can't be improved without a major public outcry against our rivers becoming toxic chemical waterways. Pennsylvania is developing its own energy field with more than its share of disaster risk. Unless we firmly control our drinkable, fishable, and swimmable waters, we may face frightening consequences as a species. Thus in the future impaired waters may in turn lead to impaired people.[27] In his film documentary, *Gasland*, for HBO, Josh Fox takes us on a "fracking" journey into the far west of Colorado and Wyoming, where he encounters many residents bitter over their ruined water supplies because of natural gas drilling. A review in the *Washington Post* called *Gasland* a dirge "shot against the chilly and bleak American expanse." The irony of this documentary is that it began when a gas company offered Josh Fox a six-figure fee for drilling rights to his Pocono farm where he was raised near the Delaware River.[28]

People like Josh Fox who want to protect their land have to contend with oil and gas interests that have some of the most powerful lobbyists in Washington. During the period of 1990 to 2004, the "oil and gas crowd" amassed $181 million in campaign contributions. Oil and gas influence is sufficient to keep state legislatures and the federal government writing statutes favorable to their drilling interests with generous tax deductions.[29]

Colorado is a cautionary example about oil and gas drilling. According to *The Denver Post*, oil and gas companies reported "almost 1,000 spills to Colorado regulators over the past 2-1/2 years totaling 5.2 million gallons of drilling liquids and oil." Fracking accounted for 80 percent of the drilling messes. "To believe that we can have lots of little spills and a lot of big spills and that we are not going to see a really big impact is to ignore the reality of the risks of this industry," said Nada Culver, senior counsel for the Wilderness Society in Denver.[30] Companies that use large quantities of water to run their businesses are seeking to lock up water supplies. One is Royal Dutch Shell, which is buying groundwater rights in Colorado as it prepares to drill for oil in the shale deposits there.

During the writing of this book, one of the worst environmental disasters to occur in the United States unfolded in the waters of the Gulf of Mexico as millions of gallons leaked from a British Petroleum well and headed towards the shores and pristine wetlands of Louisiana and Alabama. BP/Royal Dutch Shell announced at the same time that Europe's largest oil company paid $4.7 billion in cash for East Resources, a Pennsylvania company that owns more than 2,500 oil and natural gas wells in the United States. It also controls 1.25 million acres of land in the Marcellus Shale region that runs from New York to southwest Virginia. Thus, in a single deal that Shell CEO Peter Voser said was part of the company's plans to "grow and upgrade" its holdings, the stream health and forest habitats of three states are now at risk. Environmentalists worried that in the wake of the BP disaster whether BP/Royal Dutch Shell would "grow and upgrade" a similar environmental calamity.[31]

Conclusion

While a North American drought is no more than a mild distraction for some Americans, our future may be ominously dry. It has all happened before. A perspective on a long-term drought in the United States can be obtained by analysis of water data from sediment deposits in lake beds that date back as early as 1200 AD. The data reveals that there were quite a few droughts in North America, some lasting over a century. The droughts may have been the result of cycles of solar activity and fluctuations of carbon dioxide in the atmosphere. According to a recent NASA report, there is mounting concern among scientists that as levels of atmospheric carbon dioxide rise, the average global temperature rises with it. This will have profound effects on precipitation patterns and may affect oceanic circulation as well. Whatever the cause, for over 1,500 years there was a persistent pattern of drought in North America. We may be returning to that mode of climate behavior that North America experienced before 1200 AD.[32]

In 2007, the Southwest was in the grip of what climatologists called a "mega-drought," one of the worst in 500 years. Environmental writer Mike Davis summed up the long-dry of the first years of the twenty-first century rather well: "What if the prolonged drought in the southwest turns out to be on the scale of the medieval catastrophes that contributed to the notorious collapse of the complex Anasazi societies at Chaco Canyon and Mesa Verde during the twelfth century?" In one way the Anasazi were like us, argues Davis: They were little prepared to make sacrifices in their lifestyle. "In the last instance they preferred to eat one another."[33]

We have only begun to recognize our vulnerabilities when it comes to water. As water expert David Carle reminds us, the food that each of us consumes per day represents an investment of 4,500 gallons of water. This land of plenty, called the United States, would do well to keep in mind the bucket brigades of Orme, Tennessee, the garden hoses of Detroit, and the fracking explosions in Pennsylvania.

The water crisis is no longer something that affects far away developing and poorer nations. The crisis is right here in our backyard. The many failures of our public water systems have generated our new and keen interest in water and its potability. We are concerned about the service of our water companies and the dependability of their service. For too long we have taken water for granted as we turned on the tap to brush our teeth, took a shower, washed our car, or filled our swimming pool. Whether keen public interest is sufficient to bring about social and environmental change remains to be seen.

Just as the safety of our water supply increasingly grows precarious, we have seen over a century of sound public health management overturned. Specifically, during the recent George Bush presidency, the administration targeted for dismantlement laws that protect drinking water in American cities. It also proposed sharp cuts in funds to cleanup polluted waterways. The main target for the Bush Administration was the 1972 Clean Water Act, which successfully protected American waterways for over thirty years. The Bush Administration chipped away at key provisions of the Act at the behest of mining and natural gas companies and agribusiness and developers. As I write this, a new Congress in Washington is attempting to neuter the Clean Water Act even further. Thus, water problems have become an increasingly dismal chronicle. The Great Lakes are shrinking. Upstate New York's reservoirs continue to drop to new lows and in the West the Sierra Nevada snow pack is melting faster each year. The EPA can hardly keep apace with record levels of impaired or polluted water in our urban areas.

No part of the United States seems immune from water problems. Currently the state of Florida worries that its drinking water supply will be threatened by the BP Gulf oil spill. Many of Florida's lakes, streams, and rivers are part of the Florida aquifer, which supplies fresh drinking water to more than 18 million people. Florida fears oil spills will enter the wetlands and ultimately the aquifer. Oil pollution of our shores does not go away simply because it is no longer a headline feature in our newspapers. Thanks to a massive public relations campaign by British Petroleum, people think everything is back to normal. Most Americans are still unaware, reports the Natural Resource Defense Council, of the environmental damage and the financial and health stresses.[34] As oil-contaminated water percolates downward into the ground, it moves from where the water table is high to where the water table is low. Water experts in Florida fear that the consequences of aquifer contamination from the Deepwater

Horizon oil spill of 2010 will be a catastrophe for virtually all of the state and parts of Alabama as well. This fear is accompanied by other fears about the destruction of much of Florida's tourist economy because of polluted fishing grounds and oil-strewn beaches. Resort areas like Henrico County and the Tampa metropolitan area could lose untold millions of dollars to the Gulf oil spill and it may be years before these areas recover. Pristine waters like Tarpon Springs and Weeki Wachee Springs may become aquifer oil casualties. According to the Air and Waste Management Association, in the long-term, toxic materials from oil can remain in the water and on the land for many years. They can build-up in the food chain to lethal levels and destroy or disrupt an area's ecosystem.[35]

On a bright warm and sunny Memorial Day weekend my son and I cruise happily along a beautiful stretch of bikeway in Washington known as the Northwest Branch of the Anacostia Trail. Behind my son is my grandson, Anthony, happily strapped in a bike trailer and communing with the sky and nature. The bird life is stunning and we see a Baltimore Oriole for the first time in many months. To the left of us, down the bank, flows the Anacostia River, by now a stream rippling pleasantly through the watershed of the Washington suburbs. The trees bend down gently towards the river and people with picnic baskets flock the park benches and picnic tables. The only cause for apprehension comes when we turn with our bikes on a path underneath a traffic-choked bridge. On this stretch of the river we come upon some small children in the distance happily playing in the water. The stream at this point smells of sewage. Broken or cracked sewer lines that run down through the stream valley from the suburbs to sewage treatment facilities in the District are the main culprits, though a gentle wind has disguised the water's odor. Calling out is senseless as they are too far away to hear above the noise of the bridge traffic. These children and others along the stream are playing in toxic waters and could come down with gastro-intestinal problems from e-coli. For these mostly immigrant Hispanic families, the water looks clear and clean — probably far better than what they had been used to in their native land. Except for the sewage it is a touching Memorial Day scene of water, fun, and leisure. We know this scene. It is replicated everyday in developing countries where children play in dangerous waters. We have seen kids swimming in the dirty klongs of Bangkok and in the sewage-plagued rivers of India. We shake our heads, change gears, and bike on.

The question for the future in the United States is whether Americans want to live in a country polluted or parched or both. It is also a question that has the most profound implications for the developing world, especially India, which seems to be rushing headlong into one of the planet's most difficult water crises.

"If we become

rich or poor as a

nation, it's because

of water."

-- Sunita Narain

Chapter Four

India's Make or Break Water Issue

India's Big Thirst

To see India's drinking water problem in detail, one only has to visit any of India's crowded railway stations. At the Kolkata Main Railway Station a mass of people swirls out to the platform to cajole and push its way onto the railway carriages. Other passengers for future trains tend to gather near the available water cistern — a large glass or ceramic device of five to ten gallons. A turn of the faucet allows Indians to wash their hands and pat their brows with a wetted towel in the intense pre-monsoon heat. Others pour untreated water into drinking glasses of dubious sanitation. Upper-class passengers wait to get their bottled water on their train. The cistern, or a plastic bottle of water, is the closest an Indian gets in public to what he thinks will be water that will not make him ill. Or go to a country well and watch farm women draw water from a hand pump. It is often strange smelling and muddy brown. The women carry five-gallon water jugs on their heads, sometimes for long distances. On their heads, Indians also carry the weight of the world's water future. Their strength makes an American struggling with a gallon jug of milk seem puny by comparison.

It is hard to explain India's water problems to friends as they invariably raise the question: "Is not India water-drenched by monsoons?" My answer is yes, there is rainfall. Still, there is not enough good water in India. The monsoons of India, which come in the summer and late fall, are so intense that it leaves one speculating on how India could possibly have a water shortage. Ironically, these heavy rains are part of the problem. Not only are these rains often accompanied by devastating floods, but also the monsoon runoff is not well-utilized and is frequently contaminated. Rain harvesting or water management lacks national direction, so the rains fail to adequately recharge the groundwater aquifer levels that are receding alarmingly across India.

India's people need access to clean drinking water. With a current population of over 1.2 billion, India has a gigantic thirst. Current population projections suggest that India will have almost 2 billion people by the end of the twenty-first century.[1] Indians drink on the average three to five liters of water a day. Thus, by century's end, India will require six billion liters a day just for basic drinking purposes. A 2009 McKinsey Associates study on global water consumption reported that India presently consumes 740 billion cubic meters of water each year. By 2030, India's water needs will double in terms of personal, agricultural, and industrial consumption.[2]

What is happening in India is a more intense replay of what is happening elsewhere in terms of the world's water problems. Like many developing countries, India has more than its share of "magical thinking" that assumes serious problems like water shortages will be easily solved with a quick technological fix. Against this backdrop of "magical thinking" is what analysts call "the inexorable crush of demographic destiny."

At this time only five percent of India's water is reserved for drinking and domestic purposes. Three percent of the water supply goes for industrial use while agriculture gets the lion's share, 92 percent. To intellectually grasp this demand, consider India's annual water consumption. In 2006, when India's water problems received critical international scrutiny, water scientists found that between the domestic, agricultural, and industrial sectors, India used approximately 829 billion cubic meters of water every year, which in American terms is approximately the size of Lake Erie. Looking again at the McKinsey projections of 1,500 billion cubic meters of water consumed in India in 2030, it's possible India will be well on its way to consuming water at the rate of two Lake Erie's annually in the future.[3]

All of India's fourteen major river systems are heavily polluted, mostly from the 50 million cubic meters of untreated sewage discharged each year as wastewater throughout the country. Every large city in India has its own nauseating tableaux of public stench, runoff from garbage dumps, and water from faulty pit latrines. Animal waste from cows in the streets and fecal coliform bacteria in most rivers often wildly exceeds World Health Organization standards. India's troubled urban water supply is the culprit in a growing number of gastrointestinal ailments among the population. Add to this the wastewater from industrial activities that are often contaminated with toxic organic and inorganic substances as well as acidic refuse from textile plants.

In a recent report, Somni Sengupta, a *New York Times* journalist covering India, noted that foraging for water both in the city and countryside is a predicament that "testifies to the government's astonishing inability to deliver the most basic services to its citizens at a time when India asserts itself as a global power."[4] The economy of India is the eleventh largest in the world by nominal GDP and the fourth in purchasing power parity. Talk to Indian businessmen in Mumbai and they will recite the mantra of India's rise to global power. They will talk about India's IT revolution, its manufacturing base, the glorious Tata industrial complex, and India's vast human resources. Arguing that India has reached a profound economic takeoff point, they predict that the country will soon be among the leading powers of the world. Says Gurcharan Das, retired director of Proctor and Gamble, India: "To ask a poor country to slow its economic growth is immoral — it is to condemn its poor to penury."[5] What these businessmen will not talk about is how this rise to globalism will occur in a nation with major water problems.

India's growing economy and its large agricultural sector may well stretch its thinning water supply to the breaking point. Certainly clean potable water is at a premium these days. The only water one can safely trust to drink is bottled in plastic and these water bottles pose their own environmental problems.

In November 2009, I traveled to India as part of a Smithsonian-based team to teach a course on the history of water to mid-level science museum professionals in Kolkata. My purpose, ostensibly, was to show how to incorporate water history and water policy issues into exhibits at science museums across India. On the weekends, I was the guest of various regional museums where the administrators were eager to showcase some of their more popular exhibits. In conversations over tea and delicious desserts, I asked my hosts a simple question: "Where can I go to find a clean stream or tributary for drinking purposes?" My hosts were reluctant to answer. Instead they pointed out nearby lakes or ponds that had great cultural or religious significance. Finally, on a crowded overnight train from Kolkata to Siliguri in the far north, I resolved to look for clean water myself in the highlands of the Himalayas. My trip was complicated by the fact that the Indian Army had sealed off the main mountain road to Darjeeling because of "ethnic disturbances." My wife and I were comfortably ensconced in a forest bungalow complex near the Jaldhapara Wildlife Sanctuary National Park in West Bengal and personally attended to by the resident chef. This 114-square-kilometer area contains lush forests and grasslands and is cut by the Torsa River. Nestled in the Himalayan foothills, the park has great natural beauty. Though not frequently visited, the sanctuary is home to over fifty Indian-one-horned rhinoceros whose numbers have recently come under serious threat by poachers.

We drove with our guide to see rhino and elephants. I was more preoccupied, however, with the condition of the Torso River, which begins its journey southward from Tibet. I subsequently discovered that even in the highlands, the Torso was already polluted with human feces — and this was but a short distance from where the Himalaya's snow pack begins the water cycle for much of India.

Urbanization and the Water Intensive Life

Recently India's water crisis has grown as fast as its population and economy. Cities and squalid metropolitan sprawl dominate the landscape with raging speed. A thirsty urban population and agricultural regions determined to tap every available stream and aquifer for irrigation place great strains on the country's sanitation and water. Admittedly, with modernization and increasing standards of living in India, people are living more water-intensive lives, especially in the cities. Flush toilets and washing machines are becoming necessary amenities for millions of newly minted middle-class Indians. In the twenty-first century, India has made the social decision to join Western nations in the celebration of a water-intensive life — the most telling example of this commitment to the lush life with water is the irrigated lawn.

India's urban population has doubled in the past thirty years and now represents over 30 percent of the country's total population. Demographers in India anticipate that India will be 50 percent urbanized in 2025. Of course, this rate of population growth is also going to urbanize India's water crisis.

India has the world's second largest population, which is expected to overtake China's by 2050. Currently of India's 1.2 billion people, 58 million Indians lead very comfortable lives; they are the nation's primary indicator of water waste and water affluence. Social forecasters predict India's middle class will be 583 million by 2025 and, with a burgeoning industrial and agricultural base, its water supply is being stretched ever thinner.

Every Indian urban center has its litany of water woes. For many of New Delhi's middle class residents, fretting about water begins with the awakening day. Water supply in the nation's capital is unpredictable (except for the rich) and it is a rare morning when water flows rather than trickles through the public pipes of middle-class and poor Delhi. Most residents have to rely upon a private water tanker truck. Water is in such demand in the cities of India that farmers in the countryside have stopped planting crops. They have become water farmers. Writes water journalist Steve Solomon, "They simply sell it to fleets of private water tankers carrying 3,000 gallons apiece that come a dozen times each day to transport it at a tidy profit to India's desperately thirsty and unsanitary cities."[6] City residents wait for the tanker to show up. If it doesn't, then they will have to rely on the water for mandi baths they have stored in buckets in their bathrooms. Bathing and rinsing with dipper-amounts of water is preferable to being unclean. Afterwards the same water will be used to flush their toilets. This is a lot better than relying on dilapidated municipal water systems that are unreliable and frequently contaminated with sewage.

The Yamuna River, a fetid watercourse if there ever was one, flows through New Delhi. Many Delhi residents are forced to rely on the Yamuna for their drinking water; it is Delhi's major water source. The New Delhi water board extracts 229 million gallons of water a day from the river. Its residents pour 950 million gallons of sewage into the river each day. The water math problem is obvious. In ancient Hindu mythology, the Yamuna was the river that fell from heaven to earth for the benefit of man, but from a public health standpoint, scientists have pronounced the Yamuna to be clinically dead. Currently the Yamuna is also New Delhi's principal waste drain. Therefore, Delhi's residents have a great likelihood of drinking their own sewage than anything else. Smart engineers in the near future, however, may be able to capitalize on the methane gas that bubbles from all the human feces to the river's surface for cheap energy. Thus, in one the richest cities in India, many of Delhi's residents are understandably edgy about water.

Across India, urban water distribution networks are in disrepair. Many have not been updated since the British Raj. The public taps flow only at certain times of the day. Because the rivers of India are too polluted to drink and the government is unable to deliver freshwater to the cities, many urban dwellers are doing the same thing as their counterparts in rural areas — turning to groundwater. However, this is only contributing to the depletion of underground aquifers. The greatest casualty of India's raging public thirst will be the nation's poor. India's society is still deeply stratified and its poor are socially and politically marginalized. India is home to one-third of the world's poor, most of whom are young. While it is easy to point out that for India the water stakes are too high to continue in the old way, India, like many of its Western neighbors, moves along with a "politics-as-usual" approach to its water problem.

Poor Governance — High Ideals and Low Dealings

In her highly regarded study on India and its water crisis, Nina Brooks has written that "water scarcity in India is primarily a man-made problem; therefore if India makes significant changes in the way it thinks about water and manages its resources soon, it could ward off, or at least mollify the impending crisis."[7]

Water supply functions have been critically disrupted in a country that gets 80 percent of its rainfall in three to four months. Currently the water cycle in India alternates between devastating floods and droughts. Groundwater over-drafting is now widespread in parts of India's Deccan Plateau, including the states of Andhra Pradesh, Karnataka, Maharashtra, and Tamil Nadu. Since 1946 the water table in parts of Karnataka has dropped from 8 meters below ground to 48 meters. Similar developments are occurring across India — testimony to the fact that India has failed to sustain its water cycle.

However, India's problem is the same as that of the United States. Like the Americans, for too long India has been living in a fool's paradise of cheap water that has been the mainstay of agriculture, diverse manufacturing and industrial sectors as coolants, water bases for food and beverage production, textile dyes, and sewage transport. This cheap water, over which there is virtually no regulation in India, is being rapidly pumped from underground aquifers and has been a major factor, reports *Earth Trends*, in the success of India's economic growth. As India faces a decline in its groundwater and the hopeless pollution of its surface water, it also faces the supreme irony — a well-watered nation with nary a drop to drink.

During storms and monsoons India receives an average of 4,000 billion cubic meters of rainfall every year. Very little rainfall is actually captured in cisterns and open wells for drinking; instead 48 percent of the rainfall ends up in India's polluted rivers.[8] With thirteen major rivers, high rainfall, and a general preponderance of water resources, anyone on a visit to India could conclude that it has plenty of water. Despite this water advantage, the per capita water availability in India is declining: in 1952, the water availability was at 3450 cubic meters per person; in 2010, it stood at 1800 cubic meters. Hydrologists estimate that by 2025 it will fall to 1200 cubic meters per person. Many argue that the privatization of water is the only viable efficient solution to the government's management of its water resources.

Rakesh Kumar, R. D. Singh, and K. D. Sharma have conducted considerable research on the water resources of India. They worry that the hydrological cycle is being profoundly modified qualitatively and quantitatively in their country. They fear that without sustained planning and "capacity building," the country will continue to be whipsawed by the flood and drought syndrome.[9] The privatization of water is a serious concern. While I shall have more to say about water privatization elsewhere in this book, suffice it to say here that privatization of water in India will lead to more highly priced water with a profound impact on the nation's poor. As the demand for potable water starts to outstrip supply by increasing amounts in coming years, India will face a host of problems from food and water shortages. Many concerned environmentalists in India echo the refrain of

Sunita Narain, director of the Center for Science and Environment in New Delhi: "If we become rich or poor as a nation, it's because of water."

Rain Harvesting and Bore Wells

Each morning, along the sleepy Boathouse Road, the sounds of bird life and occasional cars blend with the gentle whirring of water pumps. It is time to fill the sumps and cisterns of one of Chennai's most affluent neighborhoods with water. The local waterworks can bring water to houses at ground level, but property owners have to pump the water themselves to their rooftop cisterns. Even the imposing white stucco Madras Club, the snug harbor of Chennai's elite, has to deal with sumps and pumps. In Chennai, water issues cut across class and linguistic lines; and thoughts about water are part of the local consciousness along this section of the Bay of Bengal. Chennai has problems with variable monsoons and diminishing groundwater. Since the 1970s severe dry spells have come to this tropical port.

To its significant advantage, India currently has some of the most thoughtful and innovative thinkers on solving the planet's gigantic thirst. One of the solutions to India's urban water crisis, and the best way to recycle water, is through rainwater harvesting — capturing the runoff. Rain harvesting is an ancient practice and its implementation requires no sophisticated technology. In cities like Mumbai and Chennai, municipal governments are implementing programs to capture and store rainwater for use in the city during the dry season. Basically it is a program to develop catchments and rooftop systems to charge groundwater. Chennai can receive up to 1300 mm of rainwater per year. As Chennai is heavily encased in concrete, rainwater that falls on terraces and roofs can be collected in cisterns and diverted through pipes into wells for groundwater recharge. Chennai hydrologists believe that it is possible to recover 50 percent of the lost rainwater through this type of harvesting.

In July 2002, the Chennai Rain Centre opened a model house in the Santhome Beach area to demonstrate various models of rainwater harvesting. The house is one-story and resembles most Chennai houses except that it is equipped with storage tanks and sumps that can put water into the ground from the monsoons. Sekhar Raghavan, the centre's director, says this simple technique allows homeowners and apartment dwellers "to replenish the groundwater table and enables local wells to yield in a sustained manner."

With the rise of suburbs in Chennai in the 1970s and the construction of multi-storied apartment complexes and paved parking lots and roads, the local water table declined precipitously. In 1995, local citizens, led by

Raghavan, started a groundwater campaign to create public awareness of the problem and to provide people with plumbers and masons who could do the simple technology of rain capture. Soon, local citizens saw the fruits of their labor as they were able to divert water from the annual two monsoons into the ground. Currently, says Raghavan, about 50 percent of the local community has outfitted their homes for rainwater capture. Since 2005, Chennai has compiled an excellent record of rain capture, and locally-dug bore wells have plenty of water. At the Rain Centre, Mr. Raghavan shows a simple but very effective video about how people catch rainwater in everything from inverted umbrellas to the helmets of traffic policemen. As Raghavan puts it, "water harvested is water produced."[10]

While methods of rainwater harvesting may vary from cisterns in rural areas to groundwater recharge in cities, the net effect is to increase available water supplies. Such houses with groundwater charging capability may soon be springing up all over Chennai since, in many parts of the metropolitan region, traditional wells dried up years ago and people began to dig deep bore wells to tap groundwater. Some of these urban wells go as deep as 200 feet, but, unfortunately, as bore wells increase in the region, groundwater levels continue to sink further down, requiring more sophisticated and expensive pumping mechanisms.

During a tour of the model house, I learned that rainwater harvesting involves a number of different steps, including storage for later consumption or immediate use. The simplest design consists of collecting the rainwater from building rooftops or ground level surfaces, filtering it through a chamber of bricks and sand, and then using a percolation pit to recharge it underground. Rainwater can also be stored in sumps and rain barrels. According to hydrologist Ram Krishnan, use of such a rain capture technology can easily provide clean drinking water for a water-conserving family of five.

Rainwater harvesting can also enable households, factories, schools, and offices to overcome their problems of irregular and inadequate water supply or water supply of poor quality. The process involves storing rainwater that falls within one's premises and re-using it after basic treatment. By using equipment that is easily available, rainwater is diverted towards existing underground tanks or terrace fitted tanks and then supplied to the taps. The purification methods used by households, factories and offices can be used to treat rainwater. Treated rainwater is safe not just for cleaning and washing, but also for cooking and personal consumption. The amount of rainfall notwithstanding, people living and working in various types of geographical terrains can harvest rainwater. In the long run, rainwater harvesting will replenish India's rapidly depleting groundwater levels and lead to water security and sustainability.

Mumbai's Water

Meanwhile, on the other side of India, the water problems of the city of Mumbai are so chronic that locals no longer consider it news. What is news, however, is how much worse the city's water problems can appear as a negative cultural reflection of the city's nouveau riche. Across Thane Creek from old Bombay, the planned city of Navi Mumbai sparkles in the winter sun. It was developed in 1972 as Mumbai's satellite community and is the largest planned city in the world with a total of 133 square miles and a population bordering 3 million. It has been rated by *National Geographic* as one of the Super Cities of the World because of its highly modern infrastructure, its communication and computer elites, its high standard of living, and its imaginative social planning. It is a city of magnificent automobile fly-overs, ample parking, and reliable electricity. Most of the neighborhoods have their own security forces to combat crime. The city has a lively club life and the lounge bar at the Navi Mumbai Ice n Spice has a 12,000-square-foot dance floor that throbs with the "colorful and quirky" activity of the city's affluent young.

In 2010, because of the poor monsoons, Mumbai decided to cut water supplies. In the thriving suburb of Navi Mumbai, however, real estate developers are constructing swimming pools. In a region beset with water difficulties of nearly every description, it is possible for residents to preen in the sun and enjoy a relaxing swim in one of the many residential pools in this satellite city. Swimming pools serve a symbolic function of showing the difference between well-watered wealth and the rest of the old Bombay region.

Mumbai is an old colonial city. To escape the intense pollution, rich Indians hibernate in air-filtered cocktail lounges like that of the Taj Hotel and munch peanuts and drink Kingfisher beer until they can flee by car to the fresher breezes outside the city. Alternatively, Navi Mumbai is the comfortable American-style land of India's middle and upper class business and high tech future. Navi Mumbai was once a land of rice paddies and mango and coconut orchards. The land had good irrigation. As land prices rose in the greater Mumbai area, the farmers were forced out. Industries came in, fresh food markets evaporated over time, and the overall quality of water deteriorated. Now Mumbai faces the problems of sanitation and shortages of potable water. Across Thane Creek, in Navi Mumbai, the poor and the beggars, or "Slum Dogs," are not permitted. However, riots by frustrated villagers who are being pushed off their land as the city expands are not uncommon.

Real estate agents laugh off social critics who point out the luxury of swimming pools given Mumbai's water crisis. Meanwhile, Mumbai's poor have trouble getting clean water to drink and to cook. Outside the city, women travel long distances to public wells and spigots to fill large water jugs that they have to carry back to their modest family dwellings. The news that filters down to the poor that Mumbai has water problems while Navi Mumbai has swimming pools can only intensify class antagonisms in the city over access to water.

Water and the Rural Expanse

Despite India's rapid urbanization, the country is still a vast rural expanse of small farmers. Agriculture is still an integral part of India's economy and society. Between 1947 and 1967 India underwent the Green Revolution, which enabled farmers, with the help of the United Nations and developed countries, to use new seeds and improved genetics as well as double cropping to have an agricultural base free of the specter of famine. In the period since independence, India has grown from being an importer of grain and other foodstuffs to a net exporter of food. Today India has food security and the country's rural economy sustains two-thirds of India's billion plus citizens.

Unfortunately, this surge in agriculture required the construction of irrigation projects that pumped massive amounts of groundwater from aquifers that over time have become depleted. With food security being the highest priority for Indian politicians, the state has helped to subsidize and distribute electric water pumps. This has allowed for extremely fast pumping that permits ever-larger irrigated acreages. With new technology and access to groundwater, India is now producing massive amounts of rice, wheat, and cotton — very water-intensive staples. Cotton, rice, and wheat sell easily on the world commodity market, a fact that enables many farmers to escape from a pathetic cycle of poverty and subsistence living.

However, this new way of farming has meant that fertilizers and pesticides have entered the water supply through runoffs and are leaching into the groundwater table where people get their drinking water. As groundwater becomes contaminated, people sink deeper bore wells that sometimes strike water reserves contaminated with arsenic and fluoride that have been under the soil for millennia. Arsenic is carcinogenic and many farm communities are reporting high incidences of liver cancer as a result of drinking arsenic-laced water. As farmers and rural people dig ever-deeper wells in search of retreating groundwater, arsenic awaits. Similarly fluoride in well water, not to be confused with the kind used for dental hygiene, can over time cause major crippling bone problems. In villages one can usually find a man or woman whose legs have become so bowed from fluoride poisoning that they can scarcely support themselves without the use of crutches.

In 2002, seventeen states in India were affected by severe fluorisis from consumption of contaminated aquifers. Endemic flourisis, Indian officials report, has emerged as one of the most alarming public health problems in the country.

As fertilizers become part of irrigation and storm water runoff, they enter lakes and fish ponds, where the resulting eutrophication shuts out light and kills the fish and water life. In a short time bodies of water become choked with decaying vegetative matter accumulating on a riverbed or lake and making the water unsuitable for human consumption. Very high levels of eutrophication have already been reported in areas of India like the Hyderabad in Andhra Pradesh and the Naintal in Uttar Pradesh.

Cheap water that can rapidly be pumped from underground aquifers has also been a factor in the expansion of India's industrial base, especially the garment industry in the southern state of Tamil Nadu. Given the precarious nature of surface water, India grows steadily more dependent upon groundwater at a time when aquifers are showing signs of serious depletion. Many of those aquifers cannot be replenished as they hold catchments of fossilized water thousands of years old that do not admit seepage from irrigated waters on the farmlands. This crisis is not just the disturbance in the demand and supply curve, but is also about mismanagement of water resources. It is worth repeating: India's water crisis is a man-made problem.

Water quality is now being recognized in India as a major crisis. What is ironic is how late policy makers in Delhi have come to this position given the fact that under the Indian Constitution the nation is pledged to maintain water quality. Ensuring the supply of safe drinking water in India is a Constitutional mandate, with Article 47 conferring on the nation the duty of providing clean drinking water and improving public health standards of the state. Since India's first Five-Year-Plan in 1951, when the nation began to make investments in sanitation and water, some 37 million Indians have been annually affected by water-borne diseases. Each year 1.5 million children are estimated to die of diarrhea. The over-dependency on groundwater has led to 66 million people in twenty-two states being at risk due to excessive fluoride and around 10 million at risk due to arsenic in six states.

Monitoring the groundwater remains a major challenge in rural India since it is the predominant source of drinking water. India also faces political water challenges along its borders. Two of the most vital rivers in India — the Brahmaputra and the Ganges — deserve mention at this point because they are India's principal Himalayan rivers, bringing southward the revitalizing waters from mountain glaciers upon which India depends.

The Brahmaputra flows across Tibet, cuts through the walls of the Himalayas, and tumbles down into India's Assam valley. Its rich semi-evergreen forests historically have given an Alpine quality to this part of India. Today, like its sister glacial river to the east in Pakistan, the Indus, the Brahmaputra faces the peril of melting glaciers and declining annual flow of water to its water-needy lands. In addition to nature, the Brahmaputra has a human problem: the Chinese. In November 2010, China acknowledged for the first time that it has begun damming the Yarlong Zangbo River in Tibet in order to break ground on a 510-megawatt hydropower project. This river flows into the tributaries of the Brahamaputra. There are rising concerns in India that this dam will seriously degrade the flow into the Brahmaputra. The two countries have not reached an accord over the joint sharing of river resources originating in Tibet that feed into India.

The other Himalayan river, the Ganges, is in a class by itself.

Ganga

Practically all the water problems of India can be summed up in one word: Ganga. The Ganga, or Ganges River, is the 1,557-mile-long watery spine of India. It originates in an ice cave on the slopes of the Himalayas and flows eastward until it empties into the Bay of Bengal. Given its lengthy course across the hot plains of northern India, it is hard to believe that this river is a glacial flow.

Every water problem that India has — from pollution and sedimentation to water shortages, to burial practices and food habits, and to ethnic divisiveness and irrigation politics — is associated in some way with the Ganges River. The Ganga, wrote Jawaharlal Nehru, the first Prime Minister of India, "is the river of India, beloved of her people, round which are intertwined her memories, her hopes, her songs of triumph, her victories and her defeats." The river is the most venerated body of water in India and is said to flow from the lotus feet of the god Vishnu. In global religious culture it compares in historical significance to the Nile of time-honored Egyptian civilization. Bathing in the Ganges is believed to wash away one's sins and any water that is mixed with even the tiniest drops from the Ganges becomes holy water. Devout Hindus cast the ashes of their dead into the river after cremation because they believe that Ganga will guide the souls of their loved ones straight to paradise.

Today, while the Ganges remains the important spiritual and religious core of Hindu India, it is an extremely stressed river. Since the regular scientific surveying of the Ganges commenced in 1983, the river has been found to contain one of India's most deadly fecal coliform counts: bathing in and drinking its waters is very dangerous due to the high level of fecal matter, urine, and the over one billion liters of untreated raw sewage that enters the river every day. Inadequate cremation procedures result in partially burnt or unburnt corpses floating in the river. Fortunately, the river has an unusual ability to retain oxygen, which helps to mollify some of the river's toxic brew and prevents large-scale epidemics that would otherwise occur. Despite these facts, the Ganges is considered a holy river and an estimated two million people bathe daily in its water. Thus does the Ganges offer itself to India and to the world as one of the great environmental conundrums of our age.

Perhaps a clue to solving India's river puzzle can be found in the country's ancient past. Sometime around 600 BC nomadic tribes began to develop a highly sophisticated water-based civilization in the Indus Valley west of the Indus River. Excavations around the ancient city of Harappa reveal sophisticated water management that included wells, water tanks, and public baths. Town planners of the ancient city of Mohenjo-daro connected every house with both drinking water and a drainage system for sewage. People carved large water reservoirs out of rock that were able to distribute water to the ancient cities of the Indus Valley year round. The civilization of the Indus Valley in antiquity knew how water could be used to build a stable society. Ultimately floods and wars destroyed the irrigation systems and intricate water networks, but the Indus Valley's history contains ideas for solving India's present water problems. The old cities of the Indus Valley, like Harappa, Mohenjo-daro, and Dholavira, had a reverence for water and knew that a river could make a civilization.

The Challenge of Water Policy

India's water challenges go far beyond the issues of drinking water and sanitation. Approximately 80 percent of India's water is used for agriculture, but in many areas of the country farmers are still without reliable access. Over the years, India's Ministry of Water has struggled to formulate a water policy that would address India's manifold problems. Time is of the essence as World Bank officials are already predicting that India will be severely water stressed. Since water in India is considered a "state subject" under the control of the government, it may be instructive to look at some of the water policies currently being formulated at the national level.

While not a pure government water plan per se, the "Water Policy and Action Plan 2020" was assembled by government consultants and enjoys the support of the Ministry of Water. Viewed in its entirety, it is a remarkable document and represents perhaps the very best thinking on water issues in Asia today. Water experts in India today argue that changes in water policy have to be undertaken at the "micro-level" and urge the establishment of community-based water organizations all over the country to deal with issues of water quality, sanitation, and water's agricultural and industrial use. Thus, the decentralization of water policy in India may be a major step in forestalling some of the water calamities on India's horizon — especially in the area of food shortages. Also the plan calls for new and imaginative approaches to improving water quality and to step up the recycling and re-use of water.[11]

What is bold about the Action 2020 plan is that it recognizes how central water must be for all of India's future economic and social planning. As India moves into the twenty-first century, it will have a national water information system that builds on a micro-watershed level that allows the free flow of accurate information about local water issues into government councils. The plan gives municipalities and local bodies the opportunity to manage their own water facilities in the context of local needs and problems. Action 2020 fixes a national water allotment for domestic per capita use at 30 to 60 liters a day depending on regional climates. Finally 2020 takes a strong leadership position with regard to rescuing imperiled traditional and natural wetlands and emphasizes watershed area management. The consultants urge that land swaps should be the "preferred option in those regions and states where land for resettlement is or can be made available." Until recently watershed management in India has been more rhetorical than actual; 2020 makes groundwater management the first prerogative of local municipalities. "The first right to groundwater should be to the concerned community," the report urges.

Of course, India still will face controversial issues like dam construction and hydropower. Opposition continues in the Narmada Valley in central India where thirty large dams and 3,000 small ones are slated to turn the region into a farmer subservient hydraulic empire. The government continues with its River Interlinking Project, a vast network connecting irrigation canals with dams and rivers that, if implemented, will redraw the hydrological map of India. The sheer cost of the project has been estimated at around $200 billion US, which amounts to about 40 percent of the country's gross domestic product. Throughout the nation there is a growing public resentment over the displacement of people, farms, and whole villages because of hydropower and irrigation construction programs like this, but when it comes to dams and irrigation, engineers, regardless of nationality, want to build! Their techno-hubris often transcends social and cultural reality. As India currently enjoys a period of unprecedented national prosperity, the River Interlinking Project might get the funding to unleash bulldozer construction armies across India.

In 2005, two Indian scholars, A. C. Shukla and Vadama Asthana, published what may well be the definitive assessment of the impact of the River Interlinking Project in India.[12] They conclude that the River Interlinking Project was a top-down bureaucratic decision of a government bureau, the National Water Development Agency, that was concerned little with input from the people affected by the project. Its approach to water management ignored the principle of conservation and was based solely on increasing water supply through grandiose dam and canal projects. In fact, a government study in 1996 concluded that there was "no imperative need for massive water transfers." Water needs in India could be met with more efficient use of water resources. The entire project was the creation of "political pressures." Further this project envisages the knitting together of ten major rivers across the nation, a scheme not attempted since the Chinese built the Grand Canal over 3,500 years ago. This interlinking would "inadvertently distribute pollution loads across the rivers, spreading local contamination problems," and raise significant issues about the responsibility for polluting water resources. A national water grid, environmentalists argue, is not the same as an electricity grid. Given the expense of the project, foreign capital will have to be involved, which Shukla and Asthana argue will have its own complications. This project may well lead to the commoditization of all water in India that will involve pricing mechanisms harmful to the poor in most rural areas of the country.

Ironically, Indian independence, so cherished since 1947, may very well be subverted by the capital controls of the World Bank. At this writing, there is considerable fear in India about what will happen to social welfare programs that are placed under "the logic of the market." In terms of basic technology, the problems of the River Interlinking Project are legion. Among the most obvious: the system will require a network of pumps to transport water from the Ganga-Brahmaputra to tributaries in the south. "The electric power required to pump water to such heights will be close to the current power generation of the entire nation." Further, a canal network will require dredging, which is expensive, and will involve myriad communities in prolonged debates about interstate transfer of water. Finally, this project will lock India in conflict with its neighbors, Nepal and Bangladesh.

In summary, the River Linking Project, researchers note, "serves the Promethian aspirations of bureaucrats and technocrats that form the rank and file of the government." How it will be implemented is still anyone's guess. New legislation on water laws will have to be introduced by the parliament. The regulation of groundwater, so vital to agriculture for irrigated farms and for industries like food and textiles, may well prove to be a major political battleground of vested interests. Also, it is not at all certain where all the money for a dramatic restructuring of India's water bureaucracy will come from.

The revamping of India's water policy may require a revolutionary change in social behavior with regard to water in India's future. It will require Indian farmers to switch from raising water intensive crops like cotton to vegetables and legumes more in harmony with local water availability. It certainly will require, notes India Liaison Officer of Water Aid, R. Srikanth, more strict standards regarding levels of arsenic and fluoride in Indian drinking water. "The traditional Indian food is semi-solid and contains more water and therefore, increases the probability of body burden due to fluoride and arsenic. Therefore, the adoption of stricter drinking water standards in the case of fluoride and arsenic compared to World Health Organization guidelines is highly desirable in the Indian context."[13]

Conclusion

Walking the beaches of Goa, India, is a delightful experience. The Indian Ocean splashes gently on the shore, and beyond the beach affluent communities of sun-seekers lounge at the many luxury hotels that have sprung up to service the needs of winter-weary Europeans. In February the beaches are populated with heavy-set Russians with red sunburns. At my hotel, the sun dappled palm trees are counter pointed with the soft reassuring splash of cascading fountains. In Goa, mostly good clean water is everywhere to be had. Goa, however does not reflect the reality of India's water problems. It is more an image of what India needs to be. Meanwhile, India's big thirst has driven its population into a competitive frenzy to obtain fresh potable water for its teeming cities and rural communities.

Almost half of India's 626 districts were drought-stricken in 2009. In Maharashtra, only 16 percent of the state's cultivable lands are farmed, leaving the remaining lands reliant on seasonal rains that are diminishing. The 2020 plan may well go down as one of those great efforts that came along just a little too late. India's investments in domestic water infrastructure have been inadequate.

Also, due to global warming, the country's rainfalls have become erratic and unpredictable, seriously affecting the agricultural sector. The water crisis will also have a big effect on Indian manufacturing, possibly stagnating many industries. India still has the power to avoid this dark future if people take action immediately in the following manner: start conserving water, begin to harvest rainwater, treat human, agricultural, and industrial waste effectively, and regulate how much water can be drawn out of the ground. Unfortunately such strategies have difficulty enough being implemented in prosperous Western nations let alone in a sprawling populous and diverse nation like India. In talking to Indians and reading the literature on the country's water problems, it is obvious that an informed national consensus exists on what needs to be done. From better use of groundwater, desalination-improved irrigation techniques, people participation, and capacity building, the Indians have a blueprint for meeting their country's water demands for the present without compromising the needs of future generations.[14] Implementing the technology and the information remains India's biggest problem.

The most promising development on India's water horizon is new technology to reduce waterborne arsenic in groundwater. Known as subterranean arsenic removal (SAR), this new method does not treat water with chemicals. Instead the SAR system, according to the Ecological Society of America, aerates pumped groundwater and sends it back into the aquifer to supply oxygen for bacteria that eventually allows for water to precipitate into benign forms of arsenic and iron.[15] Whether the government can afford to build SAR plants to improve the quality of life in rural India remains to be seen. India will have almost two billion people by the end of the twenty-first century. India's water problems are problems of quality, not quantity, with large amounts of water polluted and degraded. India's economic policies at best ignore the importance of water and often encourage mismanagement. Unfortunately in the short-term, India's water problems will likely get worse because of increasing urbanization, population growth, and political ineptitude.

We live in an age of "unnatural disasters" with storms, floods, droughts, and sea-level rise predicted to be more frequent and more intense. These disasters will have an unprecedented impact on India's food and water resources. With global capital markets uncertain, India's water scarcity won't just be a problem for farmers, scientists, and policy makers. It will be the defining problem for all of India and the rest of us as well. India remains a poor country, and its water problems are disproportionately faced by its poorest. However, my Chennai-based son reminds me that India and its people have proved to be resilient and innovative at a scale unmatched worldwide. India's size, geography, diversity, and growing economic clout make it the centerpiece for global economic development. World society may rise or fall with India's twenty-first century endgame.

"Water is a brutal delineator of social power."

-- Matthew Gandy

Chapter Five

Sanitation, Splendor, & Squalor

Bad Water

Thirst is a driving biological force that causes millions of people to drink contaminated water. Everyday, tens of thousands of people die from water-related illnesses that are directly related to contaminated water. In the West our basic confidence in the safety of our water blinds us to the harsher realities in other parts of the world. Most Americans are startled when they are informed that contaminated water causes 80 percent of the world's health problems. In developing countries, notoriously virulent diseases lie in wait in the water for public consumption. Among these are typhoid, diarrhea diseases, amoebic dysentery, and cholera. It's particularly ironic that these disease conditions persist in our era when technology has done so much in the world to eradicate disease. Most of these maladies in the water can be easily removed by simple water treatments.

Why are so many developing countries doing so badly in providing their citizens with good sanitation? Why are they not investing in sanitation? Because their culture, history, or government bureaucracies prevent them from thinking clean. When large numbers of people defecate in the open as they do in India and Africa, they are not thinking clean. The popular attitude in their countries is that clean is not that important. Some countries like Thailand and Malaysia have made significant strides in transforming the fetid sanitation systems of their cities and countryside into something that is healthy and socially beneficial. In the 1970s, Peru began a major effort to provide clean public drinking water and has made major strides in curbing water-borne diseases. Sanitation is often more a matter of attitude than money and it all begins with our attitude towards a common denominator — the toilet.

Flush Times

In the United States, most of us pay scant attention when we flush our toilets. "Thinking clean" for Americans is largely unreflective and automatic. Our homes are equipped with devices that whirl and whoosh efficiently as the spoil of our lives is carried on a watery highway out of our homes. Where that spoil goes is not our concern. Toilets, on the other hand, concern us greatly as symbols of status and technological efficiency. Today's American bathroom rivals the famous baths of the Roman world. We have elegant toilets and tubs with gold plated fixtures and bidets that herald a new conscience of cleanliness. One can even read, talk on the phone, or watch television while attending to one's most private affairs.

The bathrooms of today are starting to resemble the living rooms in many homes, replete with elegant carpeting, sofas, and "resting chairs." The showers and baths offer waterfalls, sprays, and Jacuzzis of delight. The water tumbles out of the shower-head glistening in either artificial or natural sunlight. In many second homes on the coasts of America, bathrooms have sliding windows and sunning terraces that bring the ambiance of the bath into direct contact with the sea. Pick up a modern bathroom design book. It is so elegantly spread with lush pictures *en toilette* that might entice the old Roman Emperor Caracalla himself![1]

No country in recent times has had quite the love affair with its toilets as Japan. It was not until after World War Two that the flush toilet was introduced mostly by the forces of military occupation. By the 1960s, the western-style toilet with a wooden high-rise seat began to replace the simple porcelain or steel squat toilet that was the bane of Western tourists and elegant Japanese women wearing the complex kimono. These toilets required some measure of physical dexterity, and people have been known to hold on to water pipes to avoid falling into the "bombsight." Aged Japanese men and women also found these toilets to be difficult.

In the twenty-first century most Japanese homes have toilets that are shrines to comfort and sanitation. They combine all the best notions of the West — the bidet, a sink, the air-conditioner, the music hall, and the electric dryer. The Japanese celebrate an unofficial holiday on November 10th of each year as "Toilet Day." November is the eleventh month of the year and the word "eleven" can be read as *ii-to-ire* or "Good Toilet." Unsurprisingly, the nation has a very active Japan Toilet Association and people talk of their yoshiki (toilet) in reverential tones.

To understand the toilet training inherent in Japanese culture, one has to visit a Japanese home. There one may experience the wonder of the Japanese super toilet. It is, from the Western view, a fairly complicated unfamiliar device. The primary function of this toilet rests with a pencil-size nozzle that squirts water from two settings for either the anus or feminine washing. The nozzle is sanitary in that it does not touch the body. On either side of the toilet seat are instruction panels alerting the user to all of the toilet's functions: angle of bidet spray, choice of music, heater for the toilet seat, and a fan for cooling and drying the body's extremities. Significantly (and this is something that I have yet to see in America and Europe), Japanese toilets have spigots with small basins on the top of the toilet that allow users to conserve water by washing their hands in water that will be the next flush of the toilet. A deluxe Japanese "elimination button" carries with it the choice of music accompaniment like Mendelssohn's *Opus 62 Song of Spring*. In Japan, a top of the range Toto toilet, with all the bells and whistles literally, sells for around $5,000. The Japanese use special toilet slippers in the toilet because they consider it an unclean area of the house. Toilet slippers have not caught on in the West.

A few years ago while in Tokyo, I was amused by a story in *The International Herald Tribune* of an innocent American foreign service officer. Newly arrived in Japan, he was the dinner guest of a well-to-do Japanese couple. When it came time for him to use the bathroom toilet, he faced a personal crisis in not knowing which buttons to press. He invariably pressed all the wrong buttons after urinating and turned his host's toilet into a gurgling Versailles-like fountain that sprayed everywhere.

Flushed with economic success, China is also now gushing over high-tech toilets. Other countries are following. Currently, the total worldwide market for these sanitary devices is more than $1 billion. TOTO, meanwhile, has invaded the United States. With its slimmer side-control panel, heralds Toto's website, "Washlet is designed to introduce you to a level of unprecedented comfort while delivering on the promise of maximum cleanliness. The specially designed contoured seat is also heated to provide maximum comfort." TOTO proclaims that its new toilet, with its soothing benefits, cleansing nozzle, and warm air dryer, "virtually eliminates the need for toilet paper."

The use of high-tech toilets is now well-advanced in the United States and in the very near future we will have toilets that measure blood sugar based on urine. Toilets that take blood pressure and determine body fat content of the user are entering the market. It may soon be possible to purchase a "talking toilet" where one can communicate directly with a doctor or specialist who can analyze your excreta. Thus, are we now living in an era of the high-end of the rear-end? Certainly the advent of this affluent expansive bathroom culture represents the merging of washing, bodily privacy, and hygiene into a new geography of social behavior and public discourse. It is probably not too far out of the question to imagine a whole new range of "water reality" television shows organized around bathroom activities.

While it is easy to dismiss deluxe toilets as amusing anthropological curiosities, these devices tell us a lot about water and our assumptions about water use. In our sanitary culture we are so far removed from developing countries that the Third World is more like a distant planet to us than a socio-economic region of the earth. The toilet is the modern metaphor of affluence and power. These devices consume a lot of energy and they use a lot more water than their predecessors. It is strange to look at toilets as a fashion phenomenon at a time when the world is entering a profound period of water scarcity.

Furthermore, the flush times of the West have more than their share of darker water secrets. One of these is that we are counting on the technological manipulation of our watercourses through sewage treatment to maintain drinking and popular water use standards. Sanitation is emerging as one of the great water issues of the twenty-first century.

In Brooklyn, New York, the upscale, million-dollar brownstones and condos of Park Slope, Cobble Hill, Carroll Gardens, and Red Hook border the Gowanus Canal, a major environmental scandal in New York City. Currently, New York City is being forced by the Environmental Protection Agency to clean up this stench-ridden cloaca of a waterway. The Gowanus Canal has been designated a Superfund site for major cleanup that will start in 2015 and last almost eleven years at an estimated cost of $300 million to $500 million. Michael Bloomberg, mayor of New York, opposed the canal's designation as a Superfund Site because he believed that it would embroil the city in legal battles and scare off developers. The canal is severely polluted with contaminants, including carcinogens like polychlorinated biphenyls or PCBs, metals like mercury, garbage, and sunken debris.

For more than a century after it was carved out of tidal wetlands, the Gowanus Canal was a major route for ships going to oil refineries, tanneries, and chemical and gas plants along its banks. The Gowanus Canal, writes Elizabeth Royte in her book *Garbage Land*, is pretty much dead with precious little dissolved oxygen in the water. "Today," she notes, "the canal is a sacrifice area, a series of brownfields zoned for industry, and not a few manufacturers want to keep it that way." However, the canal is just the beginning of New York's sanitation problems. In a city of millions, the average resident produces 1.3 annual tons of municipal waste, with a good bit of it getting into New York's waterways.[2] Thus, it is difficult to feel superior to poorer nations in the matter of sanitation when Americans can befoul a city as majestic as New York. Also, one can just as easily point an accusing finger at "tourist havens" like New Zealand that grapple with their own solid and hazardous waste problems and the pollution of its lakes and estuaries by agriculture.

Towards the end of her book, Royte quotes solid waste expert William Rathje as saying that "sorting garbage is the ultimate Zen experience of our society because you feel it, you smell it, you record it; you are in tactile intimacy with it. Some time or other, everybody ought to sort garbage." I am not so keen on the tactile intimacy side of garbage. For five years, I lived in Mito, Japan, and I could never figure out how the country managed to spin such a wonderful environmental image of itself when there was garbage everywhere but in small areas of postage stamp beauty for adoring tourists with digital cameras. When the garbage trucks came, the Japanese threw bags laden with the sordid messes on the roadside. Much of it spilled out. There was always trash. The public canals that flowed through Tokyo were black with the city's never-ending waste. My trips to the ocean were usually frustrating attempts to find a clean clear space in a beach full of rubbish, beer cans, food wrappers, and discarded chopsticks.

Sanitation's Darker Backside

Mega-cities of the global South — like New Delhi, India and Lagos, Nigeria — have acute sanitation problems. They have not enjoyed the kind of technological transformation in water treatment that has been experienced in places like Singapore, Europe, and cities in North America. When it comes to infrastructures for drinking water and public sanitation, there is no economic dynamic in developing countries to build stable, centralized water and sanitary systems.

However, Western countries are now confronting the problem of how to renew their water systems that have become old and somewhat dilapidated. In a recent study, Matthew Gandy points out that by the late 1980s over 25 percent of London's water mains were over one hundred years old and 30 percent of the water was being lost through leaks.[3] Further, cities like Washington, DC, London, and New York are struggling with rusted and corroded water supply systems. Washington, for example, grapples with an ongoing problem of lead in the drinking water from antiquated residential plumbing and storm water and sewage overflows.

What is at stake here for both the West and the developing nations is that there does not seem to be at this time a willingness of cities to support and strengthen the municipal ethos of water. Currently, urban centers are more inclined to turn water management over to private, commercially-driven enterprises. Such private water companies have come into operation in London, Buenos Aires, Manila, and other cities, often with controversial results for local populations. Thus, at a time when sanitation and the need for a dependable supply of potable water is paramount in developing countries, the old publicly-supported municipal engineering ethos is not a strong part of the water equation even in the West in the twenty-first century.

It is in this regard that we examine two cities: Washington, DC and Lagos, Nigeria. Both are large cities, urban conglomerations with millions of people in their metropolitan reach. In past times, Washington suffered many of the same sanitary problems Lagos is currently experiencing. Both cities have sanitation issues that can help us better understand the twenty-first century water dilemma.

Washington, DC, the nation's capital, has always had a sewage problem. During its founding years, the new capital endured hollowed out, wooden sewage pipes that easily decayed, overflowing outdoor privies and typhoid-producing canals. Washington built its first organized sewer system in 1810, focusing on the removal of storm and groundwater from District streets.

It was not until four decades later that the District concerned itself with building a sanitary sewage system. Outbreaks of cholera and effluvia-related maladies prompted city sanitarians to address the sewage problem. The Civil War, with its massive infusion of federal troops and refugees in Washington, created major water pollution problems, especially typhoid and malaria. Finally, in the 1870s, the city's Board of Public Works constructed an 83-mile sewer system, which eventually eliminated the fetid drainage canals and sewers.

With some control of the "dejecta" (a polite Victorian word for you know what), a sewer system allowed for an elegant expansion of mansions at DuPont Circle and other new areas of the city. The rich had the best in sewers and indoor plumbing while the poor had to rely on the periodic emptying of their overflowing privies by independent contractors with night soil carts. (Well into the 1960s many homes in Anacostia, one of the city's poorer areas, had outdoor privies and well-water subject to contamination.)

During the 1920s Washington's principal sewer system consisted of effluvia pumped directly into the Anacostia, Potomac, and Rock Creek watercourses. Sewage pollution became so bad in the DC Tidal Basin that the District banned swimming at what was once a beautiful beach dedicated to water sports overlooking the Jefferson Memorial.

One-third of Washington, predominantly in the old central parts of the city laid out in the late eighteenth century by Pierre L'Enfant, sits above a combined water and sewer system that pushes raw sewage into the Potomac during major storms and sewer overflows. Federal facilities in the District constitute 18 percent of combined sewer overflows — something that Congressmen should consider when they are next "en commode."

When the Blue Plains Sewage Treatment Plant opened in 1938, sanitarians considered it a state-of-the-art facility that was projected to serve a population of 650,000 by 1950. In 1959, it was a well-recognized secondary treatment plant removing bacteria from sewage at the rate of 240 million gallons of sewage water a day. It was around this time that the Congress, which funded the District of Columbia, began to ignore its sewage plant. For decades the plant limped along with shoddy management and a deteriorating plant facility while the tides of sewage rose. By 1995, Blue Plains was a wreck. Federal inspectors from the EPA discovered a deteriorating facility endangered by inadequate maintenance. This set the stage a year later in 1996 for a lawsuit by the Environmental Protection Agency against the Washington Area Sewer Authority, the owner of Blue Plains. Meanwhile, environmentalists worried about excess discharges of ammonia, nitrogen, and harmful bacteria in sewage sludge that would increase health risks for recreational users of the Anacostia and Potomac Rivers.

Under a federal court mandate, Blue Plains was tasked with making an $800 million upgrade of facilities. Shortly thereafter, Blue Plains was under the federal gun to work out a system for dealing with the enormous amount of water from combined sewer overflows in the District. Environmentalists routinely pointed out that because of the massive three billion gallon a year of combined sewer overflows, the Washington Area Water and Sewer Authority and Blue Plains violated the Clean Water Act so many times that its reputation was as dark as the sludge it processed. Citizens in the District and in the environmental community screamed to have Blue Plains fixed. DC residents argued that they were entitled by law to live in a community where sewage did not routinely appear in their basements during heavy "rain events." Recently, however, the record of sewage treatment at Blue Plains has been exemplary. It has excess capacity to manage the flow of wastewater, but, as John Cassidy, a Blue Plains engineer, points out, "With a major rain event or a hurricane, all bets are off."

On a rainy and dark spring afternoon I arrived at the Blue Plains Advanced Wastewater Treatment Plant. An industrial behemoth covering 150 acres of Potomac riverfront, it is the largest advanced wastewater treatment plant in the world, with a capacity of 370 million gallons a day with a peak capacity of a billion gallons a day. As I walked in the rain with Ron Bizzarii, Project Manager for WASA, I saw a vast array of miles of pipes, pumping stations, elevated storage tanks, and hydrants — all dedicated to cleaning Washington and its surrounding suburbs of their effluvia before pumping cleansed water back into the Potomac River.

Today, sewage in Washington commutes just like the ridership on local highways and subways. It travels underground and under the river through sewage tunnels 23 feet in diameter, large enough to contain railroad freight cars. Blue Plains is one part of the District water and sewage system that takes water from the upper Potomac for drinking and commercial purposes, chlorinates and purifies it, and later treats it as "clear" wastewater to be deposited downstream. The facilities at Blue Plains and the Dalecarlia water treatment plants are technological marvels. They are also extraordinarily expensive to maintain. Only a western urban middle-class tax base can sustain such an elaborate operation. Further, Blue Plains is an "advanced treatment plant," which means that it not only removes bacteria from the water, but it also removes chemicals in the water like nitrogen and phosphorus that harm the river's quality.

At Blue Plains, sewage flows into sedimentation tanks that "clarify" million gallons of water daily. These tanks remove the bad visual stuff — scum and sludge — from the water. In its secondary treatment facility the water is aerated to support the growth of "friendly" microorganisms essential to eliminate harmful bacteria from the water. Afterwards, the water courses to sedimentation basins that separate sludge. Later, the sludge is solidified in thickening tanks where it is sold as compost and field fertilizer for Virginia farms. The water that remains is now relatively free of "excess biological solids" and undergoes a denitrification process to remove excess nitrogen harmful to the Potomac and Chesapeake Bay. Now the treated sewage undergoes further action in a filtration process through beds of sand and anthracite coal. Finally, the water flows through disinfection tanks before the clean effluent is discharged into the Potomac River.

Today the Blue Plains plant faces its own unique watershed of experience. Can it adapt to continued population growth in the metropolitan area? During extreme weather events, the District sanitation system is forced to put millions of gallons of raw sewage into the river to avoid overloading it. In the District's future will its capacity continue to be adequate for protecting our water? Currently, the District is building huge underground storage tanks to keep raw sewage warehoused until the plant can treat it in better weather. Washington in the past has known what it is like to be swimming in effluvia.

Blue Plains has seen more than its share of controversy. Until *The Washington Post*, in the aftermath of the 9/11 terrorist attacks, revealed the risks of chlorine gas in Washington, Blue Plains routinely stored the deadly chemical in 90-ton rail cars. *The Post* reported that the rupture of just one of those cars would have put 1.7 million lives at risk, covering residential neighborhoods, the White House, Congress, and Bolling Air Force Base. The sewage facility switched to sodium hypochlorite bleach, which is far less dangerous. Also, until recently, Blue Plains was a notorious nitrogen dumper, annually placing 6.2 million pounds of nitrogen taken from sewage into the Potomac River.

The problems of Blue Plains have been repaired for now. Today, Washington is an example of what urban geographers and planners call "the bacteriological city." By this, they mean that an elaborate technological infrastructure of water and sanitation is now in place to enforce public demands for spatial and ideological cleanliness. This represents the successful imposition of hygienist views on urban space that began in London, Paris, and New York in the nineteenth century. According to Matthew Gandy, a University of London urban geographer, water and its infrastructure has become one of the major focal points of defining urban life in modern times. For such a water system to function, it must rely upon a "hidden city" of pipes, sewers, and treatment plants that sustain private life.[4] If even the most advanced wastewater treatment plant in the world has its problems, what does that portend for the rest of us? Meanwhile, some developing nations seem to be following the same trajectory of pollution and disease that historically plagued Washington, DC.

Once upon a time, Lagos, in southwestern Nigeria, was a small colonial capital designed by the British in 1914 to accommodate a population of about 10,000. British engineers put in a sewer system and established a local waterworks. The system still exists with improvements made in the late 1940s, but Lagos no longer has a population of 10,000. Today Lagos is a demographic nightmare: a sprawling canker of low-rise developments with 70 percent of its people living in slums. Canoes and push boats glide along the waters of stinking lagoons. The vast tarpaulin and scrap wood shacks on stilts of Lagos's major slum, Makako, are connected with precarious walkways of wooden boards over the water. Many of the residents are fisher folk and upland farmers who were lured to Lagos by the promise of better-paying jobs and a better life. Instead they have the reality of Makako, with its rampant crime, foul water, sewage, and ever-present steamy tropical stink. Raw sewage goes directly from the shacks into the fetid water below.

Lagos is the largest urban center in sub-Saharan Africa with a metropolitan population of 15 million people. Much of the city is built around coastal lagoons. With sewage that spills into the streets, Lagos is considered by public health authorities to be one of the dirtiest cities in the world. It is a city, literally, without a sanitation system. For the sake of perspective, imagine a vast mega-city of crude scrap wood and tarpaulin shacks larger than New York City without a functioning sewer system. Meanwhile, nearby on Lagos Island, site of the old colonial city and the old British waterworks, the rich and the powerful live in a kind of urban splendor with homes, cars, and cell phone lifestyles reminiscent of Miami Beach.

105

The official government line is that Lagos is changing. Police are tearing down the slums, and Lagos will soon be "the Singapore of Africa," but no one is answering these questions: Where will all the people live? How will they get fresh clean water? How will their vast sprawling community become sanitary? Currently, the World Bank is pouring close to $100 million into the city to improve sanitation and storm water drainage, but it is a relentless struggle because the rate of annual migration (10 percent) into the city is faster than the city can keep up with, leading to problems of solid waste management, water potability, sewage system management, and drainage. Put simply: The infrastructure of Lagos, in terms of sanitation, is overwhelmed. Toilets spill into open drains and plastic bags filled with defecation litter the streets. Lagos is tropical, and frequent severe flooding further compounds the city's sanitation problem.

The lagoons are also the repository of toxic waste from the nearby oil refineries and other industry. There are also wastes with high levels of iron and nitrates that have contaminated food and water supplies. Seventy percent of all the hard industry of Nigeria is located here. In Lagos, a million cars and hundreds of factories spew over three tons of lead into the air each day. Lead, a chemical toxic to the physical and mental development of children, enters the local drinking water with each rain and storm runoff. Carbon monoxide and nitric oxide complete the poisonous cloud falling on Lagos.

Currently, Lagos suffers from dramatic increases in waterborne diseases like typhus, salmonella, and dysentery, as well as increases in pathogenic bacteria that thrive in polluted water. However, provisions of safe potable water to the public by the government are rare and restricted to those areas inhabited by people of high socio-economic status. Thus, in Lagos, chlorinated drinking water that would greatly improve public health is more dream than reality. What the reality of Lagos is at this point is tragically evident: impaired people drinking severely impaired water.

Given current projections, in 2015 Lagos will be the third largest city in the world. It will also be the biggest city in the world lacking a water and sanitation infrastructure. A World Bank Report in 2006 stated, "The very poor sanitation situation is compounded by the frequent and severe flooding affecting many areas." Water does not appear in Lagos to be thought of by governing authorities as an integral part of Nigerian citizenship. This represents a break in the age-old compact between cities and government that citizens have a right to water as fundamental as any other right.

Nigeria has plenty of water, at least in the south. That is not an issue. Unfortunately the polluted lagoons and rivers of the Lagos metropolitan area do not offer much of a sustainable future to a city whose license plate reads: "Lagos, Center of Excellence." What Lagos needs is potable water. Many of its bore hole water wells have failed. Efforts to revive the near-defunct Adiyan Water Works on Lagos Island have resulted in a flow of two million gallons of water a day for its affluent thirsty citizens, but this amount is literally a drop in the bucket for an urban conglomeration of 15 million people.

Nigerian officials are working through a swamp of corruption, political apathy, and financial structure to remedy this problem. Potable water, if and when it comes, will be metered and expensive. Lagos' water and sanitation problem is Nigeria writ large. The country is rapidly urbanizing, says urban planner Charisma S. Acey, but access to improved water sources is actually declining. In a report to the US House of Representative in 2005, she noted that the Lagos Water Corporation is still mostly a system of unreliable water bucket vendors.[4]

As we look into the arena of global issues and controversies in the twenty-first century, sanitation stands out as what may well be one of the most pressing and crucial problems of our time. At present there is virtually no country on the planet that is not at some stage of sanitary crisis. Cryptosperidium, e-coli infection, and other maladies of water are now transnational. As Christmas of 2010 approached, readers of American newspapers learned that a dangerous form of water pollution, thought to be under control, had come back to haunt them. The National Environmental Working Group reported that after analyzing the drinking water in thirty-five cities across the United States, it found that most contained hexavalent chromium — a probable carcinogen made famous by the film *Erin Brockovitch*.[5] Hexavalent chromium was commonly used throughout the country as an industrial chemical added to paints in the automobile and other industries to increase bonding with metals and to give painted metal an aesthetic sheen. Scientists recently found that it causes cancer in laboratory animals when ingested and could cause stomach cancer and leukemia in humans. Such findings have not been well received by American water utilities that worry about the increased cost of controlling this contamination. At least 74 million Americans in forty-two states drink chromium-polluted tap water, much of it likely in the cancer-causing hexavalent form.

We who live in prosperous Western nations like to believe that we are living in safe and sanitary environments, but as scientists and policy experts pore over documents and laboratory tests they find that we are increasingly being exposed to health threats in our environment. We have a right to know these unsettling facts, notes the Environmental Working Group, but the truth is often hard to obtain. Meanwhile, do not think that we are living in sanitary bliss. The problems of Lagos, Nigeria, are really not that distant from us. The differences between developing nations and others are more a matter of degree rather than kind.

As I travel in the developing world, there is a picture that is etched in my mind. It is women of all ages and children congregating at water pumps to carry large water jugs on their heads to distant homes with the children innocently playing and defecating near these pumps. Often, the water that flows out is a light shade of brown. The women are taking both life-supporting water and dread water-borne diseases into their modest habitations. Water's burden falls heaviest upon women and the impact of diarrhea and dysentery is often quite gender specific. Lastly, getting water in many developing areas often means traveling a significant distance from a water source; this often translates to water travel of about two hours a day. According to one health report, "The length of time taken to fetch water indicates that the household's supply of water for hygienic purposes is unlikely to be near the level that would provide the necessary health benefits."[6]

In South Africa, the post-apartheid government became embroiled in issues involving polluted water and gender. South African women are the principal water bearers in the mostly rural areas and are the most likely to be infected by waterborne disease. The water that South African women bring to their families from public wells and pumps has a direct bearing on their families. Delays in putting waterworks systems into operation in South Africa have led to intermittent outbreaks of cholera. Despite the noble aspirations inherent in the government's passage of the Water Services Act of 1997, which outlines and defines a citizen's right to clean water and basic sanitation services, a lot of work remains to break the chain of marginalization of women and public water access.

Water delivery in South Africa is mostly in the hands of the private sector; this means that water carries a price tag for the poor. Austere rural budgets mean that women may limit the amount of water that they use from metered taps and continue to draw untreated water from streams and rivers. There are enormous and growing differentials in service and incomes between those living in the cities and the poor living in rural areas. Even in cities like Durban more than thirty percent of the population cannot afford to purchase sufficient quantities of private metered water for washing and cooking. Thus, we see that even when water is available, there is still a portion of the public living under poor hygienic conditions. When one factors in the differences between "piped households" and "unpiped households," surveys indicate much lower hygiene standards particularly in toilet use.

Far away in the councils of the South African government, though, the benefits of clean water and sanitation are assumed rather than demonstrated. Even though the delivery of water services in rural South Africa has improved markedly in the last decade, there are still some 12 million people who must travel farther than 200 meters to have access to a water standpipe. Also, local municipalities are in charge of their water and often shutoff water to those least likely to be able to afford it. In 2002, for example, many of the old Bantu homelands had standpipes with electric meters in order to extract "water tariffs" from the local citizenry. Poor people resorted to free but contaminated water to slake their thirst. This led to an outbreak of cholera in KwaZulu-Natal of over 106,000 cases. According to the World Health Organization report of that year, this was the biggest outbreak of cholera internationally for that year.

Soon after the outbreak, the South African Department of Health and Water Affairs launched a public campaign of information urging people to either boil their water or add a teaspoon of bleach to 25 liters of water. Thus, rather than addressing the root problem of water pricing in the rural districts, people were only left with emergency instructions on combating cholera, which, more than any other water malady, reveals the fault line of sanitation in the developing world.

Today urgent voices are being raised about the need for more accelerated provisions of water and sanitation in developing areas. At the same time, research indicates that there is a profound lack of political resolve in these same areas for water and sanitation delivery beyond the expensive, electronically-metered standpipe. This may well become one of the most significant development failures in the twenty-first century. The high mortality rate among children from preventable water-related diseases continues. Further, water for the poor is bedeviled by a lack of reliable statistics that can clearly illustrate who gets water and access to sanitation facilities and those who don't. Often researchers have to rely on informal guesses.

Access to clean water continues at an uneven and unequal rate at a time when many nations of the world are spending fortunes on military weaponry and general technology of war. Many of the very countries with water deprivation are those countries that find money in their budgets to purchase weapons. (High military expenditures and parsimonious spending on key water initiatives continues to be one of the main trends of the twenty-first century.) The message of the twentieth century is also the message of the twenty-first: Place the sting on the poorest. It is easy to conclude from even the most rudimentary study of water and sanitation that a positive government intervention to insure people's basic right to water is worthwhile. Intervention, however, is not happening in a large way. Given the propensity for corruption in developing countries and the many conflicts between bureaucrats and the military, it is naïve to expect that United Nations concepts like "The Decade of Water" can be translated into concrete and meaningful action.

Living Downstream: Disappearing Watersheds

Until recently the only people who concerned themselves with watersheds were hydrologists in the American West and a few concerned scientists and conservationists like Rachel Carson and Aldo Leopold. In the twenty-first century, watersheds have become part of our growing environmental consciousness and have entered the discourse of our political life. Watersheds, those basin-like formations along high points and ridge lines, descend into valleys through forests, sumps, and streams. Drop-by-drop, they channel rainfall into soil, groundwater, creeks, and streams. Watersheds affect the quality for all communities living down stream. Watersheds are the home of important fish populations, benthic critters, and friendly bacteria that help to keep water pure.

We did not think much about watersheds. We dismissed them as parcels of junk forest on the suburban fringe, scenic mountain ranges, or pasture that over time will have houses, business parks, and shopping centers built upon them. Watersheds are vibrant and protective sources of freshwater and they are slipping away at an alarming rate. The rainforests of the Amazon and Indonesia fall under the lumberman's axe and saw. The watersheds of the American Eastern Piedmont get turned into real estate developments. Absorbent wetlands and marshes get filled in and covered by the impervious surfaces of parking lots. What we do to our watersheds is of great consequence in how we deal with our global thirst for water. Unless we take our water from an underground supply, most likely we are dependent upon a watershed. For example, so dependent is the city of Washington, DC on the Potomac River for its water supply that it regularly gets water level data from the Interstate Commission for the Potomac River Basin on water flows coming out of all the tributaries that make up the Potomac watershed.

Recently the U.S. Fish and Wildlife Service documented a continuing loss of wetlands in the coastal watersheds of the Great Lakes, Atlantic Ocean, and the Gulf of Mexico. Wetlands are fish nurseries and offer habitat to many endangered species. Their loss testifies to the rampant urbanization of American life as development now on both coasts of the United States is beginning to traverse mountain ranges in a swift uphill and down valley momentum. More than half the population of the United States lives along coastal watersheds and, by building roads, homes, and businesses, they are jeopardizing future water supplies; after all, cutting down forests and paving over countryside allows for little replenishment of groundwater.

Also, as many Americans move to exurbia and beyond for their little piece of country paradise, septic systems leach into the groundwater. In areas of Appalachia with large shale formations, the porous rock allows polluted surface and septic water to contaminate drinking water wells. The state of Maryland is so concerned that it recently commissioned a study to ascertain what impact gas drilling and exurban development would have on drinking water in the Marcellus Shale formation of the western part of the state. Once a watershed has been paved over or deforested, the likelihood of its ever coming back to its former aquatic strength is nil. In many suburban areas the streams that continue to drain have become conduits for floods of storm water from parking lots and roads. The runoff gouges out streambeds, destroys fish and benthic populations, and causes major problems for wastewater treatment plants dealing with excess for which their plants were not designed. Scientists believe that climate change will only add to the stress currently being placed on our remaining wetlands. Our watersheds are ecological treasures and today we are ridding ourselves of them as if they were pieces of easily discarded costume jewelry.[7]

Disappearing watersheds are part of a larger global process brought about by a combination of government irrigation policies and dam construction, as well as the expansion of the urban metropolis into new areas that require control of both groundwater and watersheds. The Aral Sea was once a Soviet Union tourist destination and maritime center. Its beaches were a sunbather's delight as they frolicked under sunny skies and pleasant surroundings that stretched back over the millennia. The Aral Sea supported a large fishing industry that brought great prosperity to small towns that bordered on the sea. In the 1960s, the Soviet Union made a decision to dam the tributaries of the Aral Sea and grow cotton for a growing domestic and international market. Waters to the Aral Sea dried up and today this once-famous vacation spot and fisherman's paradise is now scrub desert. A few abandoned freighter ships list and rust in the sand.

Draining off the wetlands and destroying watersheds is not a new development, as historians of the subject will tell you. The famous Norfolk Broads of England were once a vast region of bogs, fens, and wetlands of myriad waterways, marshes, sand spits, and waterfowl. In the seventeenth century, the Duke of Bedford, in consort with King Charles I, brought Dutch engineers to build sluices and pumps to drain the fens. The Dutch, for centuries, had been draining the Zuider Zee in their own homeland. They proved masterfully efficient. The fens were drained and today few recall that the cathedral town of Ely was named after the eels that were once a major maritime industry there.

On a similar scale, for decades sugar farmers and developers diked, diverted, filled in, and appropriated the waters of the Everglades. Today, America's historic "river of grass" is slowly on the conservation mend, but for decades it was less a source of freshwater and waterfowl habitat and more a gigantic sump for Florida's sugar cane industry.

Mexico's largest lake, the Chapala, is the primary source of water for five million people in Guadalajara. Since the 1970s the lake has lost over 80 percent of its water due to agricultural diversions of its tributaries. Soaring municipal and industrial water demands currently exceed sustainable supply by 40 percent. On my visit to Lake Chapala, the beautiful fishing lake that I had hoped to see looked more like a vast algae pond. For American expatriates who have purchased retirement homes along the lake, it is not a pretty sight to behold algae blooms over morning coffee. Mexicans complain of the smell and lament the damage done to local fishing and tourism.

Similar processes are at work along the Mekong Delta in Vietnam and Laos and at the greatly diminished Lake Chad in central Africa. Lake Chad, because of excessive agricultural water consumption, has shrunk by 95 percent from its original 9,653 square miles to 521 square miles.

Conclusion

With the amount of time mankind has given to thoughts of water and sewage, one would think that solving global sanitation problems would be an easy matter. Archeologists have discovered urban hydraulic systems dating back to the Bronze Age (2800-1100 B.C.) in Mesopotamia. The ancient city of Eshnunna, about 80 kilometers from modern Baghdad, has excavations revealing sewers and lateral connections to individual homes. Other cities in what was Sumeria show exposed clay pipes as well as tee and angle joints for pipes.[8]

Perhaps we should take a cue from the ancient Romans, who spent a considerable amount of time providing water and sanitation for private and public purposes. The public baths and aqueducts of ancient Rome, while seemingly dwarfed by the great watercourses and dams of our present era, had a greater purpose that eludes us. Romans designed their systems for their own personal enjoyment as well as to offer the public the opportunity to lead a clean well-regulated life through public baths and latrines. While the Romans had their word for the craft, *plumbarius*, which has survived the ages, they were more comfortable with the craft of *aquarius*. The former was a pipe fitter's trade while the latter was always referred to as "the bearer of water" or the water expert who helped to design a comfortable water system in your house or town, a sort of early hydrologist who could offer a sensible sanitary view. We could use a lot of people in the *aquarius* role today. In final analysis, dealing with sanitation problems is a moral act. It is a matter of values. As Elizabeth Royte reminds us, water, garbage, and our sanitation are part of the common mix of civilization.[9]

Today, water, like sanitation, is big business. Water has become a commodity in many respects that resembles oil. What will happen with regard to water pricing in the future is any man's guess. Suffice it to say that large corporations and entrepreneurs will have a major say in water's outcome.

"The world's

water supply

is being

stolen."

-- Ben Manski,
Co-chairman,
Green Party of the
United States

Chapter Six

Big Water and Privatization

An Acrimonious Issue

W hen it comes to the subject of who owns water, locally and globally, the lines of contention are being clearly drawn between those who argue that water should be privatized and subject to the pricing mechanism of the world market and those who believe that access to water, much like air, should be a natural and inalienable right. The latter groups argue that water is part of a global commons to which people of all color and income should have access.

Those with a humanitarian bent believe that the movement for access to water, especially potable water, is part of man's fight for survival in the twenty-first century. Water has now become part of the global justice movement — an effort to preserve water as a public trust and a common heritage against those business interests seeking to turn water into a commodity that can be bought and sold much like Coca-Cola®. In many areas of the developing world, the population is growing two to four times faster than the available water supply and access to water is an acrimonious issue. In South Africa, for example, 600,000 white farmers consume 60 percent of the country's water supply for irrigation while 15 million black South Africans have no direct access to water. Water apartheid exists long after its racial variant has been outlawed.

Across the globe a market is developing around this scarce resource. Water rights and water systems are being bought, sold, and leased and brought into the private sphere of an expanding global market that has little or no patience for the world's poor and dispossessed. Water, today, is viewed as an important moneymaking opportunity. According to Water Justice writer Maude Barlow, "The global water market can conservatively be said to be a trillion-dollar-plus-per-year industry with no limit in sight."[1] Meanwhile, from Africa to India, China, and the United States, people are questioning how we currently use water and what our water priorities should be. It has long been a common saying in the American West that water flows uphill to money. Now water is flowing to money in the global marketplace. In a nutshell, water has become a major commodity and battles rage over access and control of water systems.

In a 2008 report on water privatization, David Hall and his colleagues reported that Suez and Veolia of France and RWE, a German company, controlled about 75 percent of the world's private water supply market.[2] Veolia Environment, formerly Vivendi Water, operates in seventy-four countries and employs over 312,000 people with revenues in excess of 34 billion Euros. Similarly, Suez Environment had total revenues in 2009 of over 11 billion Euros, servicing thirty-three countries and employing some 35,000 people. These two companies give meaning and dimension to the term "Big Water." RWE, the third largest water company, is a German energy and water company that recently bought Thames Water of England and now serves 70 million people worldwide.

The rise of these "Big Water" corporations comes at the time when global concern over access to water is being fueled by a warming climate that is having a major impact on forest cover and the continued existence of glacial masses that provide a lot of the water supply in Asia. The question of who really owns water these days is a thorny economic, political, and moral issue that in the words of Maude Barlow "seemed to sneak up on us, or at least those of us living in the North. Until the past decade the study of fresh water was left to highly specialized groups of experts — hydrologists, engineers, scientists, city planners, weather forecasters and others with a niche interest in what so many of us took for granted." The water problems of Third World countries, she continued, seemed to be just another side of the poverty and social justice issues being focused on by international relief agencies.[3]

In the United States, the water issue exploded on the political scene as part of America's problem with aging infrastructures. By the 2000s, aging public water systems required massive repairs at an annual cost of $17 billion projected over a twenty-year period. Aging water mains broke at the rate 240,000 a year, and more than a trillion gallons of wastewater spilled into our rivers and streams annually. Federal funds for repairs have been insufficient, requiring major increases in local taxes for many communities.

Escalating costs prompted many communities to look for alternatives, with officials in cash-strapped towns eager to sell their aging water systems to corporations because they believed that privatization of water would help lift their burden. Some municipalities sold their companies outright while others turned to private companies to buy their utilities, repair them, and then lease them back to the community in what was known as "public-private partnerships." The companies promised improvements, greater efficiency, and money up front. What communities often got once a private company bought their utility were skyrocketing rates and little public recourse.

The American Water Works Company, a corporation in the forefront of this development to privatize water, has taken over many utilities in California and other states. Recently American Water Works was acquired by Thames Water, a giant London-based corporation. In California, a subsidiary of American Water, Cal-Am, proposed a 74% increase over three years in the price of water to the California Public Utilities Commission. This sparked what has been an ongoing fight between citizens groups protesting major percentage increases in the price of their water and the private water companies. Some towns have been successful in resisting the private water giants while others have not. Behind this water privatization issue looms an even larger one: the federal government is getting out of the public water business. Before President Ronald Reagan took office in 1981, 78 percent of money for new water projects in the United States came from the federal government. Thirty years later, the proportion fell to three percent. Furthermore, during the Clinton Administration, tax-law changes made it easier to privatize local water and sewer systems and for foreign companies like Thames Water and Nestle® to enter the market.

How do people value water? The simple answer is "differently." Water is certainly linked to concepts of quantity and pricing, especially as potable water becomes scarcer, but it is also linked to both purpose and utility. Water for drinking carries a different value than water for use in the laundry or toilet. Water, when viewed on the massive scale to satisfy agricultural irrigation needs, is valued as almost a different commodity — measured in acre-feet rather than liters or gallons. Water is also measured in rivers and streams in terms of flow or millions of gallons per day. Thus, how water is valued or priced may be determined by a host of factors that include nature, morality, crop pricing, sanitation, and citizen demand. Furthermore, it is hard to develop incentives for water efficiency when for many people water either "seems" or "should be" free. Thus, it is hard to construct water policies with regard to any long-term public good.

Water principles or "benchmarks" that are within and across national and international boundaries have been largely absent until now. Water planning at the United Nations in terms of sustainable development only dates back to 1998 and discussion of terms such as "cost recovery" and "financing for accessible water supplies" for monitoring only date to 2003. Thus, water policy to address growing water needs around the planet is largely a construct of the twenty-first century and very new to international thinking.

A variety of problems relating to water use are emerging. In most areas of the world groundwater has been defined as "a common property resource with very high use value," but how can you prevent people from siphoning off all the water if they own the land above the aquifer? Further, problems abound on water sharing, particularly when water basins are in transboundary areas. Water pricing continues to be a tough issue. What is a fair price for water when there are variations in pricing that range from 47 cents per million cubic feet in South Africa to $1.23 per million cubic feet in France? The only thing that is certain in this regard has been that since the onset of the twenty-first century there has been resistance to developing a realistic pricing scale for water largely because of the complexity of human values involving water use. Lastly, regulatory institutions are not in place worldwide that are necessary to accurately apply cost to those who generate waste, inefficiencies, and water pollution. Planned water sharing and realistic water pricing have almost always come about by necessity rather than by international or national accord. The United Nations currently has developed a Water Conservation Scheme because water is now so inextricably linked to agriculture, conservation management practices, and flood control. However, the experts will tell you, water sharing is hard work on this planet.

Just about the only realistic way to save water on a large scale is to regulate irrigation subsidies in the United States and beyond to promote equity and efficiency. As Sandra Postel has noted, "Practical ways exist to give farmers an economic incentive to use water more efficiently." In India, for example, local government units are working to charge farmers for water according to the volume of water taken from an irrigation canal that services their area. This plan may succeed far better than attempts in the United States to obtain meaningful reform of the Bureau of Reclamation's irrigation policies that permits farmers to pay a small fraction of the actual cost of their water. However, as city populations continue to grow in the United States, notes Postel, farmers will be forced to realize that "meeting new demands will increasingly require shifting water among the different users — irrigators, industries, cities and the natural environment." In some areas of the American West, where farmers have clear property rights to irrigation water or rivers, they have an option of selling those rights to a willing buyer. Farmers who turn to less thirsty crops can continue their profession and at the same time profit from selling water rights to cities and municipalities. Out of this may come either a frenzied bidding for water rights reminiscent of a new issue on the stock market or the development of a new water ethic for rational water resource allocation. However, as we shall now see, the entrepreneurial pool for water has more than its share of sharks in residence.

There Will Be Water

In 2007, American moviegoers were treated to a probing film about human greed entitled, *There Will Be Blood*. Based on an Upton Sinclair 1927 novel, *Oil*, starring Daniel Day Lewis as a late nineteenth century California oilman, Daniel Plainview, the film chronicles one man's ruthless quest for wealth during an oil boom. The film concentrates on Daniel Plainview's greed, ambition, and paranoia. Both Sinclair's novel and the film show the best and worst in the ethos of rugged individualism. Plainview obtains a monopoly of oil leases from distressed farmers for hard cash. In the beginning, the locals call him their hero. Later on, they see him as an arch villain. The film even spawned a stock phrase: "I drink your milkshake"; that is, just about all the deeds of this arch capitalist are done in "plain view" as the character's name suggests. Plainview is quite open about siphoning other people's oil reserves with techniques that are perfectly legal.

Today, on the plains of west Texas, another oilman is preparing to "drink your milkshake." This time, though, the resource is water. Rugged individualism has transcended time and geography to come to Roberts, Texas, where Texas oil-billionaire and wind farmer T. Boone Pickens is attempting to control a lion's share of the Ogallala aquifer and build a 250-mile pipeline across the plains to service Dallas. If Pickens succeeds, he will make the story of Daniel Plainview in California a prelude to the greater story where domination, and not gain, is the ultimate goal. Pickens is doing everything in "plain view" with the assistance of his vast wealth and a rangy herd of land-owning neighbors, Texas lawyers, and lobbyists. Texas journalists have been quick to point out the similarities between Daniel Day Lewis' character and T. Boone Pickens, referring to the billionaire's efforts as "There Will Be Water."

However, Pickens would be the first to admit that he is a country boy capitalist who made a fortune in oil and natural gas. He has also lost over a billion dollars in the hurly-burly of the oil business. What is surprising to many people is that he also believes his water grab of the Ogallala is part of his being an environmentalist. This Roberts County oilman sees himself as having an unlimited right to draw water for free from the Ogallala aquifer and sell it to Texas cities. He feels that he is limited only by his pumping capacity. As an exponent of wind power and vast wind farms on the plains of the Texas Panhandle, Pickens argues that his wind farms and water pipeline ideas are part of the "green revolution" to give Americans better and cheaper access to increasingly expensive resources. Pickens worries that in an age of diminishing resources, America must protect its vital energy and water resources. How this translates into piping Ogallala water to Dallas across land that he does not own at great expense to the public remains to be seen.

Pickens has plenty of money, and he has given nearly $700 million away to charity. Wind and water are just chess pieces on his board of market domination. These are not new Pickens tactics. He tried before in California to establish a natural gas fuels company that would be the beneficiary of a $5 billion California bond issue. California voters shot that project down. Yet, when it comes to water, Pickens is no dilettante. A trained geologist by education, he believes that we are now at what he calls "peak oil" and starting to enter "peak water" where these resources begin to decline while they soar in value. Pickens is just a "good old boy" at heart, but he knows a few things. He knows that the population of Texas is booming and that meteorologists predict that by 2021 the state will go into perpetual draught owing to climate change. He knows that municipalities will have to protect their citizens through drought-proof, long-term access to water. Today Pickens and his investors are ready to tell Texas and the country at-large that there will be water — at a price. Even if this means draining down the Ogallala aquifer to a point where parched future generations will not be able to live on the Great Plains, at least for now there will be water.

Pickens is just one of many entrepreneurs, farmers, and opportunists seeking to exploit the Ogallala, the largest underground water system in the world; it provides drinking and irrigation water to Colorado, Kansas, Nebraska, New Mexico, Oklahoma, Texas, and Wyoming. Farmers named the aquifer after Ogallala, Nebraska, where it first came into serious use at the end of the nineteenth century.

The best way to understand the Ogallala, experts say, is to consider it to be an underground ocean comprising 174,000 square miles. By comparison, the total area of Lake Superior, the largest of the Great Lakes, is 31,820 square miles. In some areas of the Northern Plains, the Ogallala's water can be tapped at a depth of some 500 feet, but in most areas groundwater can be found at a depth of 200 feet. The Ogallala was not tapped for farm use prior to the 1930s because existing well technology was too expensive. After the Dust Bowl years of the Great Depression and the persistence of drought conditions on the plains, farmers used new cheaper water extraction technology to mine the aquifer and make the Plains green again. Since large-scale irrigation began in the 1940s, water levels in the Ogallala have dropped 100 feet in parts of Kansas, New Mexico, Texas, and Oklahoma. Recently increased efficiency in irrigation has slowed the rate of groundwater mining; however, cities rising on the plains and desert grow increasingly thirsty and eager to tap into the Ogallala's bounty.

Because of heavy irrigation usage in Kansas the part of the Ogallala water table in that state has dropped twenty-five feet in the last ten years. Corn, a crop that is very water-intensive, is the main reason for the Ogallala's disappearing act. Ethanol produced from corn is now an important component of the American gasoline industry. Unlike solar energy and wind that can be used to propel our nation's cars and electrify our homes, there is no solar or wind alternative to water.

The Ogallala is what hydrologists call an "unconfined aquifer." Virtually all of the Ogallala's recharge comes from rainwater and snow melt. Over the millennia, the Ogallala was a creation of the snow melt and glaciers of the Rocky Mountains made by deposition from streams that flowed eastward. This is not happening as much as in former centuries. Today, given the fact that the Great Plains are above this aquifer and either semi-arid or drought-stricken, water recharge of the Ogallala is minimal.

The Vanishing Drinking Fountain

During good weather, my wife and I like to take our two grandchildren to a playground in Stanton Park in Washington, DC. The kids frolic on the playground and joyfully descend the slide. After they have played and run for a suitable time, we gather them up for the homeward stroll. As we leave the park, we stop at a public drinking fountain. We lift the kids up so they can drink the cool water from the fountain that offers relief from play-generated thirst. This fountain always surprises me, mostly because it works. A lot of drinking fountains in parks, playgrounds, and public areas are defunct today. It is often a lot easier to find a store that sells bottled water than it is to find an operational public drinking fountain. Only in museums and theaters can one confidently find a drinking fountain to slake one's thirst. Even then, it is not always an easy task.

Drinking fountains used to be everywhere — in city hall lobbies, office buildings, playgrounds, and even at car dealerships — but these days the drinking fountain has gone the way of the phone booth, the record player, and the drive-in movie theater.

Suffice it to say, that in the history of our global environment, the water fountain may be one of the most important plumbing fixtures ever invented. Water fountains were important places for health and conviviality. The Bible contains many fountain metaphors. In the *Book of John*, Jesus Christ is the fountainhead who says, "Whoever drinks of the water that I shall give him will never thirst."

The drinking water fountain has a history that dates back to the ancient Greeks. One of the earliest drinking fountains was a pneumatic fountain invented by a Greek engineer, Hero of Alexandria, around A.D. 47. It used a pneumatic device based on principles somewhat like a modern siphon to create a constant stream of water from a pool or container.

The Romans valued water and went to great lengths to provide access to drinking fountains. They located their "cisternas," or fountain sites, on side streets in Rome and to this day many Italian towns have their Villa della Cisterna. One of the most famous is Rome's Villa Sciarra, which depicts two gods holding a large bowl in the form of a seashell. Below their knees water pours gently into a refreshing pool. No doubt, throughout history many a Roman slaked his or her thirst at the fountain Villa Sciarra.

The drinking fountain remained relatively unchanged until the Victorians gave it a new design and functions. In nineteenth century Britain, sanitarians sought to construct healthy drinking fountains that would wean the English poor from the town pump, which often drew up water laced with e-coli and other toxics. Also, they hoped that drinking fountains would be a public alternative to drinking from London's Thames River, which by 1858 had become a toxic sewer. In pamphlets and public art, both the Thames and the common pump were labeled "Death's Dispensary."

The public drinking fountains were attractive architectural works, the result of a determined English sanitary reformer and Member of Parliament, Samuel Gurney. Using his own funds and those of his philanthropic associates, Gurney established the Metropolitan Free Drinking Fountain Association in 1858 and soon fountains supplying pure cold water sprang up all over London. Other philanthropists joined in to create a drinking facility for the public good. Perhaps the grandest of that era was established in Victoria Park by Baroness Angela Burdett Courts at a then astonishing cost of 6,000 pounds. It was a noble piece of eclecticism that combined Venetian, Moorish, and Renaissance elements — all designed to make drinking water a popular activity linked to history and romance. The Victorians became famous for their ornamental and highly decorative drinking water fountains and, by World War I, there were over 48,000 public fountains throughout Britain.

A similar reform movement took place in the United States in the 1870s. The Women's Christian Temperance Union (WCTU) fountains were less a sanitary solution and more a device to wean men and women away from "alcohol and demon rum." In 1874, at the WCTU's annual meeting, members were urged to erect drinking fountains in their towns so that men could get a drink of water without having to enter a saloon, where they would then be tempted to stay for stronger drinks. Many of the fountains erected by the WCTU in the United States are still standing in their original locations, having been lovingly restored by local history organizations. One of the most notable can be found along the boardwalk at the seaside resort of Rehoboth Beach, Delaware. Erected in 1929, the fountain was dedicated to "temperance" — the total abstinence from alcohol.

Drinking fountains became technologically sophisticated in the twentieth century. In the early 1900s, two California men, Halsey Taylor and Luther Haws, invented a "faucet" for drinking water that was widely used. Today the Halsey Taylor Company produces wall-mounted fountains for public schools as well as refrigerated water coolers that are tailored for new building designs. Most of us know the water fountains that are the creation of what is now the Kohler Company. In 1888, the Kohler Water Works patented a device called a "bubbler" that has become a standard water fountain fixture in America. The "Bubbler" responds to the human touch of a button and shoots water into the air, creating a bubbling texture. Often the force of water shooting upwards was quite strong and Kohler had to work to regulate the flow. Today, the device is less often called a "bubbler" and more often referred to as "a water fountain."

The development of water fountains in the United States also entered the strange currents of Jim Crow. From the outset in the American post-Civil War segregated South and lasting well into the 1960s, municipalities and private businesses maintained segregated water fountains labeled "white" and "colored." White water fountains were larger and kept cleaner than their smaller "colored" counterparts. Thus, water fountains became a metaphor for the "separate but equal" argument for racial segregation and served as an early indicator of one kind of water apartheid.

In Great Britain a new reform movement has begun to campaign for drinking fountains in all public green spaces in the country. Christine Haigh of the Children's Food Campaign argues that as fountains disappear in public parks children are turning to tooth-rotting sugary drinks instead of drinking water. Haigh says: "Health professionals say water is the best thing for children to drink yet we make it hard by failing to provide fountains in parks. Drinking fountains are a cheap, easy way of improving public health. The Victorians were way ahead of us." Also Britain's Friends of the Earth leaders note that water fountains offer an opportunity to fill a reusable bottle with water, which is "an easy way to minimize waste and cut our carbon footprints."[4]

What's In the Bottle?

In the twenty-first century water fountains have fallen into disuse primarily because of false beliefs, political ineptitude, and the greed of the bottled beverage industry. Over the past two decades public water fountains have come under attack by so-called water purists (usually backed by private water companies) who have asserted that municipal tap water is contaminated. If you drink it, they assert, you will become ill. Owing to the power of advertising, people have become convinced that bottled water is better than tap water. This flies in the face of research that has consistently proven tap water in Western countries is better than bottled water, which is not scientifically monitored and often lacks key minerals.

Recently one company, Coca-Cola®, was forced to admit that its Acquafina brand of bottled water in New England was nothing more than tap water from the municipal water supply of Ayer, Massachusetts. At present more than 25 percent of all bottled water in the United States comes from a public municipal supply, including Dasani® and Nestle Pure Life.® The water is treated and sold to us with a thousand-fold markup on price. It would be the same if we boiled our tap water, put it into a bottle, slapped a label on it, and sold it to an unsuspecting public. In many areas of the United States, bottled water costs more than $4 a gallon.

Currently there is increasing controversy over access to water fountains in American sport stadiums. The National Plumbing Code requires sports facilities to offer one public drinking fountain per 1,000 fans, but these codes are rarely followed because stadium owners would rather sell $3 bottles of water and $4 soft drinks and make enormous profits. In 2003, the NFL's Philadelphia Eagles opened their brand new stadium without any drinking fountains. They later called it an oversight.

In his blog on bottled water, Pacific Institute president Peter Gleick has pointed out that stadium owners try to remove water fountains from their facilities for "health reasons." Fortunately, Gleick notes, that tactic in Cleveland produced fan outrage at Cleveland Cavalier basketball games. Fans perceived that Cavalier executives were just trying to boost bottled water sales. Similar reactions have occurred in Florida and elsewhere. Gleick sees a broader issue in this contention: "Public water fountains need to be maintained, cleaned, and made even more widely available, and the trend to eliminate water fountains needs to be fought."[5]

In New Zealand, alcohol has become cheaper than bottled water, a recent study at the University of Otago reports. University researchers in the *New Zealand Medical Journal* found that wine cost as little as 63 cents (47 cents US) per standard drink compared to 67 cents for 250 ml of bottled water and 43 cents for an equivalent amount of milk. The study also found that the relative price of alcohol had plummeted over the past decade as wages increased. With wine cheaper than water there seems less reason to refrain from binge drinking among New Zealand's youth. Inadvertently the increased consumption of expensive bottled water globally may have ramifications for public health of which we are just starting to become aware.[6]

As we bring a variety of cultural and social perceptions to the water we drink, it should not come as a surprise that young people today, guided by perceptions of higher quality, are more likely to purchase both bottled water and home-filtration systems. Purchasing bottled water carries a degree of status or snob appeal. Over the last decade the middle classes of the world have been "trading up," deciding that what they consume in terms of brands to a great extent explains who they are in terms of status. If people prefer BMWs to less classy vehicles, it is understandable that people's status requirements are defined by expensive food and drink. Evian and San Pellegrino bottled water are unreasonably expensive, costing about $2 a bottle. While cynics may point out that chic bottled water is a sucker's game, Evian and Pellegrino's mineral water cachet entrances others along with brand name clothing, first class tickets, and Rothschild wines. Just as one would not buy a Hyundai if one can afford a Lincoln Continental, one does not choose cheap water when the more expensive brand can be had.

Meanwhile, the bottled water market has never been hotter. In 2005, worldwide sales exceeded $10 billion; and people whose incomes exceed $50,000 annually purchase the lion's share of bottled water. Classy bottled water seems to be the drink of choice for the young professional class. Walking around with an expensive bottle of water shows that you have a higher status than people in the "tap water crowd." Finally, bottled water comes with evocative names and labels depicting pastoral scenes that convince the public that the liquid is the purest drink around.

The United States is the world's leading consumer of bottled water. According to a recent report from the Earth Policy Institute, Americans drink over 26 billion liters of bottled water annually. Mexico, China, and Brazil follow with 12 billion liters each. On a per capita basis, the Italians are the biggest lovers of bottled water; and other Europeans are developing a fondness for this new kind of H20 as well.[7] According to water expert Charles Fishman, "Bottled water is the food phenomenon of our times." It costs three or four times the cost of a gallon of gasoline for a product we've always gotten for free from taps in our homes.[8] According to FDA reports, if the water we use at home cost what even cheap bottled water costs, our monthly water bills would run $9,000. Meanwhile, water experts argue that where drinking water is safe, bottled water is a superfluous luxury we can do without.

Recently, George Hawkins, the general manager of DC Water, Washington's municipal water authority, voiced his dismay about bottled water consumption to the United States Congress. Despite the new frugality of Congress, the House of Representatives spends nearly $800,000 a year on bottled water — water that is not subject to strict federal regulation. According to Hawkins, "A House that buys bottled water for its members is also a House that isn't focused on the importance of municipal tap water and the need to invest in infrastructure improvements." Naturally Hawkins wanted to help. He sent the House Speaker a letter offering free reusable water bottles for all members of Congress so that high-profile politicians could demonstrate their support for inexpensive public tap water that is both safe and cheap. After all, Hawkins reasoned, Congress was the author of the Clean Water Act. Hawkins also offered to have DC Water test all the taps and water fountains in congressional buildings.[9]

Americans annually drain the aquifers of Micronesia from a distance of 9,000 kilometers in order to drink Fiji Water and other exotic brands. Fiji Water regularly sells for $3-4 a liter and costs the Fiji Water Plant 15 cents per liter to process and bottle. Meanwhile, Fiji, unknown to most visitors and consumers, is a dictatorship with a vested economic interest in producing enormous amounts of plastic waste shipped to other areas of the globe.

Two years ago, my wife and I visited Fiji as vacationing tourists homeward bound from New Zealand. Landing at Suva, the capital of Fiji, we beheld a country rundown economically and disorganized by nearly a decade of political coups and social dysfunction. A lot of Suva reminded me of Mexico at its worst in the 1960s. The Melanesians of Fiji were happy to receive us and sent us merrily on our way to one of the outer islands. It is only when we returned to the United States that I learned that 53 percent of all Fiji residents do not have access to safe drinking water. The good water, apparently, is being exported. The Fiji islanders were once cannibals. Now they cannibalize their water resources for the profit of distant masters.

Two secretive southern California billionaires, Lynda and Stewart Resnick, whose water enterprises have benefited enormously since Fiji came under martial law in 2009, own Fiji Water. Ironically, in California, the Resnicks befriend liberal organizations and give to environmental causes. Yet they make their Fiji water profits by tolerating a repressive military regime in the islands. Meanwhile, Fiji Water is hardly as good as its owners proclaim. According to an article in the *Pittsburgh Post Gazette* on July 20, 2006, in blind taste tests and water quality analysis, tap water from Cleveland, Ohio, was declared superior to Fiji water.

One man's chic water bottle is another's garbage. All of this bottled water consumption gives our local municipal government one big water hangover as they struggle to deal with all the disposable plastic containers. According to the Container Recycling Institute, 86 percent of plastic water bottles used in the United States become garbage or litter. The tsunami of plastic bottles rushes through watersheds to foul the landscape and plug sewers. Most of the trash traps on American rivers and streams have one central purpose: to catch plastic water bottles before they enter our waterways. Burning plastic bottles is hazardous because they produce toxic by-products such as chlorine gas.

Furthermore, the growth of the bottled water industry has resulted in major water extractions in communities where bottling plants are located with water shortages being reported in countries as diverse as the United States, Bolivia, and India. Bottled water extraction is also having a very negative effect on groundwater resources in the Great Lakes region and parts of the American Midwest. Peter Gleick, in his highly regarded work *Bottled and Sold*, reports that the Sedona Springs Bottled Water Company "pumped enough groundwater to dramatically alter surface water flows" in Maricopa County, Arizona — a depletion that caused the demise of local flora and fauna.[10]

Gleick also notices that we have no reliable assessment mechanism to measure the quality of bottled water, and that bottled water has not proven itself to be any better than tap water. At the price people pay for the product, bottled water should be far superior to what's on tap, but it isn't. Recently scientists in Europe, reports Maude Barlow, conducted a study of sixty-eight brands of bottled mineral water and found high levels of bacterial contamination. As long as bottled water remains unregulated by government agencies, one is better to stay with the safer and medically monitored public tap water. According to Barlow, Coca-Cola® was forced to recall all of its Dasani® bottled water in Britain in 2004 when it was discovered to have high levels of bromate, a chemical compound that can cause everything from abdominal pain to hearing loss and kidney failure.

When one factors in the water dilemmas of poorer countries, it becomes self-evident that bottled water is not the answer. According to the United Nations Millennium Development Plan, it will take about $30 billion a year to upgrade global water supplies and sanitation. This is a drop in the bucket compared to the estimated $100 billion spent globally on bottled water. As Charles Fishman has noted, "Once you understand where the water comes from, and how it got here, it's hard to look at that bottle in the same way again."[11]

Conclusion

Big Water, or the water cartel, is everywhere these days and caught up in a host of business ventures. The latest is what is euphemistically called "bulk water transfers." This normally applies to pipelines, tanker trucks, and aqueducts transferring large amounts of water mostly for agricultural purposes. The newest approach to bulk water transfer is the water bag. These are gigantic floating plastic cones capable of holding over 33,000 tons of water. As freshwater is lighter than salt, these water bags float and can be towed for considerable distances by ship. They are usually longer than the length of two football fields. Of course, when you tow such enormous amounts of water freight, there are risks. Bags have been lost at sea and are a threat to commercial shipping. Many of these bags are now equipped with homing beacons so collisions can be avoided and lost bags recovered. It is equivalent to towing an iceberg wrapped in plastic. Water bags are not very profitable, but as the century progresses and the price of water begins to escalate, this situation will change.

At the moment, the major figure in the water bag business is Nordic Water Supply. Operating out of Oslo, Norway, Nordic is currently transporting water from Turkey to Cyprus. Nordic is registered on the Oslo stock exchange and has been operating since 1979. The company has lost over $1.5 million in its operations, but is undeterred in looking to expand to other parts of a thirsty planet in order to make the business more profitable. The system is relatively simple and may well be the water transport technology of the late twenty-first century. The system works by filling a giant bag with freshwater at a coastal filling station in the supply country, which is then towed to the receiving country where the bag is unloaded. According to a Nordic spokesman, "the basic premise for this endeavor is the fact that global demand for water is increasing and that the supply of water cannot keep pace with the accelerating increase in demand in many areas of the world." There are advantages to towing water bags rather than using tanker ships. Water bags have lower port costs and have a financial advantage for short hauls. Further, the bags are strong enough — made of high-strength, lightweight, and flexible plastic — to withstand oceanic rigors. For Nordic, it has not been all smooth sailing. One of its ships lost a giant water bag in the Mediterranean and some ships narrowly avoided colliding with it. Currently, Nordic plans to expand in the Caribbean and Middle East. Further, Nordic's problems have not deterred others from entering the business.

One of the most ambitious plans for alleviating water scarcity comes out of Australia. Watertow Limited, a division of Marecon Consultancy in the business of marine application of high strength industrial fabrics, hopes to help end Australia's national water crisis in the drought-plagued Murray-Darling Basin. The Murray has not had good water flows in years because of a ten-year drought. The river, which flows from New South Wales through Victoria on to Adelaide and the sea, has virtually been sucked dry by irrigating farmers and industrial users. Watertow proposes to harvest water from northern Australian rivers in Queensland's tropical north and bring ten billion tons of water per year into the Murray-Darling basin. To do this requires a bold planning scheme that has multiple parts: First, giant water bags would be filled in Queensland from the Burdekin River along the southerly flowing East Australia current, arriving offshore at the port of Tathra. Water discharged at Tathra would be pumped over a relatively short pipeline into the Snowy River and through the Snowy Mountains and eventually into the Murray. Such a proposal is fraught with high cost and some measure of environmental delusion, critics say. Simple conservation and new alternative forms of less water intensive agriculture in the Murray basin would be far more effective.[12] This is what we have come to in the age of Big Water.

Meanwhile, the specter of droughts and dying rivers on a global scale is beginning to haunt us in ways that make our reflections on bottled water and disappearing drinking fountains seem insignificant in comparison.

"There will be no sustainable development in the future if there is no groundwater supply."

-- Liu Changming, Chinese Academy of Sciences

Chapter Seven

Droughts and Dying Rivers

Dying Rivers

I n 2007, the World Wildlife Foundation at its regular meeting in Geneva, Switzerland, called attention to the problem of dying rivers across the planet. If our major rivers die, "millions will lose their livelihoods, biodiversity will be destroyed on a massive scale, and there will be much less freshwater and agriculture resulting in less food security," said Ravi Singh, Secretary General of WWF India. The WWF report said that half the world's available supply of freshwater is already used up.[1]

In parts of Europe and North America, mention of acid rain makes people think first of dying forests, but, more importantly, acid rain is also associated with the death of fish in lakes and rivers. In Norway and other parts of Europe, thousands of trout stocks have been lost forever and many rivers are kept alive only by the massive application of lime to the water to combat acidification. Chemicals from power plants and factories spewed into the air eventually fall on the rivers as toxic rain. Acid rain now seems to be a permanent part of the geography of North America, northern Scotland, and parts of the Alps.

In Italy, the Po River cuts through Italy's prosperous manufacturing and agricultural region. Some 16 million people live in the Po Valley, nearly one-third of Italy's workforce. Its major industrial cities of Milan and Turin produce most of what Italy has to sell on the global market. Turin is a major automobile-manufacturing center for Fiat and Alpha Romeo. The Po's agricultural base permits the widespread cultivation of rice as a commercial cash crop, a staple not otherwise harvested much on the Italian peninsula. Both industry and agriculture are supported by a fan of tributary rivers descending from the Alps into the narrow mountain valley of the Po River and then ultimately to the Adriatic Sea.

Italians speak lovingly of the Po, as its affluence and beauty attracts large numbers of tourists and Italians. Its urban art galleries and universities like those in Milan are in Europe's first league, but perhaps the Italians love the Po River too much — today it is a river increasingly set with serious problems. Italians love to dump their sewage into the Po. As recently as 2002, the city of Milan had no sewage treatment plant and sent its effluent directly into the river. Because of its thriving agricultural base along the Po, groundwater resources, which supply 11 percent of the public drinking water of the region, have high concentration of nitrates.

If current climate trends continue, Italy's Po River runs the risk of running dry some 100 kilometers before reaching its delta on the Adriatic Sea. This will result in saltwater rising up the river, upsetting the Po's environmental balance and making many forms of agriculture impossible. Reduced rain and snowfall in the Italian mountains has lowered the amount of water feeding the river while higher temperatures have increased evaporation and forced farmers to draw more water from the river and ground wells for their crops. According to Italy's Environmental Protection Agency, the level of the Po River has fallen 20 to 25 percent over the last thirty years.

Meanwhile, the narrow Po Valley has a brownish yellow industrial smog that gradually wafts towards the Adriatic, putting its toxic mix into a body of water already plagued with pollution and eutrophication. Inasmuch as the Po Valley is responsible for nearly 38 percent of Italy's GDP, it is unlikely that the government in the future will clamp down very hard on its farmers and industrialists with stringent environmental regulations designed to save the Po. At this writing, there are conferences aplenty in Milan and Rome about the future of the Po, but in Italy talk is a cheap, well-worn currency.

Unlike other European rivers, the Po recently suffered a unique type of pollution in the form of the drug cocaine. In 2005, scientists found large quantities of cocaine by-product in the Po. The river was estimated to be carrying the daily equivalent of four kilos of cocaine with a street value of $150 million. According to the BBC News, scientists claim about twenty-seven daily doses of 100mg cocaine per 1,000 young adults were being consumed. Urine waste containing drug residue was flushed into the Po. This greatly exceeded national figures for the drug and led wags in Milan to speculate that young people in the valley were getting very mellow.[2]

A Water-Challenged World

It is painfully apparent that our rivers and lakes may no longer be able to respond to the crisis of a water-challenged world. The demand for water in many countries is simply outrunning supply. Also, 480 million people of the world's six billion people, says the Earth Policy Institute, are being fed with grain that raises sustainability issues. For example, the water required to produce the grain and other foodstuffs imported into North Africa and the Middle East in 2000 was roughly equal to the annual flow of the Nile River. This is equivalent to another Nile flowing into the region in the form of imported grain.[3]

In the twenty-first century, no river can satisfy the demands of the world's largest cities. New York can enjoy its prominence only by having a lock on most of the aquifer of the Catskill Mountains for its drinking water. London relies on the Thames and the Lee rivers for 80 percent of its drinking water, and changing weather patterns may force the city to rely more upon groundwater as Great Britain gets hotter and drier. Already Cairo has "black zones" in the Nile River that makes the river water unfit to drink. As the twenty-first century progresses, groundwater will play an increasingly important role for urban drinking water supplies. Rivers in many cases will be too polluted to offer much of a resource. Recycled wastewater programs that provide drinking water "from toilet to tap" have not proved popular.

Increasingly, in Europe, the challenge will be how an industrialized region can cleanup its rivers. The Rhine River's pollution derives from technological and industrial processes. Its environmental history has been one of the Rhine being one long chemical cocktail that flows some 1,300 kilometers from the Swiss Alps to the North Sea. Until well into the twentieth century, the Rhine was so polluted that it had an observable chemical froth to it. Cleanup efforts did not begin on the Rhine until after World War II when international accords between Holland, France, and Germany began to restrict the Rhine's chemical mix. Companies like Sandoz have discharged so many chemicals over the years into the Rhine that there seems to be little difference between the chemical mix of untreated Rhine river water and water that has been treated in wastewater treatment plants. The corporation Hoechst has admitted recently to a major leak of chlorbenzene into the river — this at a time when 20 million people in Europe depend on the Rhine for their drinking water.

The Rio Grande River forms a 1,200-mile border between the United States and Mexico and has figured largely in the literature and culture of the old American West. Today it bisects a lush valley of farm and industrial communities on both sides of the border. On the American side alone population in the Rio Grande Valley has increased from 1.1 million in 1970 to 2.2 million today and is set to double again by the year 2030. Warm winters and inexpensive lifestyles have fueled a migration of retirees to the region, mostly from the blizzard-plagued northern Great Plains of the Dakotas, Iowa, and Minnesota.

For years the town of Laredo, Texas, has been a prosperous farming community and tourist departure point for Americans going into Mexico. Today the town has to confront the fact that its river, already polluted with raw sewage, now contains toxic chemicals that threaten the town's future. The Rio Grande is its and other communities' sole source of drinking water. The toxins in the river became painfully apparent to Laredo's city fathers in 2000 when public health officials discovered, midst the mountain of sludge, old concrete, used automobile tires, abandoned sofas, and a number of empty industrial containers for muriatic acid, a chemical for cleaning toilets and air-conditioners that is extremely harmful when inhaled. Further, a survey of fish in the river near Laredo revealed over a dozen chemicals in the fish tissue of carp and bass. Most notable were large amounts of zinc and copper, which can cause cancerous lesions in fish. Since that time there has not been much improvement to the river. To assure the public safety of its drinking water, Laredo has committed to building a $1.6 million desalination plant that will convert the areas plentiful supply of salty and brackish groundwater into pure drinking water. Using a technology that the US Navy has long used on its ships, the desalination process will consist of boiling the salty water and putting it under pressure to separate the water from the chemicals. Thus, in the midst of what should be a reliable water source, Laredo must fall back upon water processes that date back to World War Two.

Meanwhile, in many places, the Rio Grande is drying up. In the Big Bend National Park of West Texas, for most of the year, the river is nothing more than occasional stagnant puddles that are punctuated with dry beds of gravel. Any approach to cleaning up the Rio Grande and protecting it as a water source gets tangled in the political nightmare of negotiation involving federal, Mexican, state, and local agencies. In Mexico and Texas, all the energy about the Rio Grande goes not into saving the river but into fighting over who gets what.

A different drama is playing out as Alberta, Canada, emerges as a leading petro-giant through the production of tar sands oil. Extracted from bituminous tar sand deposits, the product can be distilled into oil and, in an age where peak oil sells for $100 a barrel, this technology has become practicable. It is a messy process and the region around Fort McMurray, Alberta, is known for the odor of oil that hangs in the air, the gargantuan earth-moving vehicles that clog the highways, and the din of heavy blasting. In Alberta, a tar sands pit is less of a hole in the ground than a monstrous quarry reminiscent of the Butte, Montana, copper mine. However, the crude distillate oil needs to be refined before it finds commercial use, and Canada's tar sand oil producers would like to build an Alaska style pipeline from Canada to oil refineries in Texas. This measure has produced fierce opposition from Midwestern farmers and environmental groups.

Airborne emissions from smokestacks of the plants that convert the bitumen into crude oil are now having a significant impact on Alberta's air and water quality. David Shindler, an ecologist at the University of Alberta, has authored numerous peer-reviewed articles showing that these emissions have a toxic effect on the Athabasca, the giant river that flows through the tar sands. Many fear that the continuous mining and processing of tar sands will lead to the eventual death of the Athabasca and its fish and wildlife populations. Others worry whether there will be an increase in cancer rates down stream. Meanwhile, oilmen in Calgary, Alberta, already envision a pipeline being constructed to the Pacific so that the Chinese can have access to this new oil supply. The impact of this pipeline on Canada's forests and western waters is anyone's guess. Meanwhile, at Fort McMurray, toxic lakes of mine filings cover a distance of 66-square-miles. Canons have been placed along the shore to scare ducks, geese, and other birds away from the toxic water.[4]

China's Water Reality

China has two faces: the one that it projects outward to the world and the one that confronts its own social reality. To the tourist, China is an amazing spectacle of urban development and prosperity. Its luster city, Shanghai, rivals Hong Kong as a commercial, financial, and entertainment center. To walk along the old Bund on the Wang Po River at night is to gaze upon a neon spectacle that rivals the lights of Las Vegas. Its universities import world-class scholars and its affluent suburbs easily rival anything found in Washington, DC's metro area. Beijing, once a gray somber city with its share of slums where yesteryear cabbage was stockpiled on street corners to avoid famine, is a genteel conurbation of economic and political power. Once Beijing had a rush-hour gridlock of bicycle traffic as thousands of Chinese pedaled to and from work; today Beijing has heavy automobile traffic. At this writing, about 30,000 autos a month are being purchased by Beijing's aspiring middle class. Meanwhile, on the Yangtze River the mighty Three Gorges Dam continues to provide tourists with a spectacular upriver cruise through the five locks of the world's largest dam and hydroelectric project — a distance of some 600 feet — into a large freshwater lake that holds some of the most beautiful scenery in China. The dam itself spans a distance greater than that of the Golden Gate Bridge in San Francisco, California, and is a testimony to China's cement industry. China is the largest cement producer in the world, and its concrete complex produces more than seven times the annual output of India, its closest competitor. It took a lot of cement to make Three Gorges. Upriver tourists travel to the city of Guilin, whose river Li flowing through the city reminds visitors so much of the city of Paris along the Seine. If tourists fail to make the connection, there is a tourist boat, the *Bateau Mouche*, to help them explore the city. Meanwhile, the river Li beckons for travel upriver though verdant mountain gorges and spectacular green riverscapes with vendors hawking all kinds of tourist souvenirs. The river Li lives up to its reputation as the scenic pearl of modern China. Thus for visitors, China can seem like a water wonderland.

China has another face too, one that continually confronts the problem of water scarcity in the most populous country on earth. In February 2011, the United Nations Food Agency reported that severe drought threatened the wheat crop in China. Historically self-sufficient in food as a keystone of national security, China now faces the prospect of having to import massive amounts of grain to make up for its diminishing wheat harvest. Any response by China to drought, however, could and will have a profound impact on the global grain market. It could trigger any number of responses: it could drive grain prices, already at record prices, even higher. It could also prompt China to adopt a neo-imperialist posture in seeking safe land overseas to develop for the grain elevators of China. Either event might be enough to have a seismic impact on the world's grain market.

Currently China faces the worst drought in sixty years. Its northern plains are becoming something akin to the Great Dust Bowl of the American Great Plains during the 1930s. There are many manifest similarities for these two environmental phenomena. In the 1930s, the dust storms in Kansas and Oklahoma were so severe from over-plowing and drought that red dust settled on the Capitol building in Washington, DC, over a thousand miles away. In China, every spring the sky becomes yellow from sandstorms whipping off the dried up northern plain. On the worst days, the dirt settles on the roofs and streets of Beijing and inhabitants are advised to stay inside. In northern China and adjacent Mongolia, the sands of the Gobi desert are expanding — a process called desertification.

China, of course, is not the only country to deal with drought. It is simply the largest. Surging world wheat prices have already been cited as the reason for political unrest in Egypt and the overthrow of the Mubarak regime. In 2010, heat waves in Russia, combined with floods in Australia, have limited the capacity of these two nations to contribute grain to the world market. Thus, the impact of China's drought on global food prices could create serious problems for less affluent nations that must rely upon imported food. In the past two years the international price of wheat has doubled and many countries cannot afford the imports of food on which they depend. China, however, has $2.85 trillion in foreign currency reserves and can easily outbid anyone in the global auction for grain. China has a national obsession for self-sufficiency in food. In addition to growing wheat, China produces one-fifth of the world's corn crop, mostly in the Northern provinces where the drought is at its most extreme.

Meanwhile, China confronts the drought. The ground is dry south of Beijing through the provinces of Heibei, Henan, and Shandong. Just north of Shanghai, the trees and houses are coated in topsoil that has blown off parched fields. The Yellow River, the mainstay of water for much of China's agriculture and urban use, has been declining in recent years; in some months it does not reach the Pacific Ocean. Also, the Yellow River is now estimated to be 10 percent sewage by volume.

China needs a lot of water, and it can only build as many cities as it can supply with clean water. China has 20 percent of the world's population, but just 7 percent of its freshwater resources. Rapid urban expansion is confronting China with a crisis as to how it will use its water. Urban demand is soaring while climate change threatens further availability. It is an observation made by many China experts that Beijing has too much pollution and sewage. What it does not have is enough water. Over the next twenty years 350 million people in China — more than the current population of the United States — are expected to move from the countryside to the cities, requiring an immense build-out of infrastructure and massive cement production. Calculating the energy needs of these new conurbations and the impact of energy production on water and the atmosphere will be a major undertaking.

By 2030 China could face a monster water shortage of 201 billion cubic meters. To make matters worse, much of the available water is located in southern China while the majority of the population is in the north. In southeast China, severe drought is affecting as many as 18 million people. Drying fields ultimately spell out the rationing of drinking water. In many areas water capacity is low and a lot of the groundwater is now depleted. In southern China the shrinkage of glaciers along the Tibetan plateau is taking place at the rate of 7 percent a year owing to global warming. At this writing, western China is so bereft of water that 150 million people could migrate out of the region — a vast horde of internal environmental refugees.

The greatest culprit in China's water drama remains agriculture. Farms consume 66 percent of all of China's water resources and a major part of that water is lost to evaporation owing to poor irrigation techniques. China's agricultural water supply suffers from lax oversight and irrigation infrastructure in Chinese farm communities that is antiquated. Furthermore, the water conservation paradigm has yet to see much implementation from China's development fixated leadership.

One can see this in provincial capitals like Shijiaz Huang in northern China, which is basing its sprawling growth as a "new" city on its groundwater supply. Inhabitants of this city are using up the aquifer at a rapid rate, according to Jim Yardley, who reports, "construction of upscale housing and even artificial lakes filled with pumped groundwater." People are not thinking much about the water future in Shijiaz Huang.[5] There has never been much water sense in fast-growing urban areas, and perhaps it is too much to expect that young couples eager to buy upscale apartments will do so now. For three decades, Yardley notes, water has been indispensable in fueling and sustaining China's roaring economy, "but China's wasteful style of economic growth is pushing the country into a severe water crisis."

The water situation is further compounded by the political agenda of the Communist Party, which operates on the assumption that China be self-sufficient in grain. This is an axiom of national security, but in essence it means that China must continue full bore in grain production when other forms of less water-intensive agriculture are marginalized. Meanwhile, water pollution is widespread, largely through industrial and municipal waste flowing into rivers and tributaries on a grand scale. It is hardly surprising that scientists at the World Health Organization have noticed an increase of cancer rates in China. Air and water pollution, combined with widespread use of food additives and pesticides, made cancer the top killer in China in 2010-2011. According to a government survey of thirty cities and seventy-eight counties released by the China Ministry of Health, cancer topped the list of the ten most lethal diseases for urban residents last year, followed by cerebrovascular diseases and heart ailments. "The main reason behind the rising number of cancer cases is that pollution of the environment, water, and air is getting worse day by day," said Chen Zhizhou, a health expert with the cancer research institute affiliated with the Chinese Academy of Medical Sciences.[6]

The Joint Monitoring Program for Water and Sanitation of the World Health Organization reports that in 2008 about 100 million Chinese did not have access to an improved water source and 460 million did not have access to improved sanitation. Contamination of drinking water from feces is a critical health problem in China, as in other developing countries, that causes serious illness such as diarrhea and viral hepatitis. Currently China is engaged in what possibly will be the largest program to build wastewater treatment plants in history. Such a program requires massive expenditures and expertise that will no doubt confront many challenges. One of the ironies of this program is that as treatment plants have surged in construction, the construction of pipelines for sewage has lagged behind. Thus, many of the wastewater treatment plants in Chinese cities are operating at only 30 percent capacity.

According to Peter Gleick, "China's crippling water problems are hampered by the efforts of local government to protect local industries and jobs, government corruption, the desire to sustain rapid economic growth, as well as the weakness of environmental regulatory bodies." Further, comprehensive reliable data on water quality in China is hard to find, despite evidence of growing water contamination. Groundwater especially is being degraded through the massive dumping of untreated or partially treated wastewater. Even Beijing's water in certain sections of the city has too many contaminants to be considered safe.

Currently, according to the Organization for Economic Co-operation and Development in Paris, hundreds of millions of Chinese are drinking water contaminated with inorganic pollutants such as arsenic and fluoride as well as toxins from factory wastewater, inorganic agricultural chemicals, and leeching landfill waste. This explains in part why the cancer rate in China is beginning to increase dramatically.

Meanwhile, water disasters on the level of those that have occurred in the United States with the Love Canal and Cuyahoga River due to severe water and air contamination events, are beginning to take place in China. As in the US in the 1970s, these events are spurring environmental and political activism. In 2005, an environmental disaster occurred in China that was globally reported in the media: the explosion of a chemical treatment plant in the city of Jalin. The event put 100 tons of benzene-related materials into the Songhua River.

The resultant downstream contamination was so dangerous that the city of Harbin had to suspend its municipal water supply to its inhabitants. It also led to the contamination of tributary waters in neighboring Russia, and this is not the only major pollution incident that has occurred in China. Gleick reports, "A mere three months after this accident, a plant in Sichuan Province spilled toxins into the upper reaches of the Yuexi River, disrupting the water supply of 20,000 people in the city of Yibin." Pollution accidents of similar nature involving ammonia, lead, and nitrogen have been reported as well with urban water authorities having to ship off water supplies to inhabitants. Large-scale algae outbreaks on China's rivers that are detrimental to drinking water have become common events. Typhoid continues to be a problem in the warmer climes of south China. According to World Health authorities, where typhoid mortalities normally range in developing countries between 4 and 5 per 100,000, in China the mortality rate from typhoid in 2002 was recorded at 108.4 mortalities per 100,000 persons.

Over time, serious water pollution will become an impediment to China's rapid economic development. As its lakes and rivers continue to remain heavily charged with toxic and other pollutants China will either have to slow its growth and deal with the problem or hope for some cheap technological fix that will help it escape its water troubles. Increased environmental regulation of water consumption of populations China's size will probably not succeed in curbing the problem. Price-driven quotas for consumption of drinking water may help, but it is not certain that the Communist Party will be willing to allow public involvement in the nation's crucial water decisions. A Katrina-like disaster might stimulate more comprehensive policies, in drinking water at least, than any appeals to environmental standards. Meanwhile, China's lakes and rivers wait to be rehabilitated. For the moment, says Gleick, "Sustainable water management has long taken a backseat to the Chinese drive for economic growth."

The Chinese are now building the South-to-North Water Transfer Project to funnel 45 billion cubic meters of water a year to the northern parts of the country from the Yangtze River. The water project was approved in 2002 to address the growing needs of the cities and farms of the northern plain. It is doubtful that this project will come to fruition because of massive financial cost. However, in terms of the boldness of the plan, it is worth looking it. The plan has three main parts: an eastern route that will move water from the lower Yangtze north through a 1,200-kilometer canal; a middle route that will tap the Hanjang, a tributary of the Yangtze; and a western route that will move water from the upper reaches of the Yangtze and other rivers to augment water in the Yellow River Basin. The Chinese government claims that when this plan is fully implemented as many as 300 million people could benefit from increased water supply. The adverse impacts, much like those in the proposed River Link Project in India, are just beginning to be calculated. It is, however, worth mentioning that although projects like these may seem like pie-in-the-sky engineering schemes, they appear to others quite real.[7]

China, much like the US reclamation projects in the twentieth century, is rapidly building dams to generate a greater percentage of electricity from hydro-electric power to reduce pollution from coal-fired power plants. Anyone traveling by car or bus across China today can see the Chinese determination at work. Highways get constructed and new bridges open to traffic seemingly overnight. There has been an explosion in Chinese infrastructure over the past ten years and in a command economy like China's to initiate an activity is to get it done. There is no real problem in dealing with fractious highway contractors or truculent labor unions. China is currently in its eleventh Five-Year-Plan and will probably devote as much as a trillion yuan with a focus on water distribution systems.

Other projects as grandiose as the South-to-North Water Project have already come on line and it would be foolhardy to dismiss China's future plans on cost alone. China, with its currency reserves, can easily subsidize the increasing cost of water in the immediate future. The long-term is another matter entirely. Not even a dedicated command economy as China's can control the processes of nature. No doubt, in the coming years we shall see some draconian actions in China to curb the inefficient use of water, especially in agricultural areas. Some scientists have been so bold as to argue that northern China may have to end its production of winter wheat because of the water intensity of cultivation. This may put a severe crimp in China's doctrine of food independence and force the country to rely upon international markets for its food, a prospect that is quite unacceptable to China's leaders at this moment.

Like many countries, China suffers from extreme variability in terms of floods and droughts. To a certain extent, its climate in the northern regions has come to resemble that of Australia's Murray-Darling Basin with large flood pulses that cause extremes in runoffs followed by dry spells.

140

The problems that China faces are not unique, but China, much like India, does not like developed nations of the West giving sermons to them about water conservation, even if they are sermons that they need to hear. Caught up for the first time in the congenial atmosphere of prosperity, it is difficult to entertain notions of sustainability. On the North China Plain, 200 million people depend on 60 percent of the region's groundwater for their daily use. What applies for the fast-growing cities on the North China Plain applies as well to the cities of Las Vegas, Nevada, and Phoenix, Arizona, that can survive only by using pipes, aqueducts, and dams to transport water over a long distance. Suffice to say, some cities in China ought not to have been built because of the water problems. The fabled Yangtze River is already dying from pollution and could be dead within five years. The river's plight reflects the water crisis facing the world's most highly populated country. About 40 percent of all wastewater produced in China — some 25 billion tons per annum — flows into the river, but more than 80 percent of it is untreated beforehand. Matters have been made worse by the construction of the controversial Three Gorges Dam, which environmentalists say has changed the oxygen content of the river, as well as creating a huge rubbish dump in its reservoir.

Yuan Aiguo, a professor at the China University of Geosciences based in the Yangtze port of Wuhan, said: "Many officials think the pollution is nothing for the Yangtze, which has a large water flow and a certain capability of self-cleaning, but the pollution is very serious." Industrial waste and sewage, agricultural pollution, and shipping discharges were to blame for the river's declining health, the experts said. The river, the third longest in the world after the Nile and the Amazon, runs from Qinghai in Tibet in the remote far west, through 186 booming cities, before emptying into the sea at Shanghai. For Shanghai's 20 million residents, the death of the river could be critical. Lu Jianjian, a professor at Shanghai's East China Normal University, said: "As the river is the only source of drinking water in Shanghai, it has been a great challenge for Shanghai to get clean water."

Dying Waters, Toxic Rain, and A Hotter Countryside

The stately former Portuguese colony of Goa is queen of India's coastal tourist trade. The rustic Latin architecture of the capital at Panjin reverberates with outdoor markets and noisy honeymooners on boat rides on the Mondavi River. Restaurants are filled with British and Russian tourists fleeing the cold weather strictures of London and Moscow, and American hippies continue to eke out a tenuous but happy existence on the local beaches. Outside the tourist scene, though, Goa's rivers are dying largely because they contain much-prized sand for construction. As Mumbai continues to explode with development along the coast to the south, sand mining for construction has become rampant, often eluding legal environmental restrictions. Sand mining in Goa is a multi-million dollar business. Yet for all of Goa, sand mining has produced annually only about $30 thousand in royalty fees and taxes. The government of Goa is getting a "pittance" while the state's rivers are being destroyed, says environmental activist Nandkumar Kamat. The rivers most affected by sand mining, which clouds the water and chokes fish populations, are the Tiracol, Mandovi, and Chapora. Locals complain that sand mining causes riverbanks to collapse. They also note the disappearance of river fish such as palu. Villagers, irked by what the sand miners are doing to their rivers, often pelt laborers with stones when they come close to riverbanks. Poorly paid sand divers bring up white and brown sand to boats in buckets. Given the mammoth appetite of the Indian construction industry for good sand for its concrete mixers, there is little likelihood that environmentalists will be able to do little more than complain that Goa's rivers are dying.[8]

In Russia, the Volga River is drying up under the onslaught of drought and fiery summer temperatures. The Volga, Russia's main river and the biggest river in Europe, begins near the outskirts of Moscow and flows 2,200 miles to the Caspian Sea. The river is a constant worry for ecologists. In Tartarstan, which is midway along this riverine highway, whole fish populations died in the summer of 2010. Each day during that summer, the Volga's tributaries such as the Kazanka River were like streams that could be easily crossed by foot. Farmers tried to save their crops from the summer heat and siphoned large amounts of water from the already diminished Volga. Due to the drop in water levels, toxic waste became a major part of the river's flow and caused public health problems. Currently, 3,000 factories dump 10 billion cubic yards of contaminated waste into the river each year. Russia's black caviar industry has been affected largely by chemicals that eat away the flesh of sturgeon, the source of Russian caviar in the Volga, and toxins in the Volga constitute a greater problem for Russian municipalities than seasonal variations in flow. All in all, the Volga is rapidly becoming one of Europe's unhealthiest rivers.[9]

The Volga's problems are hardly unique. Just about any major river system in the world, from the Ganges, to the Danube, to the Nile and the Murray-Darling in Australia, faces the same host of problems. (The Murray-Darling's problems will be discussed more extensively later in this chapter.) The primary threats to these river systems are pollution, drought, rising temperatures, and over fishing. Scientists assert that these problems are correctable. There is plenty of water in the world, they say. Our rivers are a political problem that can be solved by conservation and resource management, but this is like saying that all we need to end the world's political problems is love.

Dammed If You Do

As an environmental affairs writer, I am not especially fond of dams. Yes, I recognize the good work that the United States Bureau of Reclamation has done in the building of water catchments in the American West. This spurred the agricultural and community development of the western states in the twentieth century. The previous century was the era of "The Great Dams" in the west with projects like the Boulder and Hoover dams, which harnessed the water of the Colorado River for agriculture and hydroelectric power, not to mention led to the development of diverse cities like Los Angeles and Las Vegas. These monstrous construction projects provided employment to thousands in the last century, especially during the Great Depression of the 1930s.

Dams, however, have a way of going wrong. They trap migratory fish, disrupt sensitive ecosystems, and encourage unwarranted urban development in deserts and other ecologically fragile areas. Dams today in the United States are rapidly becoming passé and each month the media carries stories concerning planned or actual dam removal rather than dam construction. I wish this trend were also true in developing nations, but it is not. Massive dams and water diversion schemes are the ruling orthodoxy for Africa, Latin America, India, and China.

About nine miles north of the mouth of the Susquehanna River along the Pennsylvania-Maryland border is an hydroelectric dam that is one of the largest non-federal dams in the United States. It serves the electricity needs of the city of Philadelphia. When it was constructed in 1928, the Conowingo Dam, named ironically for the Pennsylvania town flooded by the dam's rising waters, it was the second largest hydroelectric facility in the U.S., behind only Niagara Falls. Resulting from a history of mergers, the Exelon Corporation, a Chicago-based energy conglomerate, now operates the dam. Its current Federal Energy Regulatory Commission license for the dam will expire in 2014. The dam's fate is in the swirling vortex of environmental contention because it is silted in and its future value as a hydro facility is uncertain.

Since 1928 Conowingo has not only generated electricity, but it has become a reservoir of silt with a vast amount of sediment trapped behind its walls. The water flows through the dam into the semi-salt Chesapeake Bay and is fairly clear. However, if the vast sediment "muck" were to be unleashed from the dam, it would be a disaster for the upper reaches of the Chesapeake Bay and beyond. Today the Conowingo is a repository for all the soil, coal toxins, nitrogen, and phosphorous that has flowed downriver as a result of deforestation, suburbanization, and industrial growth. Conowingo's silt, many environmentalists believe, is a ticking time bomb. This would cause havoc in the region if a hurricane or major storm on the order of Hurricane Katrina caused the river to breach and destroy the dam. Muddy water will prevent sunlight from reaching aquatic plants and grasses. Fish and shellfish will find their gills choked with dirt and the Bay itself will suffer from increased anoxia owing to a massive outpouring of nitrogen and phosphorus. Though the dam is not expected to be completely filled with sediment until 2020, a flood or a hurricane could destabilize the structure and send massive amounts of sediment downstream at once. Meanwhile, the cost of remediation would have to be negotiated between Pennsylvania, Maryland, and the federal government.

Building a new dam downstream is prohibitively expensive. It would involve the flooding of several new towns and involve politicians in a major environmental war with the citizenry along the Susquehanna. The remaining option is to dredge the Conowingo reservoir and put the trapped sediment somewhere else, but it has to be placed out in the open along the Susquehanna River banks to dry and no one wants the stink of drying river muck in their backyard. Some people advocate trucking the muck to old coal mines and dumping it down abandoned mine shafts. Given the toxins in the sediment, any plan to deconstruct the dam and let the river run free is considered a dangerously daunting prospect. Nearly 200 million tons of sediment make up the Conowingo reservoir and dam, argues Susquehanna River Keeper Michael Helfrich. The dam, he says, is only one Hurricane Katrina away from a major environmental disaster. In fact, in public talks, Helfrich warns of a "Katrina-wingo."

A huge storm could cause the river to overwhelm the dam and send what scientists call a "catastrophic pulse" — a huge brown plume of sediment-filled water into the Bay that could smother the upper Bay's aquatic community and disrupt severely the human populations along the Chesapeake as well. Helfrich views himself as a modern day Thomas Paine, bringing a radical advocacy to the people. This time the message is not independence. It is the vision of the need for a healthy river. Helfrich wants the Conowingo muck to be mined out and turned into construction material before disaster occurs.[10]

Running on Empty: Australia's Murray River

The River Murray is Australia's longest river, flowing some 2,375 kilometers. Beginning in the high country of northeast Australia, the river meanders across thousands of acres of inland plains, flowing northwest until it turns abruptly south for its final rush to Adelaide and its mouth on the Southern Ocean. The Murray, as the principal river in the system, contributes more than 75 percent of the basin flow. In concert with another river, the Darling, the rivers form the Murray-Darling Basin, home to some 31,000 farms and the heartland of Australia's cereal production. Roughly 47 percent of Australia's grain comes out of the Murray-Darling basin, with cotton, wheat, and cattle being the principal agricultural staples. Since 1913, farmers have honeycombed the region with dams, weirs, and artificial catchments to deal with the drought that has been a constant specter since the government first started keeping water records of the region in 1895. Many of the once-river fed lakes have been turned into water catchments.

Until the extensive settlement of the region in the nineteenth and early twentieth centuries, the Murray River was a model of environmental sustainability, adapting its flood plains to the ebb and flow of water. There was an old saying about the region: add water and nature erupts — from birds like pelicans and terns to the benthic animal strata that comes to the surface of the flood pulse after long periods of being burrowed down into the mud. With agriculture has come a monstrous drain on the basin's water supply. Flood pulses, which once used to bring life to the dry outback, have been harnessed and channeled into irrigation projects in order to bring some stability to unpredictable flows to what essentially are shallow dry land rivers.

The Murray's problems do not begin in the irrigated farmlands of the Murray-Darling Basin. They begin in the Murray's high country watershed. For years that region has been decimated by bush fires, which, in addition to removing the forest cover and contributing to flooding, have a heretofore little known unwelcome development. During the process of regeneration from the bush fires, the region retains water to stimulate new growth, water that would otherwise be going downstream. Where once massive bush fires occurred about every eighty years, they are now taking place in the high country every ten years or more with distressing frequency. Because of rising temperatures in the high country that are due to global warming, the bush country is drying out at a far more rapid rate. This contributes to the boom-bust cycle of drought and rainfall that has been part of the Murray-Darling for over a century.

Today the Murray at times is nothing more than a toxic broth. In normal times, floods would cover the soil with water, but during dry spells, the mud turns to pyrite muck as it oxidizes with the atmosphere. Combined with water, the muck turns to sulphuric acid with a ph. of 1.6, roughly akin to battery acid. Small wonder then that scientists are well-clothed in swamp waders and goggles when they wade into riverbeds to sample the muck. Currently 20 percent of the wetlands of the Murray are acidic, which translates to 6,000 square miles of wetlands. Many of these are near the city of Adelaide and during high water periods the water contains both acid and arsenic — two toxins that can easily ruin Adelaide's water supply unless preventative measures like liming the streambeds are undertaken. Southeast of Adelaide, just four kilometers away, the Murray flows into the sea, mostly a stagnant spent pool of salt brine. The Australian government has to employ dredges to keep the mouth of the Murray from closing with sand and sludge. A kilometer or so upstream, a dam keeps a lake of freshwater as the final catchment. The dam and its water supply are some four feet below the sea level at the river's mouth.

The best way to look at the Murray and its problem are through scientific eyes and Anne Jensen and Keith Walker of the University of Adelaide's water and environment program offer us a cogent analysis on what has happened to the Murray River and what may well happen in the immediate future. Too circumspect to say that the river is dying, they merely say that the river, especially the lower Murray, is "a river in crisis." Today, the Murray is one of the most intensively regulated irrigated rivers in the world, rivaling the Colorado River in the United States. Government policies, especially from 1980 to 2000, "failed to counter progressive deterioration of river and flood plain." The drought over the past ten years, in addition to producing the exposure of acid sulphate soils, greatly hindered water allocations in the farm belt. River flows have been changed by the irrigation network. It is almost as if one can imagine thousands of agricultural, industrial, and metropolitan straws being placed in the river like some water milkshake. Since historically most of the region has adapted to water intensive cash crops like cotton and wheat, it may be difficult to wean farmers to less water intensive commodities. Meanwhile, a crop is at ready hand — sweet sorghum. This cereal is a drought resistant crop with a multiplicity of uses. Sorghum can be used for grain; its leaves can be fed to animals; and the stalks can be used to produce ethanol. Though sorghum can become an important biofuel, it lacks the international market cachet of wheat.

Recent floods have brought some respite to the Murray River, though its long-term problems remain. The chief problem for the future is water allocation. Under the Murray-Darling Basin Authority's Basin Plan, after 2012, the government is to return substantial amounts of water from irrigation to riverine systems and to specify sustainable diversion limits for dams. However, such a plan is not likely to work well with all the farm, industrial, and municipal interests in the basin if water levels continue to remain at their historic lows. Thus, the debate over the appropriate balance of the river in the floodplains and water sharing for farms and cities presents an enormous challenge that the Australian government may not be able to meet in other than the halfway measures of the past. Meanwhile, the Murray is running on empty. The Murray's principal problem is that it is captive to very vocal agricultural interests: farmers who have been long used to getting their way when it comes to irrigation practices. There are many irrigation streams in the Murray River these days, despite the fact that the flow regime of the river has changed markedly by diversions. How can any agricultural system last when it is based on a water-dependent system characteristic of the Middle Atlantic States or the Midwest of the United States and is located in a semi-arid landscape more characteristic of west Texas? Impoundments along the river, scientists say, are a relatively short-term way of dealing with long-term drought. Over the past thirty years, marine life on the Murray has markedly declined and twenty of the Murray's twenty-three valleys in the river basin were in "poor" or very poor health.

Four states — Queensland, New South Wales, Victoria, and South Australia — have sovereignty over the Murray-Darling basin. Attempts in 2010 to implement a strong centralized water plan that proposed "sustainable diversion limits" met with strong criticism from farm communities that protested reduced water allocations. Although the Murray River has been under some type of regulation since the nineteenth century and dams, barragements, and catchments have long been characteristic of the region, the river has never been so low for such a long period of time. Notes Keith Walker, "The effects of reduced flooding are compounded by salinization of soil and water associated with rising groundwater, land clearance, and irrigation." Further, every vested interest in the Murray-Darling Basin has its own estimates of water flow needs, which it presses with great vigor to the politicians in Canberra. Rice farmers continue to draw large amounts of water to produce this grain in what is rapidly becoming a desert climate. Naturalists get their oar in the water, too, arguing for proper amounts of water for fish passage and migratory wading birds.

Because of the drought, the mouth of the Murray River on the Southern Ocean closed in 2002 and had to be kept closed through continuous dredging until late 2010 when the floods came. This enabled the river to flush out some of its salt and sediment into the sea, but river levels in the southern portion of the Murray — over 273 kilometers of stream — are still half its normal width and shallow. It will take several years of continually good rainfall to replenish the Murray-Darling basin, but even if the lakes and catchments get to be at 90 percent of the former levels, this will be insufficient to repair all of the ecological damage that has already been done. Add to this two other salient facts: 1. There has been increased interest in the Murray River as a tourist and recreation reserve, which can only be stabilized if there is water in the river; and 2. Cities like Adelaide are turning increasingly to the Murray-Darling Basin for their drinking water supply. To a great extent the Australian government has been historically flatfooted in its attempts to deal with the Murray and its problems and has often been outmaneuvered by vested farm interests in the region, so the fact that many farmers may have to relinquish their water rights though sale to the government is a very unpleasant prospect now being discussed in Canberra. Once these rights are sold, who will get the water? Nature or water-starved urban communities in the region? The only major agreement coming out of the Murray-Darling basin these days, is that without major water source allocation agreements, the Murray River will be nothing more than a series of stagnant pools and gravel beds. If Australia is not able to come to satisfactory grips with water problems in its most important agricultural region, what hope is there for less affluent countries without a democratic base to come to grips with theirs?

By 2009, in the midst of one of its most sever droughts, the Murray-Darling basin held just 18 percent of its normal water load — the worst that it has ever experienced. Human water needs were at risk and Robert Freeman of the Murray-Darling Water Basin Authority said that although no water needs in the region would always be secure, "it's important that we don't panic here." The problem is that most of the river is lost through evaporation and seepage before it reaches urban centers. In the future, the Basin Authority will have to make some hard choices like impacting farmers with water controls and allowing water to flow without interruption into "iconic flood plains." Nearby states have offered to supply Adelaide with water during critical dry spells, but they will have to repay the debt once the drought breaks. Meanwhile, hydrologists say, though recent loads have been good for the basin, in the long-term it is just a drop in the bucket. Relief will come to rescue a dying river only when there is above-average rainfall for a sustained period of two to three years — and the chances of that happening in an age of freaky climate change are not good.

Water reduction in the Murray-Darling River will affect settlement of the region in the future. Australia's major inland cities and towns may have to depend largely on recycled water and the purchase of irrigation entitlements for future water supplies. Also, the region may continue to be overstocked with cattle and sheep capable of surviving in a semi-arid landscape. This can lead to increased erosion along river stream banks and the loss of biodiversity. By 2030, climatologists estimate that the Murray flows in the Basin will decline by about 9 percent in the north and 13 percent in the south. Under a worst-case scenario, the average annual runoff for the northern half of the basin may reduce by 30 percent and up to 40 percent for the southern portion. By 2030 the value of irrigated agricultural production in the Basin could fall by 12 percent. Long-term estimates point to the final end of irrigation agriculture in the Murray-Darling basin by the end of the twenty-first century. Scientist Keith Walker speculates that the problem of "how much water does the environment need is not a scientific question at all. The answer depends on how much the community is willing to invest in protecting our natural heritage."

Conclusion

When it comes to rivers, environmental historian J. R. McNeil has made a salient point: "One of the great divides among humankind that has arisen since 1850 separates those societies that provide safe drinking water from those that do not."[11]

Today urban complexes that continue to place increasing stresses upon what historically were agricultural rivers dominate most river water. Unfortunately, our rivers do not share Montana's fate. Until recently, this vast western American state suffered from the problems of declining water, deforestation, and toxic mineral waste spoilage from copper mining operations. Now its sheer "Big Sky" scenic beauty of mountains and snow has saved it. It is rapidly becoming a political economy driven by recreation, retirement living, and lifestyles of the rich who seek to keep what is left of Montana pristine and have the economic and political muscle to do so. Also, Montana's products, timber, and wheat cannot compete well on the national market because of its relatively severe climate. The lumber mills are closing, mining is coming under increased regulation, and cattle and wheat operations become dude ranches and nature retreats. That's fine, but it's hard to replicate Montana's experience in Africa or India.

Our rivers, beset by droughts, agricultural over-use, and industrial spoilage, now face problems of epic proportion. As rivers from China to the Rio Grande or Australia's Murray begin to either dry up or serve as little more than fetid sewage and toxic channels, one can well contemplate the poetic strains of Percy Shelley's "Ozymandias":

Look on my works, ye Mighty, and despair! Nothing beside remains. Round the decay Of that colossal wreck, boundless and bare The lone and level sands stretch far away.

Whatever fate befalls our river systems in terms of drought and flood will be determined by the new bewildering forces of climate change that are altering the planet's thermostat.

"What we are
getting now is
a first taste of
the disruption,
economic and
political, that we'll
face in a warming
world."

-- Paul Krugman

Chapter Eight

The Three-Degree Difference

The Rising Tide

S cientists are already constructing a late twenty-first century scenario in which the world is three degrees warmer than it was during the late pre-industrial period. Using this global warming temperature as a baseline, they project remarkable developments that could easily unfold. First, a more rapid Arctic Sea ice melt allows for more shipping in the Arctic Circle. The lack of summer ice also allows for drilling on the sea floor for oil and other minerals. We already have a foretaste of this in Greenland where ice has been rapidly melting to reveal a new potentially mineral-rich landscape not seen in centuries. Greenland's small indigenous population confronts the dilemma of development. Shall Greenland as an independent nation let in the big corporations and risk having its society overwhelmed by a foreign workforce recruited for the new emerging mineral industries? Or shall Greenland choose to remain primarily an agricultural and seafaring economy?

In his book *The New North: The World in 2050*, Laurence Smith writes that climate change is one of four mega-trends, along with globalization, population growth, and surging demand for oil and water, that will shape the world over the coming decades. Planet warming will affect water supplies and condition human and animal settlement patterns. It will also bring about new environmental problems like the release of methane gas into the atmosphere that heretofore was trapped in the Arctic permafrost.[1]

Sea levels can rise, though by how much is the subject of considerable debate. By the end of the twenty-first century, it is a safe assumption that we will have a global sea rise of between half a meter to a full meter. In American terms, this means a sea rise of potentially three feet, which will have a decided impact on coastal areas of the planet. On the eastern coast of the United States we are now beginning to see a major loss of wetlands due to sea intrusion. This is especially noticeable in the Chesapeake Bay, America's largest estuary, where rising sea levels are flooding long existent marshes and wetlands.

According to the Environmental Protection Agency, many coastal areas in the Mid-Atlantic States will experience a large number of storm-surge flooding and coastal erosion over the remainder of this century because of this sea level rise. Over ten percent of the population on the Mid-Atlantic coast of the United States — roughly 3 million people — live on land a few city blocks from the sea that is less than one meter above the monthly highest coastal tides. Rising sea levels coupled with record tides and hurricanes can cause increased inundation of roads, airports, and railroads. Most seawalls and bulkheads that have been constructed along the coast have been based on tides and storm surges in past history. They may be a poor defense against future rising tides.

Finally, rising sea levels can infiltrate groundwater systems, elevating water tables to a point where septic tanks can no longer function properly. In many areas this will raise the incidence of waterborne diseases. As the EPA reports suggest, how people respond to sea-level rise in the coastal zone will determine the magnitude of economic and environmental costs. Many climatologists are dismayed by the complacency of people over sea level rises and speculate that various disasters might catch them unguarded.

Rising seas are now quite evident in the Pacific region where the island nations suffer from beach erosion, inundation, and storm surges. The over-pumping of groundwater also compounds the problem as urban areas begin to collapse due to subsidence. The Pacific will be in the vortex of climate change as the century lengthens. Meanwhile, investment monies for the Pacific Islands have been in short supply. The World Bank admitted in 2005 that Pacific island nations received less than a quarter of investment dollars provided in the Caribbean. Currently Pacific freshwater resources are reduced to a point where they are insufficient to meet demand during low rainfall periods. Meanwhile, storm surges with waves up to 12 meters in height can periodically pound the islands. The cyclone of 2004, for example, destroyed or severely damaged 90 percent of the island of Yap.

The one useful development that comes out of a climate-change scenario building is that scientists now argue for large-scale political and social discussion of adaptation methods for societies to survive in the event of floods or droughts. Aside from pleas for emission controls, scientists have enlisted the support of insurance companies in developing risk assessment plans by country and region for investment as well as humanitarian purposes. This is coupled with urgent appeals by the World Health Organization for population resettlement plans to deal with the great coming transformation in climate and water cycles. There is great urgency in this regard when it comes to dealing with the over 8.7 million additional people in 2050 that will live in river deltas and are most vulnerable to droughts and flood surges. At the moment climate change is the wild card in any calculations about society and water availability in the late twenty-first century. A good example of this wild card is El Nino, a periodic sloshing of warm water that flows from west to east across the Pacific around Christmas. Its female counterpart, La Nina, flows east to west and can be equally disruptive. One alters fisheries in the Pacific and climate along the Mexican and American west coast while the "sister" is responsible for flooding in Australia and the Philippines. Such surges of warm water across oceans can result in either pelting rains or flooding in many areas of the Pacific.

The Modern Agasthya

Meanwhile, agriculture is the modern Agasthya, the mythical Indian giant who drank the seas dry. Unless careful provision is made, the expansion of agriculture with its immense need for irrigation water may gobble up what is left of the planet's groundwater in virgin lands and wilderness. To deal with "Agasthya," research into new crop yields that produce seeds tolerant of increasing temperatures and water scarcity is part of the "three degree equation." One should mention, however, that the technological innovations of the Green Revolution have run their course and there is little prospect of increasing yields as a result of new farming techniques.

Recently, there has been a major fall-off in Russian wheat harvests because temperatures in the heartland rose to 100°F. Elsewhere, in another major grain belt, the Murray River and Queensland, harvests have been severely diminished. The Murray River has been plagued for years by crop-killing drought and the recent floods in Queensland have severely diminished Australia's agricultural productivity. China's farmers need water because China needs food. Production of rice, wheat, and corn topped out at 441.4 million tons in 1998 and hasn't hit that level since. Seawater has leaked into depleted aquifers in the north of China, threatening to turn land barren. Similar developments have already happened on the Great Plains of the United States. Genetic research into more hardy grains for an uncertain future proceeds apace with the problem. The real project ahead is to get people into actually valuing water in a realistic manner, says water expert Peter Rogers.[2]

Meanwhile, 2011 unfolded as a year of food crisis. Prices for food reached record global levels, driven by increases in the price of wheat, corn, sugar, and oil. To the shock of American consumers, $3 for bread became common in supermarkets. Nobel economist Paul Krugman has argued that rising concentrations of greenhouse gases are changing our climate. Responding to assertions that climate change has no bearing on the problem, he admits that changing patterns of consumption and population growth have their influence on high food prices, but with climate change he argues that this is just a beginning. We may have had a few bad winters, but "don't let the snow fool you." In a warming world, "there will be much more and much worse to come."[3]

It is no longer a secret that there is a new wave of foreign investment in farmland, predominantly in Africa, taking place on a massive scale. In 2009, the World Bank reported that foreign investors had gobbled up more than 45 million hectares in that year alone. Similar developments are taking place in the water-rich rural areas of Latin America like Paraguay and Uruguay. Top among the investors in land in Paraguay and Uruguay are members of the George Bush family. The top four targets for investors were Sudan (4 million hectares), Mozambique (2.7 million hectares), Liberia (1.6 million hectares), and Ethiopia (1.3 million hectares). There is a culture of secrecy in which communities, and even government officials, were not consulted or informed about land deals until after they had been signed. The World Bank also found that these investment projects failed to generate employment. The motivation for this new wave of investment is strongly driven by water. States with scarce or depleted water resources are looking to outsource their water use by growing crops abroad and private investors are seizing the opportunities.[4]

In Africa, the investment value is not in the land, but in the water. Judson Hill, a fund manager from NGP Global Adaptation Co., a private equity fund, said, "When a country imports one ton of wheat it is saving about 1300 cubic meters of domestic water." In an article in the *Foreign Policy* journal, the chairman and former CEO of Nestle®, Peter Brabeck-Letmathe, called it "the great water grab." He wrote: "Purchases weren't about land, but water. For with the land comes the right to withdraw the water linked to it, in most countries essentially a freebie that increasingly could be the most valuable part of the deal."[5] His statement captures the essence of the problem: that so-called "land grabs" are in fact "water grabs." Why? First, because the countries pursuing farmland investments are deeply concerned about domestic water scarcity as a result of agriculture production; second, and more importantly, says Letmathe, "because the current global regime of investment treaties and host government agreements provide foreign investors with the legal guarantee needed to safeguard and operationalise their investment (and to take states to international arbitration if they do not honor contracts.) Yet, in many of the countries experiencing an influx of foreign investment in agriculture, these protections for investors are not counter-balanced with adequate domestic regulations to safeguard the land and water rights of citizens." When it comes to agriculture, land is only, in this sense, a financier's cynical calculation on water access.

Water Shrinkage and Autogeddon

If you stand at an observation overlook at Hoover Dam in Colorado, you can see what has happened to Lake Mead, America's largest reservoir. All along the shoreline a giant bathtub ring of mineral discoloration testifies to the great shrinkage in water levels that have occurred in the lake. Reporters regularly file news stories of Lake Mead's dry docks that stretch like fingers into a desert that was once the water line. The lake is currently only 40 percent full, a victim of a decade-long drought. Buildings and houses that were abandoned to Lake Mead's rising flood in the 1930s are now suddenly eerily visible. Meanwhile, experts like Douglas Kenney, director of Water Policy Analysis at the University of Colorado, think that water flows on the Colorado will continue to decrease by at least ten percent in the next half century. In time major parts of Lake Mead may be little more than a sand and gravel quarry.

Engineers and politicians are reacting to the West's diminishing water resources with still more plans for piping what is left of the Colorado to thirsty farm fields and exploding unplanned cities like Las Vegas. Until 2011, when the water crunch really began to be felt in Last Vegas, this desert city eschewed the desert landscape for well-watered lawns, verdant golf courses, and luxurious water fountains cascading at the gambling casinos.

However, one of the most important calculations about water and climate in the twenty-first century must focus on the automobile. Even though cars are individually cleaner than in the past, collectively, notes auto expert Daniel Lazar, "they are dirtier simply because there are so many of them."[6] The global auto explosion has been fueled by the rampant economic growth of India and China where the ownership of a car has now become the *sine qua non* of middle class identity. In the United States, the number of motor vehicles has been doubling every fifteen to twenty-five years since 1925 — four times that of the general American population — and the worldwide cost of gasoline continues to escalate (it is $4.50 a gallon in India and over $7 in Great Britain as of 2011).

The cost of gasoline, however, is irrelevant compared to the joys of auto-ownership. In India, a kind of happy-go-lucky autogeddon prevails. Traffic in cities from Kolkata to Mumbai resembles a tsunami on wheels — bumper to bumper traffic with whizzing three-wheel taxis, buses, trucks, and cars added to carts, cows, and a general petrol-based cacophony. The fact that the transportation infrastructure for cars and trucks in India is a general mess makes little difference. Autogeddon flows on. Ironically, India, the nation with a profound scarcity of water, now produces the world's cheapest automobile, the Nano, of Tata Industries. Costing only $2,000US, the Nano will no doubt spark the major paving of much of India and the further disruption of groundwater.

In 2005, China had fifteen passenger cars for every 1,000 people, close to the thirteen cars per 1,000 that Japan had in 1963. Today, Japan has 447 passenger cars per 1,000 residents, 57 million in all. If China ever reaches that point, it would have 572 million cars — 70 million shy of the number of cars in the entire world today.

In terms of use, the automobile constitutes one of the most dangerous threats to global water supplies. Simply put, auto exhaust into the atmosphere eventually comes back to earth in the form of a toxic smog of chemicals, which enter streams and rivers. Further, road construction paves the landscape with impermeable asphalt, which prevents rainwater from returning to aquifers, lakes, and ponds. Transportation critic Clay McShane argues that a rational environment is impossible without some strict control over automobile use in both developed and developing countries. Car use promotes a kind of extreme individualism that is antithetical to solving the collective problems of society. We need to overcome the disconnect people have about the automobile, water, and global warming. The car is a major factor in "the three degree equation." At the moment, though, writers like McShane believe we are overly dependent on the car because we have effectively closed off any alternatives.[7]

Rethinking Progress and Stability

While traditional definitions and measures of economic progress and enviro-stability are being rethought in Western nations like Denmark, consuming more is still the operative behavior in the developing world. This is especially true with respect to global coal production. According to the International Energy Agency, world consumption of coal will increase by 20 percent in the next twenty-five years.

A new age of coal is upon us, one that is being forced on the world by China, which, in the next quarter century, will consume as much coal for electricity production as all of the United States, Europe, and Japan put together.[8] Increasingly China's ravenous appetite for coal for its energy and steel industry has outstripped its own resources: its mines are old and outdated. The coal is located deep underground and is difficult to extract. According to *The Economist*, "For the foreseeable future the country will depend on ships laden with foreign coal."

India is also turning to foreign shores for its coal supply as Indian coal is generally of poor quality. Its new coal-fired power stations demand high-quality coal and India could well be the world's biggest importer of thermal coal by 2025. Mozambique, Australia, and South Africa are currently China and India's biggest suppliers. Russia, which has some of the world's largest coal reserves, is beefing up its infrastructure to export coal by rail and ship to energy-hungry customers. Of course, this explosion of the coal market can only bode ill for the environment as coal is the filthiest fossil fuel. Such a development makes the Kyoto Protocol on global emissions seem a cruel joke. Environmentalists point out that "rich countries that spurn coal-fired power while exporting the rocks to countries with less ambitious emissions targets are merely shifting the problem around the globe."[9] The impact of these coal emissions on the earth's air and water are obvious. What is less obvious is the environmental impact that coal mining will have on scarce water supplies in poor countries like Mozambique. Some scientists are discussing the merits of carbon sequestration, or the pumping of coal gas emissions into the ground, for permanent storage as a way to allow for energy production using coal.

Thoughts on Climate Change and Water

Water availability is the crucial factor in limiting agriculture. According to Nestle's Peter Brabeck-Letmathe, roughly 4,200 cubic kilometers of water can be used without depleting global supplies. Today consumption is higher, at 4,500 cubic kilometers a year, and agriculture takes about 70 percent. As a result water tables are plummeting. Groundwater in the Punjab in India and Pakistan has gone from just a few meters below the surface to a depth of hundreds of meters down. The situation of depleting groundwater is so acute in China that the government is beginning to worry publicly about the effects of climate change. Rivers that water some of the world's breadbaskets, such as the Murray, the Indus, and the Colorado, no longer reach the sea.

By 2030 scientists estimate that the world's farmers will need 45 percent more water. They won't get it, as cities are the second largest users of water and those in developing countries with cities like Mumbai and Chennai in India are exponential users of water. In Australia, farmers in the Murray-Darling River Basin must compete against the growing water needs of Adelaide. Using existing stocks of water, farmers can resort to using more nitrogen on their fields. However, fertilizers are expensive, can cause their own environmental problems, and are out of the financial reach of most poor farmers. Rich countries might help their poorer brethren by having policies that encourage less wastage of food. According to a recent finding, "If all rich countries waste food at the same rate as Britain and America, very roughly 100 kilograms per person per year, the total waste adds up to 100 metric tons of food a year, equivalent to one-third of the world's entire supply of meat — an astonishing quantity."[10] However, curbing waste in affluent countries is a thing easier said than done.

As the demand for water for agriculture and hydroelectric power grows, climate change is expected to increase scarcity. Already pessimistic quarters anticipate the rapid desiccation of the Great Plains and the end of grain agriculture as we know it in Iowa by the end of the century. Projections of a rise in temperature and an increase in sea levels pose threats to our organized societies, and, as our planet's climate portends to become increasingly unstable, our relationship with water is changing in dangerous and potentially catastrophic ways.

In America, well-watered urban conurbations like Boston and Washington suffer from terrifying snowstorms in the winter and dry out in water-starving summer heat. Mumbai limps along with water trucks selling expensive drinking water to its thirsty poorer inhabitants. Grain farms in Central Asia bake in the summer sun under record temperatures and have very diminished harvests. In politically volatile areas like Afghanistan and Pakistan, there has been a decrease in glacial water by as much as 50-70 percent. While shrinking glaciers increase the runoff in the short-term, the long-term effect is the decrease in available water.

Meanwhile, in Asia, climate change is liable to influence monsoon dynamics that are vital for river systems dependent upon their seasonal rains. Summer monsoon rains are particularly vital to the agricultural economies of Bangladesh, Burma, India, Nepal, and Pakistan. Currently monsoon rains are projected to move eastward causing rain to fall on the Indian Ocean rather than on land. As India, for example, gets 90 percent of its total water supply from the monsoons, this shift will become a matter of serious concern to the government.

As the effects of the climate change become more pronounced, agrarian populations dependent upon monsoons and glacial melt for irrigation will be profoundly affected. The world is already 1.3°F warmer today than it was in the past century and that is severely compromising our water supplies, management systems, and aquatic systems for agriculture and human habitat. Experts predict less alpine snow pack, earlier and larger peak stream flows, greater evaporation losses, more extreme weather events — including floods and droughts — and hotter summers.

It would be nice if we could approach the problem of global warming with a wait and see attitude, but we cannot. Changes are happening too quickly for laid-back potential climate change denial. With every rise of one degree Celsius (1.8 degrees Fahrenheit) in the American West, researchers have found, snow levels are retreating upward by 500 feet in elevation. Further, scientists predict that sea levels will rise soon by 7 to 23 inches, affecting water supplies, drowning and diminishing coastal wetlands, and exposing residents to floods reminiscent of Hurricane Katrina. Island nations in the Pacific are especially vulnerable to rising sea levels. Tuvalu, a West Pacific nation whose peak height rises just five meters above sea level, could be uninhabitable in fifty years. A similar fate could drown the Maldives and the Marshall islands as these countries continue to suffer rising sea levels and are battered by increasingly fierce tropical storms.

Thanks to improved satellite data since the 1990s, scientists now know that the average global rate of sea rise has increased 50 percent in the last twelve years — up to 3 millimeters a year. Even comparatively small increases in sea level can produce large effects especially when high tides and storm surges are factored in. Worried island nations today support the so-called Mauritius strategy that was submitted to the United Nations. In essence, the strategy suggests that "environmental vulnerability" and not income should determine island eligibility for financial assistance.

It does not take a scientific education to ascertain that something is seriously amiss with the global environment. In 2008 and 2010 food riots took place in various parts of the world — from Mexico to Mozambique to Serbia to India. These kinds of riots had not been part of the global scene since the 1940s. The cause was severe drought driving up grain prices. The planet has more hot and dry periods than yesteryear and the earth could heat up another five degrees by the end of the twenty-first century, according to the United Nations Panel on Climate. Escalating increases in world grain prices brought on by droughts and floods will continue to fuel global unrest. Inflation in food today continues at a rate of 3 percent annually in Europe and over 7 percent in India. For one billion people living on less than a dollar a day in many of the poorer regions of the world, high grain prices are a threat to their very survival.

As contention increases over grain prices, water temperatures rise. The UN Panel on Climate Change projected with 90 percent certainty that world water temperatures could increase by as much as 11°F and sea levels could rise by 50 centimeters by the end of the twenty-first century.[11] The next report due out from the United Nations in 2014 could contain an even more dismal outlook.

At this writing, no natural disasters in our lifetime have generated more powerful and destructive images than Hurricane Katrina that hit the Gulf Coast of the United States in August 2005 and the earthquake and tsunami that hit the east coast of Japan at Sendai in March 2011. Both events resulted in unbelievable and unparalleled devastation with great loss of life. These two events, in dramatic fashion, illustrated both the power of water and the vulnerability of coastal populations to major and largely unanticipated weather surges and tectonic movements. Despite early warning systems in both New Orleans and Japan, safe havens were non-existent and populations had to largely fend for themselves. Both the Federal Emergency Management Agency in the United States and the Japanese government showed gross ineptitude in dealing with the disaster, which caused profound harm. In Japan's case the earthquake moved the entire nation of Japan several feet westward.

In the late twentieth century, there were 2,200 natural disasters: 35 percent occurred in Asia, 29 percent in Africa, 20 percent in the Americas, and 13 percent in Europe. The major driver of these disasters has been extreme weather events, not geologic events. Wetter events appear to be tied to changing weather patterns due to global warming as well as droughts. Droughts in sub-Saharan Africa can easily bring destruction to some 110 million people over some seven million square kilometers. Reports the United Nations Convention on Climate Change: "Combine drought with conflict, deforestation, overgrazing and human migration and the human misery index explodes."

There are two significant things worthy of mention about climate change and natural disasters at this point. First, because they involve economics, environment, and social structure, they have a lasting impact. Second, despite the realities of such disasters, there is still very little binding consensus on what to do about climate change. Meanwhile, all parts of the political spectrum in the world look to the scientists — and what they get is not necessarily what they want. Science often makes environmental controversies worse. People can use science statistics to convince themselves that environmental conditions upon which humanity depends for its well being are not getting worse, but are actually getting better. This kind of thinking can be used to justify the continued despoliation of our global water supply. There will always be enough water, some can say.

However, it is not the supply of water that is wrong; the facts of water are just misunderstood. According to Daniel Sarewitz of the Consortium for Science, Policy, and Outcomes at Arizona State University: "The recognition that something is a 'problem' demands a pre-existing framework of values within which problems can be recognized."[12] Sarewitz is currently one of the best thinkers on the subject of how scientists "perceive" environmental problems and what follows is largely an explication of his exploration of a dense and very thorny thicket of science policy argument. Science, argues Sarewitz, for the most part creates bodies of knowledge especially to resolve political and intellectual disputes and enables effective decision-making. Thus the boundaries between science and policy or politics are constantly being renegotiated as part of the political process. Further the science that is out there on practically any topic is sufficiently rich and complex to support findings of enormous disciplinary and institutional diversity. Objectivity, the altar upon which scientists support their work is far from being objective. Science is politicized as soon as it begins to investigate a research problem. According to Sarewitz, science is often the unwitting helpmate of environmental controversy because it opens the possibility that there can be two or more sets of contradictory scientific insights that can be used to defend various positions in an environmental controversy.

Conclusion

In the Charles Dickens novel *Hard Times*, Mr. Thomas Gradgrind is a man of facts. For school children in this nineteenth century story, the character of Mr. Gradgrind sets forth his views: "Now what I want is facts. Teach these boys and girls nothing but facts. Facts alone are wanted in life." A good storyline for a Victorian novel perhaps, but what we see in our contemporary life is that facts beget competing facts and the availability of competing facts and scientific argument quickly spiral out of control.

This provides us certainly with a new angle of vision when it comes to the subject of climate change. No arguments are more sensitive than those that revolve around the planet on the subject of climate change. The fate of nations and economies, not to mention that of hapless victims caught up in the droughts and floods of climate change, hang in the balance. Is the planet warming or cooling? Is global warming a hoax, a temporary aberration that can be reasonably charted over time, or a clear and present danger that should alarm the societies of the world about their future? While admittedly there have been cases in which disinterested science such as the identification of ozone depletion in the earth's atmosphere has conformed to the orthodox model of scientific objectivity, there have been too many cases where science merely becomes politicized. Sarewitz concludes his argument with the comment that "politics helps us to decide the direction to step; science helps the eye to focus."

However, if you think that climate change is a hoax, or you don't want to believe the UN Panel on Climate Change or the science on the subject, check with the insurance companies. They are in the calamity and disaster business; currently they are backing away from insuring habitations in coastal and riparian communities. Want a house on an idyllic beach? Insure it with your own money, not theirs.

It is fitting that this chapter should end with some notions about climate problems, disaster, and insurance companies since the chapter that follows is an extended disquisition on the subject of calamity and catastrophe and how both relate to water and the times in which we live.

"We are at the end

of Nature."

-- Bill McKibben

Chapter Nine

Black Swans &
Other Water Scenarios

The Shape of Our Water Future

We don't know it yet, but our landscape is beginning to unravel in terms of available choices we have to make regarding water. Global climate change, desertification, agricultural and industrial consumption, and over-population are already taking a heavy toll on freshwater supplies. In the coming years, freshwater will become a rare and expensive commodity. Countries that already suffer from water shortages will be the hardest hit. The biggest problem that we have is the failure of group decision-making that leads societies to exploit their resources to the point where extinction becomes a reality. Peter Gleick of the Pacific Institute has studied global water problems for over three decades. He argues that management failures and political myopia are at least as responsible for water problems as shortages and population growth.

We live in an age of troubling scenarios. Whether it is the disintegration of the ice sheet on Greenland, rapid die-off of the rain forests in the Amazon, or even the perhaps far-fetched fear of shutdowns in the currents of the Atlantic Ocean, which would spell disaster for Europe's livable climate, one thing is clear: we are entering a period of non-linear disruptions in our global environment. By "non-linear" I mean rapid non-incremental disruptions that are fast and unpredictable versus changes that can be measured and anticipated over long periods of time. In 2009, Johan Rockstrom, director of the Stockholm Resilience Centre in Sweden, wrote a paper that should send shivers up the spines of most thoughtful people. It emphasized how little we can predict about the environmental changes underway across the planet.[1] The future may catch us completely by surprise in terms of environmental transformation.

The disaster bureaucrats talk about "Black Swans" — calamities from out of the blue that bring strange and terrible devastation on modern populations. The world, at this writing, is currently transfixed on Japan, which suffered a nine-point earthquake and murderous tsunami that knocked out several nuclear power plants on its eastern coast. The earthquake that struck the city of Sendai was larger than the seismologists thought could happen in that part of the country. The tsunami with thirty-foot waves easily swept over seawalls.

People in the disaster business talk of "The Big One." According to Tom O'Rourke, a Cornell University environmental engineering professor, the devastation and radiation problems of Japan are a telling illustration. "We have had an imaginative idea of what the Big One would look like if it struck a major, populated, modern society," says O'Rourke.[2] "After Sendai, this is what 'The Big One' looks like." Japan's nightmare comes hard on the heels of other 2011 disasters such as Christchurch, New Zealand, where an earthquake was triggered by a little-regarded fault, and Sumatra in Indonesia, which suffered a tsunami-spawning earthquake. While the consequences for radioactive contamination of public water supplies in Japan have yet to be fully assessed, these "black swans" were enough to panic and send people on the United States' West Coast (who were well out of harm's way) to pharmacies to stock up on medicine to thwart radiation-induced thyroid illnesses.

Today people all over the world are learning one depressing fact: We as citizens of the planet cannot make our own lifestyle changes sufficient to create a more water-conserving world. Our fate is in the hands of government officials at every level in every country who are now making decisions about the future of the world's water. They will shape our water future just as they have shaped our water past. Thus far their record has not been hopeful for the conservation of the world's most precious resource. Many countries in the developing world are caught in the impossible position, between a desire for economic growth and a need for dependable sources of freshwater. The powerful surge of people towards cities continues and in cities people invariably consume more water. Even if the population of the earth stopped rising tomorrow — an unlikely scenario — the number of people facing water shortages will continue to grow for decades. Many countries will in turn become what hydrologists call "dewatered." The world's water problems begin not in the developing nations where drought, social decline, population explosion, and violence are endemic. Our water problems begin in the Western mind-set that treats practically all life as a fungible good.

For too long the Western nations have led a careless water-intensive lifestyle, mindless until just yesterday of the looming crisis that is unfolding in this century. Now we live in an age of extreme weather events that often result in high death tolls.

The Idea of Catastrophe

As Brazilian ecotheorist Sergio Abranches reminds us: "There are no natural disasters, only social catastrophes." Carelessness and failure to plan have been the biggest enemies in the face of natural weather events. Our water catastrophe (the complete global scarcity of water) will not be a product of Mother Nature — it will be human-made. "A catastrophe happens when a high intensity or extreme natural event meets a vulnerable population with a weak, unprepared, or reckless government."[3] Most countries, Holland and Switzerland being notable exceptions, would rather pursue a policy of reconstruction and post-disaster assistance than a strategy of disaster prevention. Regardless of one's ideological position, the stark reality is that freshwater is running out in many parts of the world — be it the water in rivers, lakes, basins, aquifers, or watersheds. Therefore communities throughout the world will be seeking alternative water sources, and North America will be no exception to this looming problem.

In the summer of 2010, water levels in the Potomac River sank to record lows and much of the upper Potomac as late as September looked more like a stone-ridden stream than a majestic waterway that flows through the nation's capital. Water utility companies were dependent on water flow that had been prudently banked up by large dams upstream for release in critical times. The issue was not one of a seven-week drought in the Mid-Atlantic, but that the Potomac's water level problems were part of a "long dry" that threatened to become part of the water scene of the Mid-Atlantic seaboard. Municipalities and state governments had to scramble to assure themselves of ample water supplies.

Maryland, which has water allotment provisions in its environmental regulatory system, is better off than some states in this regard. At least Maryland can guarantee local water plants a fair share of water for drinking, sewage, and other commercial uses. New ways of using contaminated water from mine drainage are currently being considered by the Maryland Department of the Environment, but even areas of the Mid-Atlantic seaboard must concern themselves with their water future.

On the international scene, access to water will continue to be a major problem. Canada worries about the security of its water supply in the Great Lakes that straddles its thirsty neighbor to the south. Despite the existence of water-sharing agreements between the United States, Canada, and Mexico over international access to transboundary lake and river water, there has been little or no consensus about policy over removing groundwater from aquifers. For example, the United States and Mexico share at least eighteen aquifers, and both these countries are already experiencing problems with the availability and contamination of water. In the future, the United States, Mexico, and Canada face nearly insurmountable problems of sovereignty over the multiple use of water along their borders. Policy-makers recognize the need for regional, even global, water cooperation from everything from fish to wetlands, to drinking water and sewage. Global climate change will make the need for international negotiation of water agreements both imperative and increasingly problematic.

A recent British study of global drought posits the view that one-third of the planet will be desert by the year 2100. This study by Eleanor Burke and a team of researchers at England's Hadley Center models how a measure of drought known as the Palmer Drought Severity Index (PDSI) is likely to increase globally during the coming century with predicted changes in rainfall and heat around the world because of climate change. In Burke's study that carries the ponderous title, "Modeling the Recent Evolution of Global Drought and Projections for the Twenty-First Century with the Hadley Centre Climate Model," she notes the Palmer Drought Severity Index for moderated drought at 25 percent of the earth's surface, rising to 50 percent by 2100, the figure for severe drought, currently at about 8 percent rising to 40 percent, and the figure of extreme drought, currently at 3 percent rising to 30 percent.[4] Put in non-scientific terms, these figures are absolutely terrifying as they predict the possibility of 30 percent of the world's land surface becoming essentially uninhabitable. These are parts of the world, mostly in developing countries, where millions of people will no longer be able to feed themselves.

The poorest areas of the planet, especially Africa, will be the hardest hit. Andrew Pendelton of Britain's Christian Aid organization said of this kind of global drought: "It is a death sentence for many millions of people. It will mean migration off the land at levels we have not seen before, and at levels poor countries cannot cope with." Thus, the Palmer Drought Severity Index makes us visualize millions of climate and water-starved refugees clambering aboard what is left of the blue ark of the developed world. Any program for developing what the West calls the "Third World" will go straight out the window.[5]

Some climate scientists believe that these findings may actually be an underestimation. There is almost no aspect of life in the developing countries that Professor Eleanor Burke's predictive study does not show to be imperiled: the ability to grow food, the ability to have a safe sanitation system, or the availability of water. For millions of people who have to struggle everyday, global warming may well push them over the precipice, notes development expert Andrew Simms.[6] This data was released in 2006 and seemed to many at the time to be too terrifying to contemplate. Currently, scientists are reluctant to mention the Burke study in their assessment of global warming. However, as we witness the collapse of our shared atmosphere, two things are becoming apparent: 1. Climate changes are abrupt, way faster than anticipated; and 2. The impact of the increased average global temperature pales in comparison to the "global wilding" of chaotic, unpredictable weather and sea rise patterns. In the future water scarcity will also affect millions of Africans and propel them towards more secure lands. In the river delta of Egypt and the river delta of

Nigeria, millions are at risk. Melting glaciers, record floods, and drought will propel large populations in South America as climate refugees. This may affect as many as 50 million people by the year 2050.

According to recent reports from the widely respected Natural Resources Defense Council, current water demands across the globe are not sustainable. In its study on Climate Change, Water and Risk, the NRDC reported that fully one-third of all the political subdivisions (counties) in the United States Lower 48 by mid-century will face higher risks of water shortage. If scientists in the United States are beginning to worry about future renewable water supplies in their own country, what are they speculating about the rest of the world? As we have seen in an earlier chapter, China with 1.26 billion people continues to be the one area that worries water experts most of the time. In the dry areas of north China the water table is dropping one meter per year due to over-pumping; and China's three hundred major cities are beginning to run short of water. China and India resemble one another in at least one sense. Their rivers are toxic, disgraceful, stinking industrial sewers, but these countries are not alone.

Water pollution is a major problem in a global context. Water scientist Malin Falkenmark has developed concepts of water stress and water use based on an index of per capita freshwater needs. She estimates that individuals need a minimum of 100 liters per day for household use and from five to twenty-five times that amount for agricultural and industrial uses. Using this index, Dr. Falkenmark estimates severe stress in water availability as early as 2025. By water stress she refers to economic, social, or environmental problems caused by unmet water needs. The impact of this kind of water stress will fall principally upon the thirty-one countries of the developing world with a combined population of 458 million. If we look at the Middle East and North Africa, we see countries facing the most acute water scarcity problems — Jordan and Yemen, for example, draw 30 percent more from underground aquifers each year than is replenished — and experts are quick to point out that Saudi Arabia presents one of the worst cases of unsustainable water use. It now mines fossil groundwater for 75 percent of its water needs.

Nigeria and Tanzania have difficulty meeting the UN Millennium Goals for adequate water supply. Ethiopia, Niger, and Angola also suffer from water stress. However, water in all these countries is contaminated. Surface water is abundant, but undrinkable. Currently only two countries, South Africa and Egypt, have sufficient dams to keep their populations free from water stress. The Ivory Coast has had its public water systems shut down because of the civil war that disrupted the country and precipitated a cholera epidemic.

While some populations may have strong credible governments, they have been just as reckless in their usage and wastage of water as their weaker and more ignorant brethren. Ask any major national leader about water today and he/she will comment on how water is becoming the most important vector of our current civilization. What that leader is reluctant to comment on is the state of preparation for an extreme event in nature. After all, it is much easier for Japan or the United States to apologize for underrating the risk of a catastrophe that accounts for deaths due to unpreparedness than to tax and discipline their societies to anticipate disaster, argues catastrophe theorist Sergio Abranches. In the future the ability to survive extreme events like hurricanes, tsunamis, drought, or extreme pollution is going to be determined by how well we have strengthened the socioeconomic core of societies to rescue people living in poor housing on flood plains, who consume polluted water, or who employ agricultural practices that are more reminiscent of the eighteenth century than the twenty-first.

Countries with strong socioeconomic cores can survive most disasters. Even Hurricane Katrina, though it destroyed a good bit of New Orleans and parts of Louisiana and Mississippi, did not affect the American GDP all that much. A study by the Congressional Research Service on the economic impact of Hurricane Katrina reported that since Louisiana and Mississippi "account for just 2% of the total US gross domestic product, the effects on the national economy will be much less dramatic than the effects on the region." A one-time waterborne event that destroyed over 28,000 homes and cost over $60 billion in lost fixed capital stock becomes an event that amounts to little more than a shudder in the national economy.[7] Lastly, it is worth noting that the first major building to be restored in Mississippi after Hurricane Katrina was a gambling casino. Better to rebuild an edifice to chance than to deal with more pressing human needs.

In a similar vein, an earthquake in Haiti in January 2010 killed over 200,000 people, left over 100,000 people homeless, and destroyed over 280,000 homes and commercial structures. This natural event precipitated a national crisis requiring massive interventions by the United Nations and other international agencies to rescue Haitian society. The earthquake was followed by a major hurricane several months later that left the Haitian society reeling in despair. Chile suffered a powerful earthquake similar to Haiti. The death toll of Chile was 2,000 in spite of Chile being hit by a stronger quake and a larger tsunami. Haiti's death toll was 200,000. When it comes to water disasters of any kind, one can argue that affluent nations experience little long-term impact. The key to surviving rests in the per capita income of the society and the ability of people in terms of literacy and human talent to rebuild. Chile and the United States have the wherewithal to survive water disasters rather well. Haiti, Nicaragua, and Guatemala do not. The bottom line is the strength of the socioeconomic core.

Will growing water scarcity around the planet be treated as a major problem in preparedness? Or will it just become another computer simulation in the game of risk assessment? We have a tendency in the West to overlook risk in the maintenance of our societies that we export as an attitudinal value to poorer nations. The tragedy of this kind of behavior can unfold for decades. Since the advent of the Industrial Revolution, we have been playing a kind of Russian Roulette with our natural resources, hoping that the fatal barrel of destruction will not discharge based on the odds. Transforming this behavior may well be a task more suited for psychologists than climatologists.

Planning for episodes that are so far down the road is a thankless task because it is difficult to convince people that they will happen. At this writing the drought in the United States has been eclipsed by periods of good rainfalls in many places. This convinces people that the long planning view for catastrophe in the form of record droughts may be unnecessary. There are so many environmental concerns that occupy our rather limited attention. Furthermore, we tend to construct a mythology of our environmental worries about water. For example, we concern ourselves about how much water we use when we brush our teeth, wash our cars, wash our clothes, flush our toilets, or take a bath or shower. This is part of the myth because these things really do not address the reality of water shortages. The problem of our water supply is rooted in the realities of how we manufacture food, paper, and cotton. It is rooted in how banks and governments force farmers to grow wheat, roses, corn, and other profitable commodities for the global market when they should be raising crops to feed themselves in a subsistence economy.

Climate Change and Environmental Refugees

Despite one's position on climate change, the earth does seem to be getting noticeably warmer. Spring in North America is arriving four days earlier per decade and plant species and animal life are migrating northward. A warming world is likely to cause high-latitude land farthest from the equator to become desirable. In the future, areas like Canada, Greenland, Russia, Scandinavia, and parts of the northern United States will become a climatic boom belt while countries in the "south" will be plagued by desertification and intense water scarcity.

In 1973, the prize-winning French novelist Jean Raspail published the novel *The Camp of the Saints*, a dystopian view of our social and environmental future. The book shocked many readers worldwide when it first came out because it chronicles the end of European civilization under a flood of immigrants from environmentally ruined countries. Raspail's story begins with the arrival on the coast of the French Riviera of an armada of one hundred decrepit ships carrying 800,000 Indians. The French government, paralyzed by "white guilt" and inaction, stands ultimately aside as the 800,000 Indians come ashore unopposed. Others from ruined lands follow. France disappears under an alien tide and later all of Europe. Near the end of the story, the hordes come to North America: Gracie Mansion in New York City, the residence of the mayor, is turned into a hovel; the Queen of England is forced to have her son marry a Pakistani woman. Switzerland remains the last hold out and does not open its borders, but it too succumbs in the end. If a social compact that is politically and environmentally sustainable is to survive under these gigantic demographic pressures, how will these populations be assimilated? Raspail, with his probing insights, charted a disturbing future.

Whether the fictive dystopia of Raspail becomes true or not, the fact is that climate refugees will be a major problem in the future. In an important paper published by the Royal Society of London, Norman Myers speculates that out of the total of all refugees fleeing their homelands, 25 million could be classified as "environmental refugees." There will be steady increases, largely because "growing numbers of impoverished people press ever harder on overloaded environments. When global warming takes hold, there could be as many as 200 million people overtaken by sea-level rise and coastal flooding … and by droughts of unprecedented severity and duration." Asia, Africa, Latin America, and the small island states have the largest populations that are at risk of becoming climate refugees.

Asia's problem is its highly populated low coastal regions and vulnerability to rising tides and cyclones. Consider Bangladesh. Its low easily flooded shores and landscape might produce record numbers of climate refugees that could outnumber all climate refugees worldwide. In light of this growing problem, nations should be developing strategies and programs to protect climate refugees. Unfortunately, little has been done in this area. The current mandate of the United Nations deals primarily with political refugees. Environmental problems are still mostly outside the thinking and planning processes of a highly bureaucratized United Nations. Further, climate refugees for the most part are fleeing environmental conditions, not repressive political regimes. They still enjoy the protection of their home countries as citizens, even though they have fled a cruel landscape. As climate refugees cross borders, they bring with them a host of cultural, political, and environmental mind-sets that can result in major conflict and social instability. Also, developing nations like India, Nigeria, and Bolivia may have strong objections to seeing their climate-induced expatriate citizens supervised and controlled by international relief agencies.

Water scarcity in the twenty-first century will produce problems of ethnic and political resettlement that have not been witnessed since the end of World War Two, when the Western society had to deal with millions of "displaced persons." At this writing it is doubtful that even Western water-rich nations will be capable of rising to the challenge of developing coherent and workable resettling and protection programs.

Will any western nation be able to absorb one million climate refugees from drought-stricken or submerged regions of the world? Protocols for dealing with this problem are either non-existent or in a very weak formulation strategy that is beset with problems of national survival and political hegemony. Practically anyone who has worked with refugee populations will tell you that a major problem in dealing with climate refugees is that we have not extended the definition of the term "refugees" in the United Nations since 1951! What kind of travel and political documentation will we offer these climate refugees?[8] Norman Meyers identifies the recent environmental calamities in Haiti as a notable instance of the environmental refugee issue. Although 300,000 Haitian boat people have landed on the shores of the United States, they have not been particularly welcomed. Americans have a hard time believing that welcoming Haitians is something that they must do. The Haitian migration posed high destination costs for communities in Florida and local governments spent up to $250 million a year for Haitian environmental refugees. This is seventeen times what the United States spends on environmental safeguards in the Caribbean.

There are limits to any host country's capacity to absorb environmental refugees. Immigrants, particularly poor ones from developing countries, offer abundant reasons for popular resentment. As we move forward in a century unceasingly marked with environmental calamity, almost one-third of all developed countries are taking steps to further restrict immigrant flows from developing countries. When Jean Raspail's fictive French leaders stood bewildered on the beaches of the Riviera and watched 800,000 Indians come ashore, they knew what they were up against.

The Tragedy of the Commons

Since 1998 the population depending on groundwater across the planet has increased from about 5 million to 12 million. If the current level of consumption continues, land subsidence will worsen and contamination problems already faced by millions will deteriorate further, ultimately rendering urban aquifers unusable. Meanwhile, urban households in developing countries are turning to aquifers for their fresh water. There are no clear property rights to this kind of water in most cases. Urban underground water tables are open-access resources — subject to the kind of indiscriminate use that Garrett Hardin predicted in his influential article "The Tragedy of the Commons." Most of the developing world mirrors the urban groundwater problems of cities like New Delhi and Jakarta in Indonesia.

In the next two decades practically every country in the world will have to address some dimension of the water scarcity problem. Will water planning be part of every piece of strategic planning? Will water shortages shift public perception on the value of water prompting governments to view water less as a commodity and more as precious resource?

In 1981, in an important article in *Progressive Magazine*, environmental historian John Opie wrote, "It is not entirely coincidental that our water and energy are drying up at the same time." Opie noted that "the lower the water tables, the more fuel or electricity are needed to pump the water from deeper wells." The water may be there at very deep levels but there won't be cheap oil-based energy to pump it up. Rather than develop continued broad-based programs to maximize aquifer utilization, Opie concluded that it just might be better to limit consumption.[9] Therein lies the trouble. There are sustainable remedies available to conserve water resources, but they won't come without pain and some degree of political shock.

Coping with Water Scarcity
What Does Not Work & What Might Work

What follows is a critical commentary on what kinds of sustainable water options we will be pursuing in the twenty-first century. Some options won't work. Others will work imperfectly. And some options that work splendidly will encounter major political, economic, and cultural opposition from a host of powerful global communities.

1. Building international frameworks and institutional cooperation.

At the heart of this premise is the 2009 United Nations Climate Change Conference in Copenhagen that called for international agreements on a growing global freshwater crisis. The conference ended on the note that comprehensive global strategies are possible to help solve the water scarcity problem. Unfortunately the one organization, the United Nations, capable of taking the lead on this issue is dysfunctional. At the moment, the United Nations appears to be incapable of coordinating multilateral action. From peace talks in the Middle East to environmental issues and nuclear power, UN diplomats are little more than bit players on the international scene. Edward Luck, a historian at the International Peace Institute, has said that efforts for the UN to lead in world affairs have been complicated by a "geopolitical situation that is very, very murky." This was a polite way of saying that UN initiatives often get overwhelmed by the politics of the Security Council, which has become a sounding board for political tantrums from the Moslem world, especially Iran. As new nations join the council such as Brazil, South Africa, Turkey, and Nigeria, they will pursue their own localized issues that have more political and cultural content than environmental awareness. Further, major countries like Russia, for example, can block any UN water initiative. If Russia can block a UN peacekeeping force from entering Kyrgystan to halt violence against Uzbeks, what are the chances of comprehensive international water planning under UN initiatives? The growing assertiveness of powers like China makes it harder to reach international compromise. And problems of financial shortfalls and corruption within the UN bureaucracy have led to the conclusion of one UN observer that "the United Nations is hobbled by failures and distractions of its own making."[10]

2. Desalination

With predictions that more than 3.5 billion people will live in areas facing severe water shortages by the year 2025, the challenge is to find an environmentally benign and economical way to have fresh drinkable water. A popular response to this challenge is desalination technology. Desalination currently is an energy intensive process and over the long term desalination with fossil energy resources is not compatible with sustainable development. Fossil fuels are finite and should be conserved for other essential uses, whereas demands for desalted water will increase. A way out of this dilemma is renewable energy sources such as wind, solar and wave power to provide energy for desalination. Indian scientist Meenahshi Jain of CDM & Environmental Services and Positive Climate Care Ltd in Jaipur suggests the most promising development for sustainable desalination. Says Jain: "Nuclear energy seawater desalination has tremendous potential for the production of fresh water." What Indian scientists like Jain and others envision are small floating nuclear power plants that will produce electrical energy for desalination processes with minimal environmental pollution and greenhouse gas emissions. Such plants could be sited offshore anywhere there is dense coastal population. These plants would provide cheap electricity to power a desalination plant. Compared with wind and solar, nuclear power in the desalination equation is more viable for the kind of large-scale freshwater production that an increasingly industrial and growing population needs. India, meanwhile, already has plans for the rapid expansion of its nuclear power industry. As B. M. Misra, a physicist at the Bhabha Atomic Research Centre in Trombay, India, suggests, "The development of advanced reactors providing heat for hydrogen production and large amounts of waste heat will catalyze the large-scale seawater desalination for economic production of freshwater."[11] Unfortunately, the recent tsunami disaster with nuclear power plants in Japan has negatively reframed the issue of nuclear power. The nuclear solution, even under the best of circumstances, however, has problematic consequences. Even if the poorer nations can afford nuclear reactors for desalination plants, what in fact will become of spent fuel rods from these reactors? Will they end up poisoning the sea, fall into the hands of nuclear terrorists or will they be safely stored in leaded caves far beneath the earth's surface?

3. A Fortress of Flood Gates

Currently international panels on climate change are predicting a sea rise of three feet by the end of this century. Every coastline will be experiencing the kind of tides that drowned the city of New Orleans during hurricane Katrina. As thirteen of the world's largest fifteen cities are on coastal plains, it is prudent for these communities to look to building dikes and water fortifications. Washington's famous tourist mall near the monuments is ringed discretely with dikes and grassy abutments to prevent flood penetrating the capital. Along the Georgetown waterfront, an elaborate fortress of floodgates protects Georgetown's waterfront restaurants and office buildings. Outside the capital, communities near Bladensburg, Maryland, are secured by large levees that are the counterpart of their Mississippi cousins.

Today anyone arriving in Tokyo by train cannot fail to notice the elaborate network of concrete dikes, promenades, and abutments designed to protect the capital of Japan from floods and tsunamis. Most of these dikes have been constructed since World War II, largely in response to Tokyo's urban water and riverfront expansion. Tokyo, home to over 12 million people and sitting right on the Pacific Ocean, is highly susceptible to tsunami and flood damage if there is a major storm. To protect against that possible catastrophe, the Japanese government has created an incredible flood control and storage system to drain the city and transport the water away if the city was at risk of going underwater. Visiting these flood control systems, one sees a huge maze of tunnels and underground pumping facilities capable, the government hopes, of rescuing Tokyo's teeming urban metropolis. The dikes and drainage fields blend into a kind of gray cityscape and visitors concentrate their vision on the numerous ball fields, soccer pitches and golf driving ranges that are the more decorative part of the flood plain of the Tokyo River. The many pathways along the river are dotted with sky blue tarpaulins that have been given to Tokyo's homeless citizens to shelter them from the elements as they build crude cardboard camps along the waterways.

When Hurricane Katrina devastated New Orleans and much of the Gulf Coast in 2005, there were a lot of nervous government officials in Japan wondering what would happen if Tokyo was ever hit by a typhoon of similar magnitude to Katrina. Now with recent tsunami events in Sendai and Fukushima, they worry even more. It seems that every time there is a torrential downpour or a few snowflakes in Tokyo, the transport system is thrown into confusion, schools close and TV networks start posting bulletins. So what would happen to Tokyo and the rest of the Kanto region in the event of a major flood and what countermeasures are in place to enable a quick response from the government?

According to the Cabinet Office, which oversees the various ministries and bodies in charge of disaster management in Japan, one-half of the entire country's population is concentrated in low-lying inundation areas and the basins of 248 major rivers are designated as potential flood hazards. In the Tokyo metropolitan region, those rivers include the Sumida, Tama, Tone, Arakawa, Kanda, Ayase, Naka, and Daiba. Most of these waterways are relatively steep with a short distance from the source to the sea, resulting in rapid flow. In the Tokyo area, an estimated 116 square kilometers of land lies below sea level, which means these areas would be inundated should embankments collapse. The good news is that Japan has never had a typhoon as strong as Hurricane Katrina in its recorded history. The most destructive typhoon was Typhoon Kathleen in 1947, which claimed 3,769 lives. Nevertheless, smaller floods and sediment-related disasters have occurred in more than 90 percent of municipalities throughout Japan in the past ten years. A deluge in Tokyo in October 2004, for example, flooded the Azabu-Juban subway station. In September 2009, Typhoon No. 9 hit the Kanto region, stopping Japan Rail lines and stranding 1.2 million commuters. The Tama River reached a dangerous level and some residents had to be evacuated from near its banks.

Experts in the U.S. and Japan have said that a disaster like Katrina only happens once every four hundred years. The mind-set has been to prepare for disasters based on recent history rather than on the worst-case scenario. However, the Japanese are beginning to realize that they cannot take anything for granted. The events of 2011 have been too painful to ignore. The Ministry of Land, Infrastructure and Transport has been shoring up embankments and simulating the flow of water in the likelihood of a major flood through computer analysis. Also Japan has to predict what would happen if an earthquake caused an embankment to break in Tokyo similar to the tsunami of 2011 in the Sendai area.

Tokyo has the same problem as New York City — a vast maze of subway and railroad tunnels exists beneath their urban surface. Water from a Katrina-like storm would engulf many of the subway tunnels in two to three hours and paralyze the city. Moreover, if the dike along the Arakawa River were to break, the water would reach Ginza, Tokyo's famous shopping district, in twenty hours and put it under two meters of water. Making matters worse, a flood analysis report warned that Tokyo's sewage system would be overwhelmed. There would be outbreaks of disease and the death toll would rapidly swell into the thousands.[12] In the United States and Japan, traditional disaster planning revolves around anticipation of a 7.5 earthquake on the Richter scale. As we have seen at Fukushima, Japan, an earthquake of 9.0 crumbled the city like tissue and the resulting tsunami leapt all storm retention barriers. So-called "once in a hundred years events" now seem to be on the border of becoming commonplace.

4. New Water Conservation Technologies

In areas where aquifers are drying up and rainwater is increasingly unpredictable, there is a critical need for innovation. As we have already seen, desalination has its problems. Further it takes large amounts of energy to pump water through irrigation systems or tunnels. While some specialists urge a greater use of wind-power to create the electricity necessary to pump water over distance, this technology has yet to earn its stripes as a mass scale energy provider.

Of course, there are tried and true technologies of water use that have demonstrated their efficacy such as modern water pricing techniques and drip agriculture and diversification into lower water use agriculture. Limitations on water consumption are a valuable tool, though one would be reluctant to identify it as a technology. However, imagine a society where water use was shut off for two to three hours a day. Or a society where one paid for the true cost of water, say $3,000 for 100,000 gallons of drinking water per year, at three cents a gallon. Writing from India, Emeritus Geology Professor V. O. Rao suggests the practical tactic of using oil and gas pipelines during certain days of the year to transport water. It is not necessary to run these pipelines with gas and oil 365 days a year, says Dr. Rao. "Such pipelines can transport fresh water from water rich countries to water deficient countries during some days of the year."

To continue, imagine a society without car washes, irrigated cotton and rice fields in the desert, cattle and corn agriculture, and per capita license fees for water consumption. Say one license paid at city hall would entitle one to 100,000 gallons of water per annum. Above that limit surcharges would apply. This is not a happy prospect to dwell on, but it does address the problem. The basic fact is that people tend to find these proposals too draconian for their liking. Better to waste water and let the next generation grapple with the problem. Americans, especially, don't like limitations on things they use.

5. Recycle Wastewater

To recycle wastewater is a wise technology that is beginning to come into its own. Graywater, as it is termed, is plentiful and can be used in many applications — from providing water for the desert casinos of Las Vegas to enabling countries like Singapore to reuse wastewater for everything from drinking water to industrial applications. Graywater is water of lesser quality than potable water, but of higher quality than black water. Blackwater is water flushed from toilets. Graywater is generally the water from baths, showers, washing machines, and sinks. The greatest source of gray water for multiple applications comes from hotels and recreational resorts, which can use gray water for a variety of activities — from watering golf courses to irrigation of non-edible plants. Through the use of settling tanks and sand filters, graywater can be used again and again. Coupled with simple methods of rain harvesting, usually in 600 foot plastic lined catchment areas, these technologies go a long way towards reusing and augmenting scarce water in arid climates. The one main problem is that globally there is little regulation of graywater use. Less wealthy countries that cannot afford treatment facilities could easily have difficulty with graywater mixing with effluvial waters producing very negative sanitation results. More affluent countries will soon be getting used to "From Toilet to Tap" water technologies, but poorer countries will have problems monitoring the quality of graywater.

6. Develop and enact better policies and regulation

As water scarcity complicates food security and pollution, government needs to redefine their roles in terms of enacting water legislation like the American Clean Water Act. Other countries currently are discussing ways to craft legislation that will keep pollution discharges out of fresh water sources. While most political leaders are quick to admit that it is up to government to insure that communities have access to clean water, there is no consensus as to how this might be done on a global scale. Water politics varies greatly from country to country; and local and tribal issues in poorer nations can easily stymie even the most determined efforts to enact legislation that will build healthier communities. A better alternative may be to enact water strategies locally. Expanding on what successes have already been demonstrated, laws that provide economic incentives for improved irrigation techniques have a greater chance of succeeding than attempts to change lifestyles and cultural attitudes towards water.

7. Shrink Corporate Water Footprints

It is well known in the field of water management that industrial water usage accounts for approximately 22 percent of global consumption. In the future sustainable manufacturing will become an important part of the water equation. Efficient business use of water, as the new water orthodoxy, may well be one possible solution to the problem of disappearing ground water supplies. In the future water scarcity will penetrate almost every aspect of operations in the food and beverage industry. For instance, executives contemplating locating plants in China may be more likely to consider the consequences of melting Himalayan glaciers on the Tibetan plateau that feed some of China's important rivers. According to Jeff Erikson, an environmentally oriented business consultant and vice president of Sustain Ability, a business strategy think tank, water shortage in the future will be heavily considered in plant sitings in the developing world, along with capital requirements and rate of return. Companies that want to stay in business will have to add expertise in water management. Says Erikson: "Companies will need to anticipate market pressure to appropriately price water."[13] As stresses in water supply make it increasingly difficult for communities and regional and national governments, business leaders will have to have well-developed water policies that take into consideration supply line pricing as well as impacts that might cause political and economic disruptions.

Thus far the record of companies in developing strategic business policies around water that will be mutually beneficial to both the company and the host community has not been good. Coca-Cola® literally raided aquifers in

India for the sake of making a beverage for India's upper class at the expense of poor farmers and villagers. Similar developments have occurred elsewhere with takeovers of water plants by private companies concerned with maximizing profits at community expense. While there is sentiment in the business community that water is not fairly priced and that governments everywhere are giving away water for free, there is plenty of opposition to water pricing. According to Milwaukee water student Renata Sjoblom, the business approach to water scarcity is pathetic. "As long as large companies like Nestle are allowed to consume (steal) water at a rate of 312,000 gallons a day (in the United States) and sell at 300 percent profit with no regulation from the EPA or FDA, the shortage and war for water will continue."[14]

Urban Development

A nation's water problems can often be disguised by the public relations of urban development. On a flat floodplain on the coast of the island of Java, glittering office towers dominate the skyline of Jakarta. The skyscrapers lend the city an aura of prosperity and power. Unfortunately, like many urban capitals today, Jakarta does not have a reliable water supply from surface streams and rivers and must rely on aquifers for water. Development and population pressure has caused Jakarta's groundwater to be overdrawn and today there is saltwater intrusion from the sea polluting what is left. As groundwater is withdrawn, the soil becomes unstable and the land begins to subside. Cracked, damaged and collapsing buildings are becoming the inevitable result of Jakarta's groundwater decisions. The majority of the world's sixteen mega-cities — those with 10 million or more inhabitants — lie within regions experiencing mild to severe water stress. As urban water demands increase, the pressure on agricultural and rural areas to sell or surrender their water rights will intensify.

Conclusion

The challenge of water scarcity in the twenty-first century could be most critical in terms of the survival of communities. In the past one hundred years we have seen a radical transformation in the relationship of man and water. Subsistence societies have become developing nations thirsty for irrigated agriculture and hydroelectric plants. Some have irrigation systems closer to antiquity than the present. When public water systems are insufficient in developing countries, everyone turns to wells and groundwater for their needs. In terms of urban groundwater use, many cities in developing countries seem to be in a race to the bottom. Meanwhile, the developed world's voracious appetite for water prevails in its farms, suburbs and cities.

In the nineteenth century, historian Frederick Jackson Turner highlighted the historic western frontier as one of the most elemental forces conditioning American culture and politics. Now in the twenty-first century, we again can see that history will have a driving environmental force. This time it will be water and we are about to enter a new era of thirst.

"Good as drink is,

it ends in thirst."

-- Irish Proverb

Chapter Ten
Global Thirst

T oday we share a water legacy that links us to antiquity in many respects. Industrial nations have evolved into intense consumer and service economies whose lifestyle marshals water resources that would astonish the hydraulic emperors of Babylon. Certainly much of the planet today is as dependent on irrigation as the ancient civilizations of Egypt, Babylon, and the Indus Valley. Also, like the hydraulic systems of old, we continue to press forward with massive dam and irrigation projects that often get us in the same fix as antiquity. Water conflict between nations and problems of water salinity are just as pressing today as they were thousands of years ago. The only thing that separates our current water dilemma from that of yesterday is the magnitude of the problem forced on us by population growth and technological hubris.

In a 1957 work, the historian Karl Wittfogel argued that there was a causal link between specialized irrigation agriculture and the rise of authoritarianism. He referred to these early irrigation societies as hydraulic states.[1] As water problems continue to escalate across the planet, one can speculate that a new variation of Wittfogel's theory might emerge: international water authorities that are just as controlling and potentially despotic as the hydraulic state of Babylon. Certainly, in the future, water will become one of those pressing problems that are too important to be left to the whims and ministrations of the nation-state. As we enter an era of water scarcity this resource may well come under an international rationing process. California and Egypt may be forced to cease raising rice. India may be required to adapt itself to new locovar agricultural economies. Cattle culture, which is so water and crop intensive, may be reduced to a small boutique industry. Cotton may once again be grown extensively in the American south and large parts of well-watered Africa. The landscapes of many countries may be dotted with fish farms — large industrial enterprises raising commercial fish like talapia in tanks. Electricity and the cost of drinking water will both be linked to the price of oil, which will be based on actual rather than nation-subsidized cost. The richer nations will notice these transformations as an irritant. The poorer nations will see these events as social and environmental triage, in which they are the losers.

At this writing the United States and other developed nations have not fully awakened to the growing water challenge of this century. Sure, there is constant talk about "drip irrigation," water trading, and urban water conservation. But the world seldom conforms to our wishes, and current water initiatives are but a drop in the bucket when we confront the enormity of the problems that face us with regard to water. Inertia as well as cultural and sociopolitical forces prevents the development of coherent water policies. High-energy costs stand in the way of alternative water processes like desalination. Only well-to-do nations like Israel, the United States and the Arab Emirates can afford to take fresh water from the sea through desalination. When the crisis threatens to overwhelm us is at hand, then, and only then, will the kind of international water accords be put in place for the distribution and use of this precious resource. When it comes, international water sharing won't be democratic in process, and it will not be fair to weaker nations. Food shortages, energy shortages and climate change in conjunction with water scarcity combine to form a perfect storm for global calamity. Furthermore, as the earth warms, we may well have extreme precipitation events that bring with it flooding on a massive scale. Already in the American Midwest we are seeing Mississippi flood events not experienced since the 1930s; and flooding in Pakistan and other developing nations destroys the best irrigation plans and contaminates public drinking water supplies. Small mud dams built over the decades by hand are swept away leaving no supply source for water during drought. Typhus and cholera, the twin evils of poor sanitation, will raise their ugly heads as the torrents come to engulf societies.

As we look back into history we can see how the human community has surmounted a host of water problems. The deserts of the American west and elsewhere became fruitful through irrigation. Cities rose on the sand through hydroelectric power, bringing simultaneously drinking water and electricity. But that was then. The old technologies of dam building and massive irrigation projects don't seem to work anymore.

Suffice it to say that water scarcity is an issue that is driving societies towards a tipping point in history. That point is one of growing conflict and instability in the future among water-resource deprived nations. The Center for Strategic and International Studies argues "on the one hand global water challenges are the result of too many people demanding too much water." On the other, these challenges are brought about by "weak institutions and poor governmental frameworks" that are unable to manage water supplies for countries and their populations.[2] Poor governance exacerbates water scarcity problems. Massive river diversion schemes to bring water to dry lands have not worked well in India and China. Currently the most farcical of these schemes is the Great Manmade River Project in Libya. This is a five-phase project to move 2 billion cubic meters of water beneath the Sahara Desert of southern Libya to agricultural fields along the coastal areas of the north at a cost of $US 25 billion. So far, only Phase 1 delivering 700 million cubic meters of water has gone into effect. The water, however, has high salinity and can only be used for agricultural purposes. Critics argue that it would be far cheaper for Libya to buy food from water-rich regions than destroy an aquifer in the name of national self-delusion. The current Civil War and overthrow of President Kadafi's regime in Libya complicates further all of that nation's water issues.

In his epilogue on water, the journalist Steven Solomon notes that in this troubling new century "no technological panacea that extracts more renewable water from nature is available or on the near-term horizon to answer the call."[3] Until societies are prepared to confront their hydrological reality, there can be no transformation in the ways that people use water.

Social science research finds water salvation in the evolution of lower consumption societies in terms of energy, food, and water, but this does not mean that we shall heed the wisdom of our experts. Of a world population of over 6 billion, more than one billion lack access to potable water. Sanitation problems will be more problematic than access to drinking water, as public water systems decline in their ability to provide clean water. Environmental diseases like diarrhea, schistosomaisis, and guinea worm will emerge because of poor water and sanitation. Bad water, bad sanitation, and bad home environments take an annual toll of 5 million. In this sense, water becomes the grim reaper rather than the sustainer of life.

Looking forward, it is safe to say that the new era of water difficulties presents important foreign policy risks for the United States and other resource-sufficient nations. Developed countries, for their own interest, should initiate robust capability programs to improve the economies and infrastructures of their water-poor brethren. It is doubtful that the United States and others will be willing to share a substantial part of their national wealth in order to prevent these countries from lapsing into a kind of water anarchy.

As I said earlier in this book, water informs and shapes society. No one can do without it, but the historical and cultural mind-set on water as a disposable commodity stifles the ability to think strategically about this one key problem. Water is a human right, a spiritual force that animates life. It is the touchstone of planetary survival. We readily acknowledge that in an intellectual sense, but then we continue our old ways. Perhaps one day soon we will get the message as we turn on the tap and no water comes. Today we no longer subscribe to the progressive view of human history — the idea that each era is better than the one that precedes it. However, that does not mean that one should plunge wholeheartedly into embracing history as humanity's downward spiral.

As we conclude our thoughts on global thirst, the only strategy that makes sense to me is one that is based on the assumption that all across the planet we can do with less water and just about less consumption of everything. Certainly, in the developed nations, a reduction of 10 percent in our standard of living would hardly inconvenience us, but the Western culture has a problem with accepting limits, whether it is with automobiles, urban design, or water. Most water authorities that I have consulted say that the way out of our water difficulties will be extremely messy, fraught with international conflict, social dysfunction, and environmental problems of disease not seen since the nineteenth century.

Many people hope that there will be social forces in the coming years that will touch and form mind and heart and pull us back from the environmental abyss at the eleventh hour. As I said earlier in this book, though, hope is not a strategy; and the eleventh hour is upon us.

Endnotes

Chapter One
1 James E. Salzman, "A Short History of Drinking Water," *Yale Journal of Law and Humanities*, Vol. 17, No. 3, March 2006.
2 "Fresh Water: A Brief History," http://www.nutriteam.com/history.
3 M. J. Ongerth, William H. Bruvold, and A. L. Knutson, "The Taste of Water," *Public Health Reports*, Vol. 79, April 1964.
4 Interview with Jill Klein Rone, June 29, 2010; Berkeley Springs International Water Tasting Awards, February 27, 2010, Press Release.
5 Water is cited in many places in the Bible: *Genesis 1:2, Exodus 15:23, Psalm 45, Second Kings 5:1*, and extensively in the *New Testament* books of Matthew, Mark, and John 4:10 and John 3:5.
6 Frederick Zugibe, *The Crucifixion of Jesus: A Forensic Inquiry*, New York, New York: M. Evans Publishing, 2005.
7 Helen Blavatasky, *The Key to Theosophy*, Pasadena, California: 1995 (reprint).
8 Ruth Levy Guyer, "The Power of Water," National Public Radio, February 26, 2006.
9 Masuru Emoto, *The Hidden Messages in Water*, Hillsboro, Oregon: Beyond Words Publishing, 2004.
10 www.spiritofma'at.com, vol. 3 no. 5.
11 Quoted in Colin Lorback's "Water Experience." www.phenomenologyonline.com/articles.lorback.html.
12 Mays, L. W., D. Koutsoyiannis, and A. N. Angelakis, "A brief history of urban water supply in antiquity," *Water Science and Technology* 7 (1), 1-12, 2007.
13 "Using Water to Understand Human Society – from the Industrial Revolution to Global Trade," European Science Foundation, November 26, 2008, Press Release; Terje Tvedt and Terje Oestgaard, *A History of Water, Ancient Society to the Modern World, Vol. 2*, (New York, New York: I B Taurus and Company, 2010). See "A History of the Ideas of Water: Deconstructing Nature and Constructing Society," pp. 1-17.
14 Charles Hadfield, *World Canals: Inland Navigations Past and Present*, London, England: David and Charles, 1986.
15 Donald Worster, *Rivers of Empire, Water, Aridity and the Growth of the American West*, New York, New York: Oxford University Press, 1985, 7.

Chapter Two
1 "Interview with Dr. Ismail Serageldin, Senior Vice President, World Bank," *Frontline: India's National Magazine*, April 24-May 7, 1999.
2 United National Global Development Research Center, "The Dublin Statement on Water and Sustainable Development," January 1992.
3 Thomas F. Homer-Dixon, "Environmental Scarcity, Mass Violence, and the Limits to Ingenuity," *Current History*, November 1996; Thomas F. Homer Dixon, "Environmental Scarcity and Violent Conflict: Evidence from Cases," *International Security*, vol. 19, Summer 1991, pp.5-40.
4 Kathryn Gregory, "Shining Path Backgrounder," Council on Foreign Relations, August 27, 2009
5 "The Euphrates Triangle: Security Implications of the Southeastern Anatolia Project," Institute for Strategic Studies, November 1999.
6 Robert V. Percival, "Water Pollution Control: Lessons from Transnational Experience," Congreso Iternacional de Derecho del Medio Ambiente, 1998, 277, 280.
7 *Book of Genesis*, "Chapter 26."

8 Reisner, M., *Cadillac Desert: The American West and Its Disappearing Water*, New York, New York: Penguin Books, 1993.

9 Donals Hansen, "Royal Building Activity at Sumerian Lagash in the early Dynastic Period," *Archeologist*, vol. 55, 1992, 206211; J. E. Hoover, "Water Supply Facilities and National Defense," *Journal of the American Water Works Association*, vol. 33, no. 11 (1941), 1861.

10 David Isenberg, "Securing U.S. Water Supplies," CDI Terrorism Project, Center For Defense Analysis, July 19, 2002. See also Dan Kroll et al, "Terrorism Vulnerabilities to the Water Supply and the Role of the Consumer," *Water World*, Pennwell Publishing, 2006; www.waterworld.com.

11 "Armed Forces Are Put on Standby to Tackle Threat of Wars Over Water," *The Independent*, February 28, 2006.

12 Gaby Hinsliff, "MI5 Seeks Power Over Travel Records," *Sunday Observer*, London, March 16, 2008.

13 Research Institute for Peace and Security, New Delhi, "India's Policy on Terrorism Since 9/11," 2008.

14 Caitlin Talmadge, "Deterring A Nuclear 9/11," *Washington Quarterly*, vol. 30, Spring 2007, 21-34.

15 Dan Kroll, *Securing Our Water Supply, Protecting a Valuable Resource*, Tulsa, Oklahoma: Pennwell Publishers, 2006, 1-150.

16 Nadine Gurr and Benjamin Cole, *New Face of Terrorism: Threats From Weapons of Mass Destruction*, London, England: I. B. Taurus, 2002, 276.

17 Claudia Copeland, "Terrorism and Security Issues Facing the Water Infrastructure Sector," Congressional Research Service, May 26, 2009.

18 See Pacific Institute's Water Conflict Chronology (www.worldwater.org).

19 James A. Lewis, "Assessing the Risks of Cyber Terrorism, Cyber War and Other Cyber Threats," Center for Strategic & International Studies, Washington, DC, December 2002; Guy De Nileon, "The Who What Why and How of Counter-terrorism Issues," *American Water Works Association Journal*, No. 5, May 2001, 78-85.

20 Peter H. Gleick, "Water and Terrorism," *Water Policy* (2006), 483-484.

21 Gleick, "Water and Terrorism," 491.

22 US Congress, Public Health Security and Bioterrorism Preparedness and Response Act (2002).

23 Mithat Rende, "Water Transfer from Turkey to Water-Stressed Countries in the Middle East," Occasional Papers, Ministry of Foreign Affairs, Ankara 2002; "Israel, Turkey Join Forces Against al-Qaeda," Israeli News Agency Release, January 10, 2003.

24 "How Safe Is Our Water – The Threat of Terrorism," www.ionizers/water-terrorism.html.

25 Claudia Copeland, "Terrorism and Security Issues Facing the Water Infrastructure Sector," Congressional Research Service, May 26, 2009.

26 Janine Zacharia, "A Sacred But Sullied Spot?" *The Washington Post*, July 30, 2010.

27 Sara Reguer, "Controversial Waters: Exploitation of the Jordan River, 1950-1980," *Middle Eastern Studies*, vol. 29, No. 1, January, 1993, 53-90.

28 Sharif S. Elmusa, "The Water Issue and the Palestinian-Israeli Conflict," Information Paper No. 2, DC Center for Policy Analysis on Palestine, 1993.

29 Jan Selby, *Water, Power, and Politics in the Middle East: The Other Israel-Palestine Conflict*, Library of the Middle East, (London, England: I. B. Taurus, 2004); Mark Zeitun, *Power and Water in the Middle East: The Hidden Politics of the Palestinian-Israeli Conflict*, Library of the Middle East, (London, England: I. B. Taurus, 2008).

30 Grant Slater, "Israel Dedicates Huge Sea-water Purification plan," Associated Press News Dispatch, May 9, 2010.

Chapter Three

1 John R. Wennersten, "The Parched East," *Bay Journal News Service*, May 3, 2007.

2 Those cities are: Albuquerque, Atlanta, Baltimore, Boston, Chicago, Denver, Detroit, Fresno, Chicago, Philadelphia, San Diego, San Francisco, Houston, Los Angeles, Phoenix, Seattle, Newark, and Washington, DC.

3 Robert McCartney, "A Champion of Truth About Lead-tainted Tap Water," *The Washington Post*, Metro Section, May 23, 2010.

4 "Health Effects of Chlorine in Drinking Water," *Journal of Public Health*, vol. 82, 955-963

5 "Drinking Water of 41 Million Americans Contaminated with Pharmaceuticals," *Environmental News Network*, August 26, 2008.

6 Theo Colborn, et al, *Our Stolen Future: How We are Threatening Our Fertility, Intelligence and Survival – A Scientific Detective Story*, New York, New York: Penguin, 1997, Introduction.

7 "Drinking Water of 41 Million Americans Contaminated with Pharmaceuticals," *Environmental News Network*, August 26, 2008.

8 US Geological Survey, "Contaminants in Groundwater Used for Public Supply," News Release. May 21, 2010.

9 KP Kantor et al, "Bladder Cancer, drinking water source, and tap water consumption: a case-control study," *Journal of the National Cancer Institute*, December 1987, vol. 79: 1269-79.

10 Nancy Kaffer, "Detroit's Shrinking Population Deepens Water Department Problems," *Crain's Detroit Business*, May 2, 2010. Brett Walton, "In Detroit: No Money No Water," *Circle of Blue Water News*, April 19, 2010.

11 Steve Angers, Trout Unlimited Press Release, "Water Withdrawals Threaten New England Streams," December 12, 2006; Commonwealth of Massachusetts, *Interim Report on the Water Management Act Blue Ribbon Panel*, Office of Commonwealth Development, December 31, 2006.

12 Tom Horton, *Bay Country*, Baltimore, Maryland: Johns Hopkins University Press, 2006; p. 81.

13 US Department of Agriculture, Natural Resource Conservation Service, Water Supply Forecast Reports, "Water Supply Outlook For the Western United States."

14 David Carle, "Introduction," *Water in California*, Berkeley, California: University of California Press, 2004.

15 Karisa King, "State Climatologist Talks Global Warming," *San Antonio Express News*, June 7, 2009.

16 North Carolina Conservation Network, 2009, "Water Allocation: It's Time to Update Our Water Laws for the 21st Century."

17 Quoted in John Manuel, "Drought in the Southeast: Lessons for Water Management," *Environmental Health Perspective*, vol. 116, April, 2008.

18 Matthew Bigg, "Water Runs Dry in Rural Tennessee Town," *Reuters News Service*, November 21, 2007.

19 "The Town Without Water," *People*, vol. 68, December 3, 2007

20 Sandra Postel, "Facing a Future of Water Scarcity,"Society for the Advancement of Education Report, September 1993.

21 Lester R. Brown, *Plan B 2.0: Rescuing a Planet Under Stress and a Civilization in Trouble*, New York, New York: Norton, 2006; 57.

22 Wertheim, F. *The Potomac*, Baltimore, Maryland: Johns Hopkins University Press, 1977; American Rivers Association, 1998: "Potomac River Named One of the Nation's Most Endangered Rivers."

23 Ted Williams, "Gas Pains," *Audubon Magazine*, May-June 2010.

24 Abraham Lustgarten, "Officials in Three States Pin Water Woes on Gas Drilling," *Pro Publica*, April 26, 2009.

25 Joaquin Sapien, "With Natural Gas Drilling Boom, Pennsylvania Faces an Onslaught of Wastewater," *Pro Publica*, October 4, 2009.

26 Natural Resources Defense Council, "Finding the Balance: The Role of Natural Gas in America's Energy Future," January 2010.

27 John R. Wennersten, "The Parched East," *Bay Journal News Service*, May 3, 2007.

28 Hank Stuever, "Beyond BP: Documentary Sees a Crisis in Natural Gas," *The Washington Post*, June 21, 2010.

29 Brown, Plan B, 21-40.

30 Bert Hubbard, "Millions of gallons spilled in Colorado over 2-1/2 year period," *Denver Post*, June 28, 2010.

31 "Shell Buys Marcellus Holdings," *Times-Tribune*, May 29, 2010.

32 "Dry Times in North America," NASA Earth Observatory, www.earthobservatory.nasa.gov/features.

33 Mike Davis, "Denial in the Desert," *The Nation*, April 16, 2007.

34 NRDC, "The Gulf's Untold Stories," *One Earth*, Spring 2011.

35 "Oil Spills," Air and Waste Management Association, May 1, 2000.

Chapter Four

1 Population Foundation of India, "The Future Population of India: A Long Range Demographic View," 2007.

2 McKinsey Associates, "Charting our Water Future," Washington, DC, 2009

3 Nina Brooks, "Immanent Water Crisis in India," *Arlington Institute Report*, August 2007.

4 Somni Sengupta, "In Teeming India, Water Crisis Means Dry Pipes and Foul Sludge," *The New York Times*, September 29, 2006.

5 Interview, *Sunday Times of India*, March 6, 2011

6 Steven Solomon, *Water, The Epic Struggle for Wealth, Power, and Civilization*, New York, New York: Harper-Collins, 2010, 424.

7 Nina Brooks, "Imminent Water Crisis in India, Arlington Institute, August 2007.

8 "The Water Crisis in India," Earth Trends, World Resources Institute,

9 Rakesh Kumar, R. D. Singh, and K. D. Sharma, "Water Resources of India," *Current Science*, vol. 89, No.5 September 2005, 794-811.

10 Interview with Sekhar Raghavan, Director, Rain Center of Chennai, India, February 8, 2011.

11 R. Srikanth, "Challenges of sustainable water quality management in rural India," *Current Science*, Vol. 97, No. 3 August 2009.

12 A. C. Shukla and Vandama Asthana, "Anatomy of Interlinking Rivers in India, A Decision in Doubt," Program in Arms Control Disarmament and International Security, University of Illinois at Champaign-Urbana, November 2005.

13 R. Srikanth, "Challenge of Sustainable Water Quality Management in Rural India," *Current Science*, vol. 97, no. 3, August 2009.

14 Rakesh Kumar, et. al, "Water Resources of India," 2005.

15 Noreen Parks, "New System Removes Arsenic from Groundwater," *Frontiers in Ecology and the Environment*," Vol. 9, April 2011, 145.

Chapter Five

1 The Baths of Caracalla in Rome lasted from 212 AD till they were destroyed by the Ostrogoths in sixth century AD.

2 Elizabeth Royte, *Garbage Land: On the Secret Trail of Trash*, New York, New York: Little Brown and Company, 2005, 3-10.

3 Matthew Gandy, "Rethinking urban metabolism: Water, space, and the modern city," City Vol. 8 No.3, 364-378.

4 Charisma S. Acey, "Access to Water in Nigerian Cities," Report to the US House of Representatives, Washington, DC, 2005.

5 Environmental Working Group, "Chromium-6 is Widespread in US Tap Water: Cancer-causing chemical found in 89 percent of cities sampled," National Press Release, December 20, 2010.

6 World Health Organization, "Review of the On-Gong Cholera Outbreak in the KwaZulu-Natal," Unpublished Report, 2001; John Thompson et al, "Summary: Drawers of Water II, Thirty Years of Domestic Water Use in East Africa," International Institute for Environment and Development, 2001.

7 National Oceanic and Atmospheric Administration, "Coastal Wetlands in Eastern US Disappearing," *Science Daily*, December 17, 2010.

8 L.W/ Mays, et al. "A Brief History of Urban Water Supply in Antiquity," *Water Science and Technology: Water Supply*, Vol.1, pp.1-12, 2007.

9 Elizabeth Royte, *Garbage Land*, 276-277.

Chapter Six

1 Maude Barlow, *Blue Covenant, The Global Water Crisis and the Coming Battle for the Right to Water*, New York, New York: The New Press, 2007; 91.

2 David Hall and Emmanuele Lobina, "Water Privatization," London Public Services International Research Unit, April 2008; 6.

3 Maude Barlow and Tony Clarke, "Who Owns Water," *The Nation*, September 2, 2002.

4 Rachel Williams, "Drinking fountains shortage 'bad' for child health," *The Guardian*, May 31, 2010.

5 Peter Glieck, blog: "Water Fountains victory: the Cavs cave," www.sfgate.com/gleick

6 News Release, Department of Public Health, University of Otago, "Alcohol often cheaper than bottled water and nearly as cheap as milk," October 15, 2010.

7 Emily Arnold, "Bottled Water: Pouring Resources Down the Drain," Earth Policy Institute, February 2, 2006.

8 Charles Fishman, "Message in a Bottle," Fast Company.com, December 19, 2007.

9 "What's On Tap?", *News for DC Water Customers*, Vol. 12, Issue 2.

10 Peter Gleick, *Bottled and Sold: The Story Behind Our Obsession with Bottled Water*, Washington, DC: Island Press, 2010.

11 Fishman, "Message in a Bottle," op.cit.

12 Ian Edmonds, "Murray River Drought Mitigation Using Burdekin River Water," www.solartran.com.

Chapter Seven

1 "Many Rivers re in Danger of Dying," *Express India*, March 21, 2007.

2 "An Italian River Full of Cocaine," *BBC News*, August 5, 2005.

3 "Population Growth Sentencing Millions to Hydrological Poverty," Earth Policy Institute, June 21, 2000.

4 "Briefing Canada's Tar Sands," *The Economist*, January 22, 2011.

5 Jim Yardley, "Beneath Boom Cities China's Future is Drying Up," *New York Times*, September 28, 2007.

6 Quoted in Xie Chuanjial's "Pollution Makes China the Top Killer," *China Daily*, May 21, 2007. See also Peter Gleick, "China and Water," World's Water, 2008-2009, (Washington, DC: Island Press) 2010.

7 "Pollution has put Yangtze on brink of catastrophe," *The Times*, London, May 11, 2006.

8 Paul Fernandez, "Dying Waters," *The Times of India*, Goa, February 17, 2011.

9 "Russia's Troubled Waters Flow with the Mighty Volga," National Public Radio Program, November 1, 2010.

10 Scott Fisher, "Muck Raker: Riverkeeper's Crusade to Save Chesapeake Bay from Sediment," *The Daily Record*, York, Pennsylvania, September 12, 2009.

11 J. R. McNeill, *Something New Under the Sun, An Environmental History of the 21st Century World*, New York, New York: Norton, 2007, 127.

Chapter Eight

1 Laurence Smith, *The New North: The World in 2050*, London, England: Profile Press, 2011.

2 Peter Rogers and Susan Leal, *Running Out of Water, The Looming Crisis and Solutions to Conserve Our Most Precious Resource*, New York, New York: Macmillan, 2010, p.152.

3 Paul Krugman, "Droughts, Floods, and Food," *The New York Times*, February 6, 2011.

4 "Global Thirst: How Water is Driving the New Wave of Foreign Investment in Farm Land," *Investment Treaty News*, December 16, 2010.

5 Peter Brabeck Letmathe, "The Next Big Thing: H2O," *Foreign Policy*, April 2009.

6 Daniel Lazar, *America's Undeclared War: What's Killing Our Cities and How to Stop It*, New York, New York: Harcourt, 2001; 291.

7 Clay McShane, *Down the Asphalt Path, The Automobile and the American City*, New York, New York: Columbia University Press, 1994, 217-283.

8 "Burning Ambitions," *The Economist*, January 29-February 4, 2011, 62.

9 Ibid.

10 "Waste not, want not," *The Economist*, February 26-March 4, 2011.

11 United Nations Panel on Climate Change, 2007 Assessment Report.

12 Daniel Sarewitz, "How Science Makes environmental controversies worse," *Environmental Science and Policy*, vol. 7, 2004.

Chapter Nine

1 Johan Rockstrom, "To Tip or Not To Tip," *Huffington Post*, October 20, 2009.

2 Associated Press Newswire, March 18, 2011.

3 Sergio Abranches, "There are no natural disasters, only social catastrophes," http://www.ecopolity, March 1, 2010.

4 Eleanor Burke, et al., "Modeling the Recent Evolution of Global Drought and Projections for the Twenty-First Century with the Hadley Centre Climate Model," *Journal of Hydrometeorology*, Vol. 7, October 2006, 1113-1125.

5 Michael McCarthy, "The Century of Drought," *The Independent* (London), October 4, 2006.

6 Ibid.

7 Brian W. Cashell and Marc Labonte, "The Macroeconomic Effects of Hurricane Katrina," CRS Report for Congress, September 13, 2005.

8 See Norman Meyers, "Environmental Refugees: A Growing Phenomenon of the 21st Century," *Philosophical Transactions: Biological Sciences*, vol. 357, no 1420 (20002) 609-613.

9 John Opie, "Draining America Dry," *Progressive Magazine*, July 1981.

10 Colum Lynch, "U.N. is at a critical juncture as it struggles to assert its relevance," *The Washington Post*, September 20, 2010.

11 B. M. Misra, "Sustainable Desalination Technologies for the Future," *International Journal of Nuclear Desalination*, Vol. 4, July 2010.

12 See Tokyo Metropolitan Government Disaster Home Page; and the simulation of Tokyo flooded on www.Japanprobe.com/flood-in-Tokyo.

13 "Transformation according to Survey of International Experts," www.circleofblue.org/waternews, March 16, 2010

14 Ibid.

Chapter Ten

1 Karl Wittfogel, *Oriental Despotism*, New York, New York: Random House, 1957.

2 "Global Water Futures," Center for Strategic and International Studies, Sandia National Laboratories, September 30, 2005, p. 22.

3 Steven Solomon, *Water, The Epic Struggle fro Wealth, Power, and Civilization*, New York, New York: Harper Collins, 2010, 489.

Index